THE
RV
HANDBOOK

Bill Estes

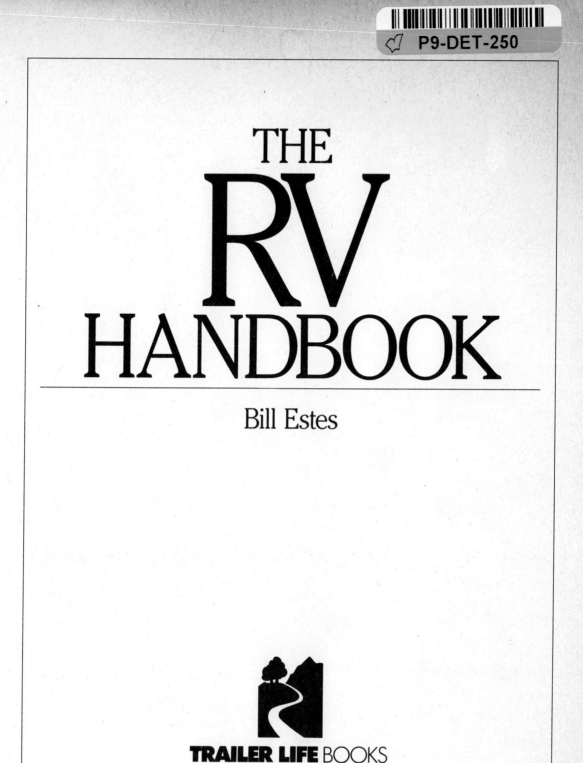

TRAILER LIFE BOOKS
AGOURA, CALIFORNIA

Trailer Life Book Division

President: Richard Rouse
Vice President/General Manager: Ted Binder
Vice President/Publisher, Book Division: Michael Schneider
Associate Publisher, Book Division: Joe Daquino
General Manager, Book Division: Rena Copperman
Assistant Manager, Book Division: Cindy Halley
Bulk Sales/Distribution Manager, Book Division: Judy Klein

Editor/Production manager: Rena Copperman
Production coordinator: Robert S. Tinnon
Cover design: Hespenheide Design
Interior design: Robert S. Tinnon
Illustrations: Miyake Illustrations
Assistant editor: Martha Weiler
Indexer: Barbara Wurf
Cover separations: Western Laser Graphics

This book was set in ITC Cheltenham Light by Andresen Typographics,
Tucson, Arizona, and printed on 50-pound Edition Matte by Ringier America,
Olathe, Kansas.

ISBN 0-934798-28-1

Library of Congress Cataloging-in-Publication Data

Estes, Bill, 1938-
    The RV handbook / Bill Estes.
       p.   cm.
    ISBN 0-934798-28-1
        1. Recreational vehicles—Handbook, manuals, etc.   I. Title.
TL298.E87   1990
629.226—dc20   90-10926
                                CIP

Contents

Preface

Even though many people do it, using an RV with little knowledge of how the various systems work seems similar to traveling without a road map. You'll probably get there, but the trip may be less predictable and more expensive.

This book is a road map to RVing, ranging in coverage from ways to improve fuel economy and performance to living without hookups—from vehicle handling and stability to propane safety. Just as different kinds of maps are available to help us locate travel destinations, also there are different kinds of books to explain and illustrate the various aspects of RVs. *The RV Handbook* is designed to help you *understand* a wide variety of RV topics, rather than to tell you in step-by-step fashion how to make repairs. That's the approach taken by another book, *Trailer Life's RV Repair & Maintenance Manual.* The two books are designed to complement each other, with *The RV Handbook* taking the more theoretical approach.

As one of my early mentors said about twenty-five years ago when RVs first caught my interest as excellent adventure-travel vehicles, "If you know how it works, you can fix it." While that's obviously an oversimplification, it is indeed difficult to repair or modify a mechanical device or system unless you know how it works. Of course, if we were to include specific data on each and every mechanical aspect of RVs in this book, it would be as thick as the New York and Los Angeles telephones books combined.

Based on more than twenty years of contact with the readers of *Trailer Life* and *MotorHome* magazines, I have selected topics that I know are of interest to RV owners—topic coverage that readers of those magazines have repeatedly requested. I trust that you will find information here that you did not discover anywhere else, and that it will help you enjoy your RV. The RV hobby easily becomes a life-style, and more expertise means more enjoyment. On the practical side, being able to diagnose problems not only reduce hassles, it can cut costs.

Trailer Life's Towing Guide, which is provided as a supplement to *The RV Handbook,* is a unique collection of data that has been in heavy demand for many years. Not only does the guide contain official trailer-weight ratings for tow vehicles, it includes suitability data on compact cars and light trucks for towing behind motorhomes. Also, there is a complete listing of specifications on motorhome chassis.

How did all this come together? With a good deal of help. Rena Copperman, general manager of Trailer Life Books, did an excellent job of editing and production management, and Bob Tinnon, production coordinator/art director, created a meticulous, attractive design. We hope you like the presentation as well as the material.

Speaking of material, I had help from several other RV experts who contributed information and, in some cases, entire chapters. My thanks to Gale Banks, Wes Caughlan, Ken Freund, John Geraghty, Bob Kovacik, Bob Livingston, Bob Longsdorf, Jerry Lyle, Brian Robertson, Dick Thatcher, Lee Weinmann, and several engineers from Detroit automotive companies and firms that refine motor oil.

As a dedicated long-term RV tinkerer—one who enjoys the mechanical aspects almost as much as rolling along the open road—it's my best hope that this book will help you find a new, heightened level of RV mechanical expertise that will make your RV travels more enjoyable.

CHAPTER 1

How to Make an Engine Last Longer

Owners of RVs have long been in search of the mechanical fountain of youth—the secrets to extended engine life. We hear boasts that vehicles have been driven for 150,000 miles or more without significant repairs, and we wonder why we can't do it—why our engines grow tired and require valve work and/or major overhaul much earlier.

Indeed, it would appear that some people get outrageously good service from their engines. Some of these people don't perform any special feats of maintenance, nor do they use any mysterious, special lubricants or additives. Others use gimmicks and believe that the gimmicks make a critical difference even though it's very difficult to find any clinically valid supportive evidence. The driving habits of owners whose vehicles appear to be immune to wear may be exemplary. Also, in most cases, these people appear to own vehicles that are the best of the crop. Despite the quality-control efforts of vehicle manufacturers, quality does vary. We've all heard of the proverbial Monday morning and Friday afternoon engines and other automotive components—ones that never perform right and don't last as long as they should. For example, a defective function in a computer-controlled ignition or carburetion system could cause reduced performance and excessive combustion temperatures that cut engine life. With that kind of vehicle, even the best of care will not get it to the 100,000-mile mark before overhaul is needed.

The engine durability equation involves many factors, any one of which can dramatically affect the outcome. Let's examine these factors, beginning with the fundamentals, and pave the way toward extended gasoline- and diesel-engine life and better efficiency, which means better fuel economy and fewer repairs.

GASOLINE ENGINES

Driving Habits

Although the basic quality of the engine has a dramatic effect on engine durability, even engines of the highest quality can be adversely affected by poor driving habits. A common bad habit is a tendency to start the engine, rev it a couple of times, drop the transmission into gear, and go. An engine needs a few seconds for oil to get into full circulation, particularly to the valve train, which is the last to see oil flow. When the engine is revved right after starting, the valve train, as well as other surfaces, may be marginally lubricated (Figure 1.1). Engine oil is supposed to prevent metal-to-metal contact, but cold starts are a particularly vulnerable time. Revving the engine creates more metal-to-metal contact during this period, and thousands of cold starts accumulate to cause serious wear.

The type of driving we do usually cannot be altered significantly, but it's interesting to note that city driving is estimated to be about 17% less efficient than steady highway cruising; short trips of three miles or less increase fuel consumption due to the fact that the engine has not had time to fully come up to normal operating temperature; and that about 2.4 MPG is lost for every 10 MPH increase over 40 MPH.

The use of cruise control often reduces mileage in mountainous terrain when we don't think ahead and increase speed a few more miles per hour while descending one hill and facing another. Cruise control also may apply heavy throttle to maintain a set speed, whereas the driver may choose to let speed drop a few miles per hour and use less throttle.

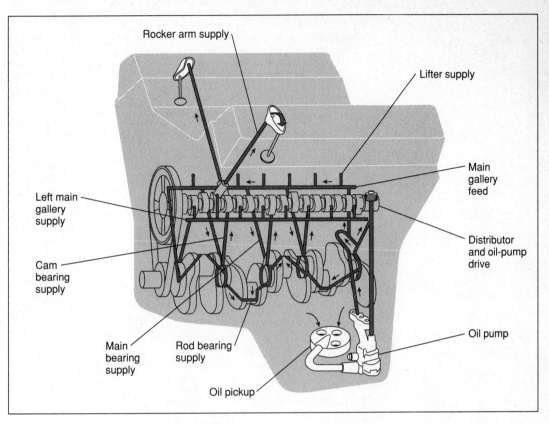

Figure 1.1
The valve train is the last engine system to receive lubrication after a
cold start.

Cold Starts

The proper method of cold-starting an engine is to depress the
accelerator pedal about halfway to set the choke (carbureted
engine), and back off to a point that will result in fast idle
(about 1,000 RPM) when the engine starts. Giving the engine
about half throttle while cranking usually will result in an initial
rev to 2,000 or higher, which is hard on an engine.

With an electronically fuel-injected (EFI) engine, there is no
choke to set; the system includes an enrichment system that

functions automatically—not actuated by the accelerator pedal. The driver should start the engine without touching the accelerator pedal.

Regardless of the type of fuel system or engine, when cold-starting an engine, run it at a fast idle for about 20 seconds, allowing oil to circulate to the most remote sections of the engine (valve train), before placing the transmission in gear. This small delay will assure good oil circulation. Keep engine RPM low and avoid heavy acceleration until the engine has reached its normal operating temperature.

Extended idling of the engine during warmup is not a good practice because fuel vaporization is poor and cylinder pressures are relatively low. Warmup occurs more rapidly if the vehicle is driven soon after being started.

Stop-and-go driving creates many more opportunities for wear, especially in cold weather when fuel enrichment occurs with each restart. This kind of driving is known to be hardest on engines.

Stop-and-go driving creates many more opportunities for wear, especially in cold weather when fuel enrichment occurs with each restart. This kind of driving is known to be hardest on engines. The driving situation that creates the least engine wear is light-load cruising. RV driving undoubtedly qualifies somewhere in between those two extremes, at least in moderate weather. When weather is hot, RV trips can produce high engine-oil temperatures and an increased tendency for the engine to spark-knock (ping). RVing typically is classified by motor companies as heavy-duty service, requiring accelerated engine-oil change intervals.

Cylinder Washdown

A significant cause of accelerated wear during cold starts is gasoline—too much of it. Chokes of many carbureted vehicles are set to produce excessively rich fuel mixtures—raw gasoline that floods into cylinders and washes the microscopically thin film of oil from the cylinder walls. This allows metal-to-metal contact between piston rings and cylinder walls. Cylinder washdown can cause accelerated piston ring and cylinder wear, leading to the loss of the ring seal, the reduction of compression, and excessive oil consumption.

During a cold start, the engine should not falter, stumble, and produce black smoke from the tail pipe. If it does, readjust the choke to a leaner setting, saving fuel as well as piston rings.

With fuel-injected vehicles, cold-start enrichment circuits are not designed for external adjustment, but waiting about 20 seconds for oil to circulate and avoiding heavy acceleration until the temperature is up are equally important.

Another fairly uncommon but very serious cause of cylinder washdown in carbureted engines is fuel percolation after hot shutdown. If the carburetor-float level is too high or the fuel-inlet valve tends to leak, fuel may drip into the intake manifold after the engine is shut off. This washes oil from the cylinders and causes partial flooding that requires excessive cranking to restart the engine. Cranking the engine under this condition causes rapid wear of piston rings.

Avoid extended engine idling, during which fuel vaporization and combustion temperatures are not ideal. The result is a higher level of cylinder washdown, causing accelerated wear, as well as an increase in carbon deposits.

On the Road

Few RV owners are street racers, so use of excessive throttle is not common. In fact, engines are designed to be operated at RPM levels up to their peak horsepower RPM, such as in passing situations when the accelerator pedal is floored and the transmission downshifts. Boat engines, which are adaptations of car and light-truck engines, are designated as suitable for sustained operation at their horsepower peaks, 4,000 to 4,600 RPM—a far cry from what most RV owners would deem tolerable while driving. Most of us become uncomfortable when RPM exceeds 3,500. High RPM does have some effect on the rate of engine wear, particularly in high-heat situations that boat engines do not encounter, so it's best to hold RPM to reasonable limits where possible. However, operation in the 3,000- to 3,500-RPM range that most of us regard as high is, in fact, moderate.

The important factor that heavily stressed boat engines don't usually have to contend with is high temperature. Although typical hill-climbing RPM in RVs (3,000 to 3,500 RPM) is not very high compared to boat engines, the complicating factor is heat. A boat has a *very* large cooling system—the entire body of water in which it is running—whereas RV engines must dissipate engine heat into the air, which is much more difficult. Engine-operating temperature may climb to 230°F or higher, and engine-oil temperature may approach 300°F. Heat also raises the engine's fuel-octane requirements, leading to another serious factor, preignition/detonation (engine ping), which drives combustion-chamber temperatures to extremes. In this manner, heat may bring an engine into a crisis situation that might be repeated several times a day.

Engine Cooling

High temperatures create tremendous heat loads on lubricants, which may thin to the point where they no longer can properly prevent metal-to-metal contact.

The need for adequate engine cooling cannot be over-emphasized, despite the fact that engine oils have been greatly improved during the past decade to withstand more heat. In the 1970s, it was not uncommon for heat to cause oils to thicken (due to oxidation) into something resembling hot asphalt that would not drain from crankcases. Good-quality oils (identified by the API rating SG) do not do that any more, but quality still varies. High temperatures create tremendous heat loads on lubricants, which may thin to the point where they no longer can properly prevent metal-to-metal contact. It's wise to make sure our cooling systems are in the best possible condition.

Late-model engines are designed to operate at relatively high temperatures, 195°F to 205°F, to help vaporize fuel and reduce emissions. These temperature levels are intended for control of emissions and aren't necessarily the best for engine durability and control of oil temperatures. It's often possible to slightly reduce an engine's fuel-octane requirements by replacing a 190°F thermostat with one rated at 180°F. Unless the cooling system is already operating at its limit, the lower-rated thermostat will cut temperatures on moderate terrain a few degrees. This helps lower oil temperatures and generally reduce demands on lubricants. Under more arduous conditions, the thermostat will open fully, and under that condition it doesn't make any difference what the rating is because the two thermostats are the same size when fully open.

The thermostat is regarded as a component of the emissions system, which means that it is covered by general prohibitions against altering components of an emissions system. In vehicles with electronic fuel-injection systems, some of these systems are programmed to regard the engine as not fully warmed up until coolant temperature reaches about 180°F. Thus, a 180°F thermostat could cause an engine to operate on enriched air–fuel mixtures.

Even with high levels of normal operating temperature, most cooling systems of late-model vehicles are able to restrain temperature rise under severe operating conditions. Most keep engine-coolant temperatures from exceeding about 230°F (diesels are lower) through use of engine fans designed to go into high-speed modes when temperatures reach 215°F to 225°F. The fans partially freewheel until engine temperature reaches a certain point, and then the fan clutches fully engage, raising fan RPM to the maximum.

Gauges on cars and light trucks are not usually calibrated in degrees, so the owner does not know exactly where the temperature is. Installation of a gauge calibrated in degrees Fahrenheit is a wise move (Figure 1.2). An engine that tends to incur a

Figure 1.2
An engine-coolant temperature gauge, preferably one calibrated in degrees Fahrenheit, is important to monitor normal operation as well as diagnose overheating.

noticeable temperature rise, accompanied by a tendency to spark-knock, needs additional cooling efficiency, a slight reduction in initial spark timing, or higher octane gasoline to prevent ping, which greatly accelerates temperature rise.

The ingredients of a healthy cooling system include:

- Radiator of adequate size, maintained properly
- 50-50% mix of antifreeze and distilled water, changed every two years
- Engine fan of adequate size that goes into lockup (makes more noise) when engine temperature rises to 225°F to 230°F
- Effective fan shroud
- Unrestricted airflow through radiator

Inoperative fan clutches are a common cause of excessive operating temperatures. When engine-coolant temperature exceeds 210° to 230° (calibration differs according to type of engine), the fan should go into its high-speed mode, dramatically increasing airflow through the radiator. Higher fan noise should be audible. If it isn't, and if temperature climbs steadily, the fan clutch may be defective or worn out.

It's important that cooling-system maintenance *never* be neglected because the effects are difficult or impossible to reverse. Certainly, the radiator can be reconditioned. But corrosion inside the block may remain until the engine eventually is "hot-tanked" during overhaul, despite efforts to remove it with cooling-system cleansers.

The reason for mixing distilled water in equal amounts with antifreeze in cooling-system maintenance every two years is that most water contains minerals. When the water is heated in the cooling system, the minerals deposit on the surfaces of the cooling system, particularly on water passages inside cylinder heads. Thus, the engine gradually builds up a coating of mineral deposits that retards the transfer of heat from the cylinder head into the coolant, increasing combustion-chamber heat and the tendency of the engine to spark-knock. Mineral deposits also impede the ability of the radiator to transfer heat to the air passing through its core.

Figure 1.3
The correct function of the viscous fan clutch is critical to proper engine cooling.

Most cooling systems designed for 14 to 17 pounds of pressure will not boil out (release pressure from the radiator cap) until temperature reaches approximately 260°F to 270°F. But that's far too hot if you expect the engine to live very long. Operating temperature even under very high ambient conditions should not exceed about 230°F, and even that is high enough to push many engines to spark-knock. Approximately 230°F coolant temperature is the highest point at which the engine fan should go into its high-speed mode to arrest temperature rise. When the fan locks in, a higher level of fan noise should be audible. If it isn't, and if temperature climbs steadily, the fan clutch (Figure 1.3) may be in need of replacement. Most engine fans are calibrated to go into their high-speed modes between temperatures of 215°F and 225°F.

Engine Oil

The search for the best engine oils has led in many different directions and has been in progress for about as long as vehicles have occupied America's roadways. Advertising claims ballyhoo one oil against another. Oils are rated by the American Petroleum Institute (API) for quality and performance, and it's an API rating such as SG you see on the top or sides of the container (Figure 1.4). **Multigrade oils** include a complex package of additives designed to extend suitability for operation in widely varying temperatures as well as other performance functions (see below for a description of additives).

In order for an oil to qualify for the highest rating (SG) by the American Petroleum Institute, it must pass a series of perfor-

---

What a Multiple-Oil Additive Package Includes

A multiple-oil additive package includes the following:

- **Pour-point depressants.** Straight mineral oils tend to congeal into waxlike consistency in low temperatures. Special additives keep the oil molecules from joining, thereby keeping the oil liquid.
- **Oxidation and bearing-corrosion inhibitors.** These compounds are designed to slow the rate of oxidation and to provide a coating for bearings.
- **Rust and corrosion inhibitors.** Water-laden air enters engine crankcases, and the water condensates when the engine cools. It mixes with the oil and causes formation of acids. Additives are needed to neutralize the acids and help coat metal surfaces to keep acids from attacking them.
- **Detergent/dispersant additives.** Combustion byproducts must be kept in suspension so they can be drained out with the oil. It's important to note that these additives will not clean sludge and varnish out of an engine; their primary role is to prevent sludge formation. The role of these additives is one of the reasons new oil tends to darken soon after an oil change.
- **Foam inhibitors.** Oil is subjected to high pressure and engine components that are rotating at high speeds, so it mixes and becomes aerated. Because aerated oil does not work very well, these inhibitors, mainly silicones, are used to reduce foaming.
- **Viscosity.** Oil viscosity (thickness) changes with temperature, and since many engines are operated in widely varying temperatures, oils that maintain fairly consistent viscosity can provide good oil circulation during cold starts, while also affording proper lubrication under high temperatures. Polymers are used to provide this versatility in multigrade oils. For example, SAE 10W-30 is listed by many motor companies as suitable for use in an ambient temperature range from zero to in excess of 100°F, while SAE 30 is listed as suitable for a range of 40° to in excess of 100°.
- **Extreme pressure additives.** Certain chemicals that tend to be attracted to metal surfaces are known as **boundary lubricants**. They help prevent metals from **galling** or from welding to each other under high temperatures when the oil film is very thin, such as in the cam-to-lifter contact area.

Figure 1.4
The quality of oil is indicated by the API rating, which should include the letters SG.

mance tests. Each test is used to evaluate a specific characteristic of oil, such as protection against wear, corrosion rust, and oxidation due to heat. For example, the oxidation test is conducted at 300°F to measure the oil's tendency to create engine sludge and varnish and to evaluate oil thickening, which are important aspects of the SG classification. All SG oils are supposed to have passed the 300°F test, although independent tests have indicated that some SG-rated samples of major-brand oils don't meet qualifications for the rating. Oil in RV engines generally runs 260°F to 280°F during normal summertime driving and may exceed 300°F on grades in hot weather.

Multigrade Versus Single-Grade Oils

Is one SG-rated oil as good as another for high-temperature operating conditions? Can multigrade oils equal the performance of single grades in severe service since the multigrade oil contains more chemicals and less base-stock oil? The additive package makes up 10% to 20% of a multigrade oil, but less of a straight-grade oil. Thus, the performance of a multigrade is heavily dependent on the quality of the additive package to create oil-film strength that separates metal parts.

Widely conflicting approaches to this question are taken by vehicle manufacturers and the companies that convert automotive engines to marine use. Automotive companies universally specify multigrades in owners' manuals, and most do not even list single grades such as SAE 30 as suitable. The owner's manual for the GM motorhome chassis lists 10W-30 as the preferred oil, but does list SAE 30 as an alternate (Figure 1.5).

In contrast, two major marine-engine producers specify the use of single-grade oils because they do not contain the viscosity improvers used in multigrade oils, which can shear down, causing loss of viscosity. Although marine engines share design similarities with car and light-truck engines, their duty cycle is considerably more severe.

For vehicles, oils as light as SAE 5W-30 are recommended by at least one major motor company for driving in ambient temperatures up to 100°F, and 10W-30 for conditions over 100°F in an owner's manual that covers vehicles rated to tow as much as

Figure 1.5
Most owners' manuals,
including this one for the
GM motorhome chassis, list
multigrade oils as preferred
choices.

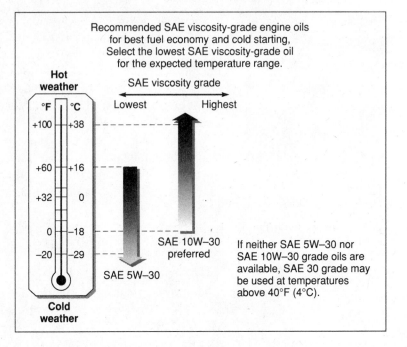

12,000 pounds. In support of the recommendations, engineers say that the engines are tested under extreme conditions that exceed the worst situations encountered by vehicle owners, and that a top-quality 10W-30 oil has all the viscosity the engine needs for maximum durability under severe use.

Motivating the motor companies to recommend relatively low-viscosity multigrades that offer fuel-economy benefits are federal fuel-economy regulations. Also there is the possibility that the vehicle owner who uses a heavier oil may neglect to change to a lighter oil for cold-weather driving. Single-grade oils such as SAE 30 do not circulate well immediately after a cold-engine startup in temperatures below 40°F, creating the possibility of accelerated wear. Oil companies do not believe most motorists are conscientious enough to avoid misusing single-grade oils.

Single-grade oils create additional resistance to movements of engine components under all conditions, compared to multigrades with lower reference numbers (SAE 30 versus SAE 10-30,

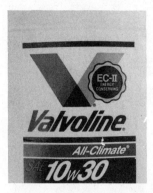
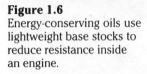

Figure 1.6
Energy-conserving oils use lightweight base stocks to reduce resistance inside an engine.

for example). Use of oils labeled Energy Conserving are estimated to improve fuel economy 1.5% or more over standard oils, and those labeled Energy Conserving II are estimated to produce fuel-economy improvement of 2.7% or greater (Figure 1.6). The estimates apparently refer to passenger-car driving; whether or not they are accurate in severe service is not clear. Certainly there would be some fuel-economy benefit from using lower-viscosity oils in RV engines. But most RV owners probably would trade the short-term benefit for the best possible oil durability under severe operating conditions.

Shear Stability

Oils that are subjected to extreme heat and pressure situations must maintain their rated viscosity and resist shearing, which is viscosity breakdown. Single-grade oils do not have to rely on viscosity improvers to maintain their specific viscosity levels, whereas some viscosity improvers used in multigrades may be affected by shear stresses. The viscosity-improver molecules are designed to contract at low temperatures and expand at high temperatures (Figure 1.7). The large size of the molecules makes them susceptible to temporary or permanent viscosity loss. Permanent loss occurs when the shear forces in the engine actually break the viscosity-improver molecules apart. Temporary viscosity loss may occur only when heavy shear forces are being applied and the molecules line up with the oil's direction of flow (Figure 1.8). When high forces and temperatures are removed, the oil returns to its original viscosity. Resistance to

Figure 1.7
Oil molecules prevent metal-to-metal contact inside an engine; viscosity-improver molecules contract when oil cools and expand with heat.

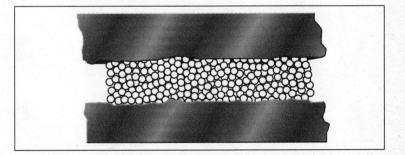

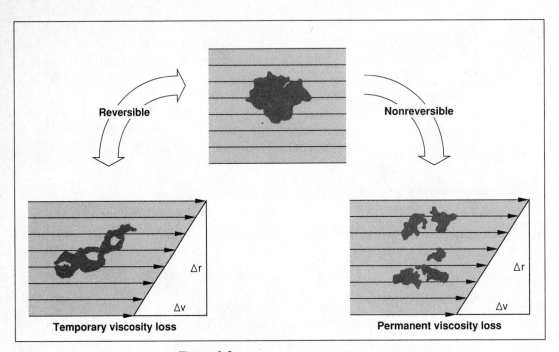

Figure 1.8
Temporary loss of oil viscosity occurs when viscosity-improver molecules
line up in the direction of oil flow; permanent loss occurs when molecules
break apart.

shear is only one measure of an oil's quality, but it's an important one for owners of vehicles that are subjected to severe
service.

Evidence of oil breakdown is difficult to detect, even when
the oil loses a substantial portion of its viscosity, because
engine-oil pumps usually have excess capacity. Pressure may
remain the same even though the oil has lost some of its viscosity. When the oil-pressure-gauge reading drops during a long
hill climb in hot weather and increases when the vehicle returns
to level terrain, the integrity of the oil is suspect.

Because boat engines often are operated continuously under
heavy loads at very high RPM—and because they're usually not
subject to operation in cold weather, which necessitates use of
multigrades—their manufacturers insist on single-grade oils,

with the exception of one marine manufacturer who markets a premium marine oil consisting of a mixture of SAE-25 and SAE-40 oils. This technically makes it a multigrade, but the oil does not rely on viscosity-improver additives. The company prefers oils that do not rely on viscosity improvers. (Except for that specific oil, the company recommends conventional SAE 30 and SAE 40). Although RV engines are not operated under continuous heavy loads at such high RPM levels, they often are subjected to heavy loads with much higher engine-operating temperatures than occur in boat engines.

Favoring multigrades, Castrol, an oil-marketing company that maintains a high profile in racing, acknowledges that SAE 30 may have an advantage over 5W-30 and 10W-30 in oil-film thickness, which is important for bearing life under high-stress conditions, but insists that their 20W-50 multigrade offers better protection than either the lighter multigrades or SAE 30 under high-temperature, high-load operation. A nationally known engine rebuilder and diagnostician agrees. He says he has found that engines using SAE 20W-50 are in better shape when he tears them down for overhaul than those using other multigrades or SAE 30.

The critical factor appears to be the quality of the additive package in a multigrade oil. Reports of variances in quality of SG-rated multigrade oils have been presented to the Society of Automotive Engineers (SAE), but for the consumer there are no reliable means of telling the difference between a nationally advertised multigrade that meets or exceeds requirements for the SG rating and one that falls below the standards.

Our conclusion is that the heavier multigrade oils such as 20W-50 are suitable for hot-weather driving and that the lighter multigrades are suitable for winter use, providing the RV owner has confidence in a particular brand of multigrade oil. Lacking such confidence, use of an SG-rated SAE-30 oil for hot-weather travel will provide insurance against viscosity loss under severe operating conditions.

The choice of SAE 30 for summertime driving requires that the vehicle owner make sure that oil does not remain in the engine when the temperature falls below about 40°F.

The choice of SAE 30 for summertime driving requires that the vehicle owner make sure that oil does not remain in the engine when the temperature falls below about 40°F.

Synthetic Oils

None of the engine manufacturers specifically recommends synthetics, although they include them in lists of approved oils if they carry the SG rating—and providing the vehicle manufacturer's oil-change intervals are observed. Motor companies insist that regular oil changes are mandatory for normal engine durability because contaminants that are absorbed by the oil must be flushed from the engine. Good synthetics are generally recognized as having better high-temperature tolerance than the best petroleum-based oils. Engineers caution, however, that the quality of synthetic oils may vary from one brand to another. Mobil 1 synthetic oil has built a good reputation in racing circles and is offered in SAE 5W-30, 10W-30, and 15W-50.

Oil Additives

With the complex package of additives present in modern SG-rated oils, no additional ones are needed—despite the advertising claims for a broad variety of oil additives. Some additives are merely viscosity improvers and others claim to reduce friction. Engineers at the motor companies consistently maintain that modern oils have all the additives they need, and that additional additives serve no useful purpose. Manufacturers of aftermarket oil-improver products usually are not able to provide authoritative analyses by independent testing laboratories to back up their claims of reduced engine wear.

Oil Cooling

Any oil can benefit from operation under reasonable temperatures. An oil film only .0001 inch thick must lubricate, seal, and cool engine components in areas where combustion temperatures range from 2,000°F to 3,000°F. The oil must soak up as much as 20% of the engine's heat output (Figure 1.9). While the antifreeze–water mixture circulating through the engine's water jacket cools the upper part of the engine, including cylinder heads, cylinders, and valves, the oil must cool the crankshaft

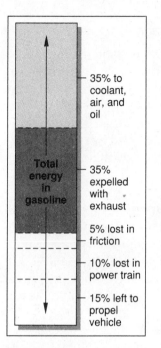

35% to coolant, air, and oil

Total energy in gasoline

35% expelled with exhaust

5% lost in friction

10% lost in power train

15% left to propel vehicle

Figure 1.9
Oil must absorb up to 20% of the engine's heat output.

and connecting-rod bearings, the camshaft and its bearings, the timing gears, the pistons, and other components.

In racing situations, coolers are used to keep temperatures in the low 200s, helping engine components withstand extreme high RPM levels under full-throttle conditions.

In contrast, oil temperature in RV engines usually runs 250°F to 270°F during summertime driving and may exceed 300°F on grades in hot weather. Modern oils are designed to resist breakdown at high temperatures, but the fact that oil in most RVs will approach or exceed 300°F under hot-weather hill-climbing conditions provides a severe test for an oil's ability to resist breakdown. Engine manufacturers say that temperatures up to about 285°F are within their design limits.

Oil cooling has obvious benefits for RV engines, but the vehicle owner must weigh the cost of adding an oil cooler against the amount of driving that will be done under hot-weather conditions. Owners who frequently drive mountainous terrain in hot weather and routinely see temperatures that exceed 275°F (in the sump) are prime candidates for additional oil cooling. Oil coolers that are suitable for most RV engines are available at performance-equipment stores and RV-supply stores.

Transmission-Oil Cooling

Motor companies usually apply the same temperature criteria to transmission oil, although the best possible transmission durability demands that temperatures under the worst conditions be held below about 250°F (measured in the transmission sump; the temperature in the transmission output line to cooler will be higher). Transmission oil is not changed as often as is engine oil, and it has more time to oxidize, hence the lower suggested oil-temperature maximums. To keep worst-case temperatures from exceeding 250°F, typical operating temperature should not exceed about 225°F. Even with proper cooling, the transmission oil and filter should be changed about every 20,000 miles. If cooling is marginal, the transmission oil should be changed every 10,000 miles during the period when high temperatures occur.

Detonation and Preignition

Although detonation and preignition (engine ping) can be caused by two different conditions, the results are similar: extreme stress and extreme heat. Detonation occurs when the rapid rise in compression creates heat that ignites the air–fuel mixture, causing a flame front that travels across the combustion chamber and meets a flame front created by the spark plug. When the two flame fronts meet, shock waves are created (Figure 1.10). Preignition has the same result, but the abnormal flame front may be ignited by a hot piece of carbon.

Engine ping typically occurs when operating conditions already are at their worst. As the combustion-chamber temperature increases beyond normal in an engine that has a tendency to ping, higher fuel octane may be needed. If octane is not changed, the ping that results can produce enough heat in severe cases to burn holes in tops of pistons. Piston-ring seal is disturbed, and valve and valve-seat wear is accelerated.

In addition to excessive temperature and inadequate fuel octane, excessively lean air–fuel ratios can cause ping. Whatever the cause, the problem must be avoided because it is one of the greatest accelerators of engine wear when allowed to continue for the duration of more than a few seconds.

Figure 1.10
Detonation occurs when two flame fronts meet, creating shock waves inside the engine. Preignition is similar, but the abnormal flame front is ignited rather than being spontaneous.

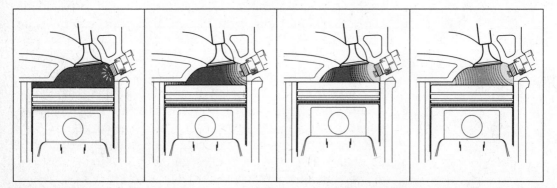

Cures include improved engine cooling, improved exhaust flow, higher fuel octane, and reduction of initial spark advance.

Engine Service

Even while most vehicle owners search for the magical fountain of youth for their engines, engineers say that one of the primary causes of engine wear is staring them in the face: poor engine maintenance. Many owners apparently stretch service intervals through inattention or by misreading their owners' manuals. Most manufacturers of gasoline engines specify two sets of maintenance intervals—one for typical use and another for severe use. General Motors, for example, recommends oil changes every 3,000 miles or three months for severe service rather than the 7,500 miles or 12 months prescribed for normal driving. The GM diesel schedule calls for oil and filter changes every 5,000 miles or 12 months under normal driving conditions, and every 2,500 miles or 3 months for severe service. Oil-change intervals for automatic transmissions also are shortened when the vehicle is subjected to severe service.

Severe service is defined as operating in dusty areas, towing a trailer, extended idling and/or frequent low-speed operation such as in stop-and-go traffic, operating when outside temperatures remains below freezing, and when most trips are less than four miles. Engineers list improper maintenance as the most common cause of accelerated engine wear.

Extended idling of gasoline or diesel engines is not recommended because it allows excessive compression **blow-by,** acceleration contamination of the engine oil. Diesels are believed to be well suited to extended idling, based on the fact that lots of diesel rigs are seen idling for extended periods at truck stops. But engineers maintain that the light-duty diesels in light trucks are not well suited to extended idling.

In fuel-injected engines, proper maintenance of the air filter (Figure 1.11) is crucial, especially on engines where fresh-air ducting is used. Although carbureted engines are also affected by restricted air filters, filter maintenance is much more critical in fuel-injected engines because fuel flow is controlled mainly

Figure 1.11
Regular replacement of the air filter is critical, especially in fuel-injected engines.

by throttle position rather than airflow through the venturi of a carburetor. Therefore, any restrictions in the air filter will dramatically affect fuel mileage. The air-filter element should be inspected every 10,000 miles. Also, look for restrictions in the fresh-air inlet tube. Hoses sometimes collapse, and foreign matter can partially block the inlet.

Oil Filters

Filtration of oil is critical to remove abrasive particles that come from engine components, as well as those that may leak through the air-filtration system. The standard pleated paper filters do not remove all contaminants, but the good ones are designed to catch particles down to about 25 microns in size (Figure 1.12). A micron is about $\frac{1}{25,000}$ inch.

Most name-brand filters, including those offered by auto manufacturers, are known to perform well. For best performance, use a name-brand filter and change it according to the vehicle manufacturer's recommendation.

Figure 1.12
Pleated-paper oil filters
remove contaminants down
to about 25 microns in size.

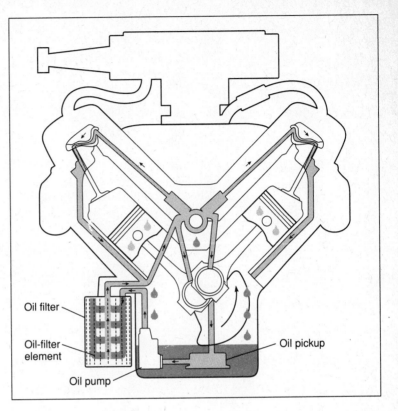

Oil filter

Oil-filter
element

Oil pump

Oil pickup

Lead in Gasoline

With lead having virtually disappeared from gasoline, owners of
vehicles equipped with engines designed for use of leaded fuel
are understandably concerned. Accelerated valve and valve-seat
wear occur when an engine with "soft" valves and valve seats is
subjected to heavy-duty usage on unleaded fuel. In fact, even
so-called regular leaded fuel is virtually unleaded, with the lead
content officially having dropped to .1 gram per gallon, and .5
gram regarded as the minimum amount of lead necessary for
adequate protection of soft valves. Fewer companies are mar-
keting leaded fuel due to reduced demand, leading to the total
demise of leaded gasoline.

The primary risk occurs during heavy-duty usage, which involve situations requiring the use of heavy throttle for extended periods, such as climbing mountain grades with RV weights high enough to require downshifting and more than three-quarter throttle. Hot weather adds to the risk by adding more of a heat load to a situation that already creates high combustion-chamber temperatures.

Even engines with hard valves and valve seats (Figure 1.13)—those designed for use with unleaded fuel—are subject to higher than normal valve wear under severe usage, according to tests conducted by the Environmental Protection Agency.

However, the situation is not cause for panic and immediate engine modifications to forestall possible catastrophic problems. Valve wear occurs very gradually, even when unleaded fuel is used in an engine with soft valves. Such wear doesn't usually lead to immediate failures, but it does lead to valve leakage, which is noticeable in reduction of power and engine smoothness. A simple cylinder-compression test is a good

Figure 1.13
Even engines with hardened valves and seats may be subjected to accelerated wear in severe service with unleaded fuel.

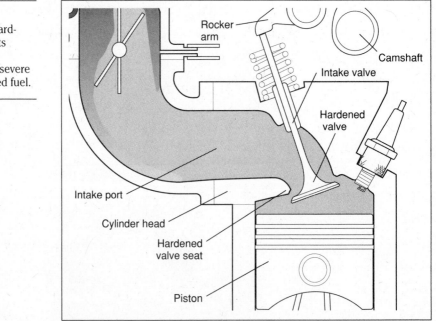

monitor of valve wear. If one or more cylinders varies more than 10% from others, valve wear has caused excessive leakage. A valve job is necessary to repair such leakage, and at that time hardened valves and valve seats can be installed. The special equipment usually adds about $200 to the cost of the job, but greatly improves valve and valve-seat durability.

When it's necessary to use unleaded fuel in an engine designed for leaded fuel, it's best to use a valve-protecting additive. Many additives are offered, and there is no comparative testing for effectiveness. Good choices include ValveTect, offered in auto-parts stores; the General Motors additive, sold in GM dealerships; and the additive offered by Restoration Products of Tucson, Arizona. Other additives that use ingredients made by Lubrizol Corporation usually are good choices.

Always use fuel of sufficient octane to prevent the engine from pinging, which is particularly harmful to engines with soft valves.

The major builders of vehicles used in RV service have identified those engines that have little or no valve hardening as follows:

- *General Motors:* These gasoline-fueled engines were designed to use unleaded gasoline and are said by GM to be unaffected by lead reduction: (a) passenger cars starting in 1971; (b) 1971–1978 trucks less than 6,000 pounds gross vehicle weight rating (GVWR); (c) 1979–1986 trucks less than 8,500 pounds GVWR; (d) all applications, 1987 and newer.

   General Motors cautions that some engines designed to use leaded gasoline may experience exhaust-valve recession if operated at high speeds and heavy loads with unleaded gasoline. The company recommends its Anti-Valve Recession Additive, Part Number 12345492.

- *Ford*: All engines made by Ford Motor Company are said to be suitable for unleaded fuel under normal driving conditions. Under heavy loads and prolonged heavy throttle, any Ford vehicle not equipped with a catalytic converter is at risk of valve recession. Catalytic converters were used in conjunction with hardened valves and valve seats.

• *Chrysler Corporation:* Engines *not* designed specifically for unleaded fuel generally are those without catalytic converters.

When in doubt about a specific vehicle, check the owner's manual. If leaded or low-lead fuels are recommended, the valves usually risk accelerated wear with unleaded fuel, and an additive is a good investment at least for the most severe service periods.

Pumping Losses

Engine efficiency affects more than fuel economy and performance, it also affects longevity. Conditions known as **pumping losses** (parasytic losses) add considerably to stress inside an engine. Pumping losses occur when there is excessive suction on the intake side of an engine and excessive backpressure in the exhaust. When a piston must act against a partial vacuum while attempting to draw air and fuel into the cylinder, the engine's efficiency is less than ideal, and the partial vacuum adds to the load of the piston. Horsepower from the crankshaft must be used to move the piston on its intake stroke.

Likewise, exhaust backpressure causes pumping losses as the piston exerts pressure on the gases to force them out the exhaust. Again, horsepower from the crankshaft must be used to overcome backpressure and create exhaust flow. The energy for these pumping losses must be provided by fuel. The pumping losses add to loads on pistons, cylinders, and bearings. Reducing pumping losses allows the engine to devote more energy to propelling the vehicle. Methods of checking for excessive pumping losses and correcting them are discussed on pages 51 and 53.

The engine oil and filter should be changed immediately before the vehicle is put into storage.

The Effect of Storage on RVs

Some RVs, particularly motorhomes, are stored for long periods during winter months. Long-term storage can be hard on an engine if preventive maintenance is not performed.

The engine oil and filter should be changed immediately before the vehicle is put into storage. This prevents the acids in the oil from doing their corrosive work on bearings during the storage period. Also, proper amounts of fuel additive should be poured into the gasoline tank to prevent fuel deterioration and formation of varnishes on surfaces in fuel systems, particularly injector nozzles and carburetor components. Fuel-storage additives are sold in auto-parts stores.

The vehicle should be driven for a few minutes to circulate the oil and the additive-protected fuel. Just prior to parking the vehicle, idle the engine and inject enough light oil into the carburetor or EFI intake to produce smoke from the exhaust. This coats cylinders to prevent rust. Boating-supply stores sell oil designed for this purpose. Shut the engine down after the smoke appears. During a storage period of four to six months, the engine should *not* be started periodically for short periods because this wipes away the oil coating in the cylinders and also will cause formation of water in the crankcase due to condensation.

Be sure to use enough fuel additive to protect the entire content of the tank. It's best to store the vehicle with the fuel tank full to minimize water formation due to condensation. A complete chassis lubrication and check-out should also be performed. Tires should be inflated to normal pressures for travel. Provisions should be made for battery charging about once a month.

DIESEL ENGINES

Dependability, durability, and economy of the diesel engine is unquestioned. The heavy-duty diesels in commercial truck service routinely go beyond the 400,000-mile mark before major overhaul. Many of the engines used in motorhomes—Detroit Diesel, Cummins, and Caterpillar—have the same kind of longevity. The lighter-duty engines, such as the GM 6.2 liter, the Ford/Navistar 7.3 liter (formerly 6.9 liters), and the gutsy turbocharged Cummins 5.9 liter used in Dodge pickups, should provide 250,000 or more miles before major repair is needed.

This longevity does not occur from simply owning a diesel; a strict regimen of thoughtful preventive maintenance, coupled with sensible operating habits, are essential to realize this potential.

Fuel Systems

Preventive maintenance of diesel-fuel systems is basically simple, but very small tolerances are used in injector pumps and components. For example, if you were to separate the plunger and bushing from a Detroit Diesel injector in a room with 65° ambient temperature, hold the plunger in your hand for two minutes, then try to re-insert it into the bushing, it would not fit, due to thermal expansion. And the sweat from your hand could damage the lapped surface if not cleaned off within a few minutes. This may sound pretty far out, but it serves to illustrate why the cardinal rule in fuel system care is *clean*. A microscopic bit of sand can render a $200 injector useless. Yet this same injector could last the service life of the engine with good preventive maintenance.

Most diesel-fuel systems include at least two filters for protecting the injection pump and the injectors (Figure 1.14). Late-model Ford/Navistar 6.9- and 7.3-liter engines and the 5.9-liter Cummins have only one, a combination water separator and final filter. Owners of those engines should have an aftermarket sediment filter installed to avoid problems.

Other engines have water separator/primary filters in the suction side of the fuel-transfer pump, and a final filter between the fuel-transfer pump and injection pump. In the case of the Detroit Diesel engines, except for the 8.2, the final filter is between the transfer pump and the injector-supply manifold.

Sediment filters (Figure 1.15) have the capability of removing particles as small as 80 to 100 microns (.0032 inch to .004 inch), and the final filter can be as fine as 5 microns (.0002 inch). The better sediment filters have a glass or clear plastic bowl that enables you to see how much water or other crud has accumulated. The only problem with the plastic bowls is when

Figure 1.14
In two-filter systems, the sediment filter precedes the final filter and usually has a glass or plastic bowl that allows inspection of contaminants.

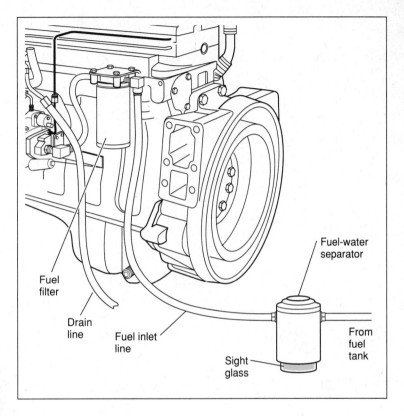

Fuel filter

Drain line

Fuel inlet line

Fuel-water separator

Sight glass

From fuel tank

Figure 1.15
A single unit may serve as the diesel engine's fuel filter as well as water separator.

the sediment filter is mounted outside the frame rail and near the ground, road debris can abrade the plastic so badly it becomes opaque. If you do have one mounted, place it where it is protected and visible. "Out of sight, out of mind" can apply when a sediment filter is hidden from view.

Some sediment filters also have sensing devices that trigger a light on the dash, warning of high water level. Don't rely on the light to tell you when to drain or clean the filter. It should be checked, either by visual inspection or draining, at least weekly. If you travel in the boondocks and must buy fuel from the Toonerville corner grocery, check it daily, preferably at the day's end, at least an hour after shutdown. You may be surprised how much trash you find in it.

A word of caution on the sediment filter found on the earlier Ford/Navistar 6.9-liter engine: The sediment filter was mounted on the engine fire wall and was drained by pulling a lift ring on the top. As long as you drained it on a regular basis, no problem; if you did not, relying instead on the dash warning light, trash could become lodged under the plastic valve seat when you pulled up on the ring. When this occurred, it continued to drip when you thought the valve was closed. Or, the next time the engine was started, air was drawn into the system, causing the engine to shut down.

The Final Filter

Most diesel engines have a final filter, and some have two. These usually are spin-on filters, although the older engines may have the type of filter that is encased in a container. The container must be removed, thoroughly cleaned, and then the new element installed and primed. The engine manual will give you a suggested change interval, usually in miles or hours, followed by, "or more often as necessary." You could take on a load of contaminated fuel twelve miles or twenty-two minutes after a scheduled filter change. Carry a couple of spares, know how to install them, and know how to bleed the fuel system. Changing a filter need not be a frustrating experience. Just remember, *clean*.

Most manufacturers do not recommend filling a new filter with fuel prior to installation, to reduce the chance of fuel contamination. However, when done right, there is little chance of getting dirt in the fuel. Priming a new filter can make a restart much easier. Some engines will reprime their fuel systems easily; some will not. Carrying a gallon of clean fuel for filter priming is a good idea.

To prime a filter, fill a clear plastic container with fuel, cover it, and let it set for at least an hour to allow any sediment or water to settle to the bottom. Then slowly pour this fuel through a clean, drip coffee filter into another clean, nonmetallic container. After removing the old filter, clean the filter base to reduce the chance of any dirt falling into the new filter, then

Figure 1.16
Priming the filter can make a diesel restart much easier.

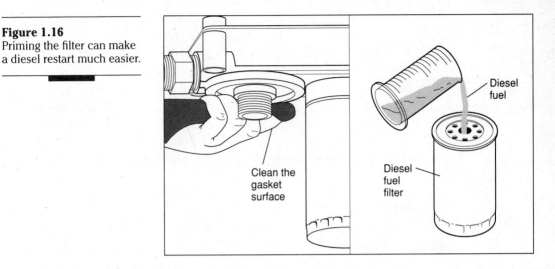

Clean the gasket surface

Diesel fuel

Diesel fuel filter

remove the old filter. Unwrap the new filter, fill it with the priming fuel (Figure 1.16), wait a few seconds to let the filter media absorb the fuel, then finish filling it. Coat the filter gasket with clean grease or Vaseline and install the filter. Do not over-tighten, or you may crush the gasket and cause a leak. Fire it up and check for leaks. You may get a burp or two, then the engine should run smoothly. If it does not start, loosen the vent on top of the filter base and have your helper crank the engine until an uninterrupted stream of fuel comes from the vent, then close it. The engine should now run smoothly.

Bacteria

Warm, humid weather can cause fuel problems. A bacterial growth nicknamed "fuel fungus" grows in the interface between the fuel and any water that may be in the tanks or filters. This is not algae, as algae needs light to grow, but it closely resembles it. A slimy mess that can completely plug a filter, it causes power loss and can even shut down the engine. Once formed, it is difficult to eradicate and is more prevalent in storage or fuel tanks that sit idle for a week or more.

The best prevention is not getting water into the tanks in the first place, but this is sometimes inevitable. The next best solution is addition of a fungicide formulated for diesel fuel. Regular fuel additives, or antigel agents, usually do not have a fungicide in them, and the fungicide can be hard to find on the open market. The addition of kerosene, gasoline, or acceptable alcohols does not help. If you plan on going into the boondocks, you may have to buy fuel wherever you can get it, and your chances of getting water and other contaminants in the fuel are good. Be prepared: Find a supply of the fungicide and carry it with you.

Regarding fuel quality, you can usually find good fuel on the major highways and in larger towns; on more remote roads and in small towns, it's necessary to take whatever you can get, and this could be diesel mixed with gasoline, used crankcase oil, furnace oil—you name it. Used crankcase oil contains a lot of sulfur and sulfuric acid, which is murder on fuel systems and metals in general. Here is where a good general diesel additive is needed. These additives keep water in suspension, inhibit the formation of soft carbon on injector tips, reduce smoking, and usually will lower the gel point. Injector-tip coking interferes with proper fuel-spray pattern, which in turn leads to incomplete combustion and power loss. Again, stay away from ethanol, methanol, or harmful alcohols.

A couple of additives with good track records are Power Service and FPPF. They are not cheap, but considering what they do, they are inexpensive insurance. Mix or add these additives in the recommended proportions; they can measurably improve performance.

Lubrication Systems

Diesel engines are much harder on oils than gasoline engines due to the larger amounts of carbon that get into the oil. Carbon is responsible for the dirty, black appearance of the oil and the sulfur/sulfuric acids formed during the combustion process. The carbon is from unburned fuel, and the sulfur comes from incomplete combustion. The carbon is not, in itself, very harmful to the engine, other than building up in the various nooks and crannies in the engine and leading to more rapid filter clogging. The sulfur, on the other hand, corrodes iron and bearing metals. The only way to combat these contaminants is through frequent oil and filter changes and by using the best oils money can buy.

Engine condition is also a factor in how fast your oil gets cruddy. An engine with well-seated rings that does not burn a lot of oil doesn't have the ring blow-by that leads to rapid oil contamination. The recommended oil change for the smaller diesel engines, such as the GM, Ford/Navistar, and Cummins light-truck engines, is 3,000 miles in severe service. (Pulling a trailer or propelling a motorhome is severe service.) The big Detroit Diesels have a factory recommendation of 20,000 miles, which seems like an awfully long interval, even for an engine of 30 quarts capacity. But the manufacturer has devoted a great deal of study to oil-change intervals.

Some folks incorrectly use the appearance of the oil and oil pressure as criteria for oil change. The oil on the dipstick of an engine that burns fairly clean may look okay after 3,000 or more miles, and if the pressure has not changed, they assume the oil is still good and put another 1,000 miles or so on it. Granted, there may not be excessive carbon in it, but the sulfur count probably is way up there. If the filter has filled with sludge, its bypass valve may have opened and the oil is not going through the filter.

Ford service engineers offer this general rule regarding oil-change intervals: Multiply the vehicle's miles per gallon by 250 to 300 to get the approximate oil-change interval.

Ford service engineers offer this general rule regarding oil-change intervals: Multiply the vehicle's miles per gallon by 250 to 300 to get the approximate oil-change interval.

Choosing Oil

What brand of oil you use is pretty much up to you, as long as the API rating and viscosity are correct. Oils may vary a bit in their additive packages, and these may vary by locality. Oils with the API rating SG/CE are preferred (Figure 1.17); if you can't find that rating, oil rated SG/CD or SF/CD will do. Do not use oils rated SE/CC or SF/CC. The SG/CE oils will probably read Energy Conserving and/or Turbo-Approved and have been approved for use by major diesel-engine manufacturers.

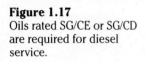

Figure 1.17
Oils rated SG/CE or SG/CD
are required for diesel
service.

As is the case with gasoline engines, some manufacturers may recommend lighter multigrade oils than we find comfortable. GM recommends 15W-40 or 10W-30 for the 6.2-liter diesel, and Ford recommends SAE 30 for use down to 32°F for the 7.3 and 15W-40 down to 0°F for the 7.3-liter diesel.

The factory fill in Caterpillar is 15W-40. If you're more comfortable with an oil that uses a heavier base stock, 20W-50 is popular and is widely available. If you plan to travel in cold weather, a change to a lighter viscosity may be necessary; check your owner's manual.

Use quality filters. Filter quality varies; Caterpillar, Cummins, Navistar, Ford, and General Motors all assure the effectiveness of their filters. When in doubt about filter quality, use the OEM filter.

The quality oils of today need no miracle additives to enhance their performance, and using additives to stretch change interval is poor economy, not to mention poor preventive maintenance. If you drain at the proper interval, while the oil is warm, no flushing agent is needed. Some flushes may be harmful to seals or other engine components. If you have an engine with a lot of sludge buildup in it, using a flushing agent will break loose all this accumulated crud and may plug some of the oil passages.

Air-Intake Systems

Any engine requires a given volume of air to burn a given amount of fuel. If that air supply is impeded, performance suffers. The biggest engine found in motorhomes today is the Detroit Diesel 8V92TA; this behemoth is 736 cubic inches and at full load and speed, gulps a lot of air. The air-intake filter must clean this air without starving the engine, and this takes a big, efficient filter.

Filter types and cleaning methods vary, but regardless of which kind you have, it must be serviced according to the conditions under which the vehicle is used. Many filters have indicators that signal when service is needed. Most owners' manuals list a cleaning interval, either in miles, hours, or both.

In regular service, this interval may be good enough. But drive through a Texas dust storm and the recommended interval goes out the window. Frequent inspection is the most foolproof method. If the filter looks dirty, service it; if it doesn't look dirty, but it has been some time since it was last cleaned, clean it anyway. If you have the disposable type, carry at least one spare.

Some of the cleanable diesel-engine air filters that come with some aftermarket turbo kits are supplied with one aerosol can of a special oil to re-oil the element. This aerosol can last about three cleanings, then you must locate more. If that proves difficult, make your own oil: Mix your favorite engine oil 50-50 with diesel fuel, and use an empty Windex spray bottle to apply it. Whatever type of cleanable filter you have, handle it gently; it is somewhat fragile, and banging it on a picnic table to dislodge the bugs can distort it or damage the gasket, causing an improper fit, with resultant leakage. Compressed air should not be used. A leaking filter is the same as no filter.

ON THE ROAD

Anyone who believes in good preventive maintenance knows that a thorough prestart check can prevent a lot of headaches. If the rig is used every day, there should be a daily "kick-the-tires" routine. The checklist on page 34 is not all-inclusive, since all rigs are not the same.

Startup

If everything is okay in the engine house, let's fire it up. Diesels, especially turbocharged diesels, should be run at the slowest speed at which they will idle smoothly until oil pressure stabilizes. Some of the turbos are mounted so they are the last component to receive oil. As the turbo may spin at startup, high startup RPM may spin the turbo at excessive speed, and premature wear will result. It doesn't do rods or main bearings any good either.

A Prestart Engine Checklist

- Perform an engine-oil check, ideally when the engine is cold, using the dipstick scale for a cold engine. The rig should be level (very important with Ford/Navistar engines). If the oil level is below the bottom marker, add enough oil slowly to bring it to, but not above, the top marker. In some engines, or in cold weather, it takes a long time for the level to stabilize.

- A coolant check should be done with the engine cold. If you have an overflow tank, check the level there; if not, slowly turn the radiator cap to relieve any pressure in the system, then remove it; the coolant should be at least ½ inch over the core; add coolant as needed. If you do not have any coolant mix handy and you must use water, add the same amount of antifreeze at the earliest opportunity; if you have a small leak and must continually add water, you are weakening the coolant protection. If you let small external leaks go until you get around to it, they have a nasty habit of becoming gushers.

- Check the automatic transmission. Most manufacturers recommend checking fluid levels while the transmission is hot, and this is good advice. Most dipsticks have a hot and cold level on them, but some folks overlook this (Figure 1.18). If you look at the wrong marker at a cold check, you may add fluid when it's not needed; the fluid expands quite a bit as it reaches operating temperature and has been known to boil out of the dipstick tube onto a hot exhaust pipe or the manifold with sometimes disastrous results.

- Perform a power-steering-fluid check: On dipstick-equipped systems, the stick will have hot and cold levels; again don't overfill the reservoir. If your system calls for automatic transmission fluid (ATF), fine; if it calls for power-steering fluid, use power-steering fluid. ATF and steering fluid have different additives.

- Check all drive belts and hoses. Loose belts cause slippage; overtightened belts can cause bearing damage. Proper tension is important, especially in the serpentine belts that do not have a self-tensioning idler pulley. If you have a loose belt, and you have the correct gauge for measuring tension, great; most folks don't. If you must make a field adjustment, tensioning the belt to ½-inch deflection of the belt between two pulleys will allow you to go on until you can have the belt adjusted properly. Check coolant and any hydraulic hoses for leaks, bulging, soft spots, loose clamps, or leaking fittings. Carrying a spare set of belts and coolant hoses is also considered good preventive maintenance.

- Check for leaks. Drips on the ground mean something; any leak is a cause for concern. If you have an engine that is a habitual dribbler and you know the leak source and how often you need to attend to it, fine. But don't be lulled into a false sense of security by the old familiar dribble.

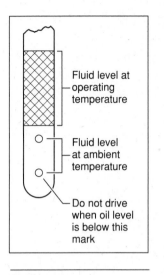

Figure 1.18
The oil dipstick may have different levels for hot and cold conditions.

Now, let's talk about idling. Contrary to legend, extended idling of a diesel engine is detrimental to longevity. At idle, the fuel is not burned completely, and the unburnt fuel washes the oil film off the cylinder walls, accelerating ring and liner wear. The unburnt fuel gets into the oil. Some idling is inevitable, but letting the engine sit outside a restaurant while you have lunch is not conducive to long engine life. Ideally, you should start the engine, check your instruments to insure everything is A-okay, let the engine idle for a minute to stabilize pressures, then take off at reduced load until temperatures reach operating level; now you can put the hammer down. In very cold temperatures, it may be necessary to let the engine idle; common sense will dictate.

Cold Weather

Starting a diesel in cold weather can present some unique problems, particularly at subzero temperatures. The glow-plug-equipped engines, such as Ford/Navistar and General Motors, usually will start at −20°F with little trouble if the engine is in good condition. An engine with low compression may have a problem. The direct-starting engines, Detroit Diesel, Caterpillar, and Cummins, may not have cold-starting devices. In these instances, other starting aids may be required if a 120-volt AC preheater cannot be used. Ether-based starting aids, sold in aerosol cans, will get the engine started, but they must be used with care. Even when used properly, they put a lot of strain on engine parts. There are right and wrong ways to use ether. Removing the air-cleaner cover, firing a long squirt of ether down the engine's throat, then racing back to the cab to hit the starter is not the right way. In this method, you may get a heavy dose of ether into one or two cylinders whose intake valves are open, and little, if any, in the other cylinders. Have someone crank the engine while you fire short bursts of ether into the air cleaner. This will give each cylinder a more balanced dose. You may have to give the engine a couple more short bursts to keep it running.

There are other ways to get the balky engine started in an emergency. If you have 120-volt AC power available, using a hair dryer can help; set it on the hottest setting and direct the airflow into the air intake. Hair spray may help; some hair sprays are made from some pretty volatile stuff, and they can replace ether to a degree.

Storage

Some folks "lay up" their rig in winter for three to six months with little preventive care. An antigel agent should be added to diesel fuel before storage. The oil and filter should be changed, and tire pressure should be checked. The fuel tanks should be topped off to minimize air space with resultant condensation. With the engine and oil warm, run the engine at about half speed, and while still running, squirt a liberal quantity of a light oil, preferably a preservative oil, into the intake. Shut the engine down while it is still smoking to create a thin film of oil on the cylinder walls and exhaust system to prevent rust. Seal off the intake and exhaust pipes before the engine cools.

Charge batteries in the vehicle once a month, or remove them for storage in a heated area. Use a trickle charger to keep the batteries up.

In summary, getting the best longevity, dependability, and fuel economy from an engine requires effort. If you give the engine the care it deserves, it will repay you with trouble-free, dependable performance.

CHAPTER 2

Improving Fuel Economy and Performance

T he quest for improved fuel economy for gasoline engines has been intense over the past two decades—since the gas crisis of the early 1970s—and it has taken on some bizarre twists. While the vehicle manufacturers pursued technological advances such as computerized ignition systems, electronic fuel injection, and multiple valves, the aftermarket came up with everything from cow magnets that were said to give gasoline more energy to miracle carburetors that supposedly doubled gas mileage.

In between the factory approach and the miracle inventions are aftermarket specialty products, such as exhaust systems, fresh-air intake systems, mufflers, aluminum intake manifolds, ignition-enhancer systems, replacement carburetors, specialty cams, special spark plugs, oil additives, and many more items.

It may be difficult to separate the valid systems from those that produce little, if any, improvement, but some products offer significant advances, at least in performance. The mileage and performance claims made by manufacturers of many products are exaggerated and, in some cases, are ridiculously optimistic. While some of the products can correct factory deficiencies, they may conflict with emissions laws. In states where such laws are not enforced through regular inspections, altering an engine with an aftermarket product may not cause immediate problems. However, many states are gradually increasing their vigilance, and the owner of an illegally modified vehicle may face penalties or the task of returning the vehicle to its original condition sometime in the future.

California has the most stringent laws and conducts biennial inspections of all vehicles, including motorhomes. A few manufacturers of some relatively sophisticated aftermarket engine-modifying products have gone to the trouble and expense of qualifying under the state's strict emissions laws, and they declare their products' legality in brochures and advertising. While such companies may not be the only ones offering products that really work, chances are good that they are among the most effective.

Because few products designed to improve fuel economy actually meet their advertising claims, the RV owner is wise to examine the claims made for such products very carefully—especially in California—and to check closely on refund and warranty policies, as well as the company's reputation. While the manufacturer of a miracle gas-saver gadget may offer what appears to be a very solid customer-satisfaction money-back guarantee, getting your money back may be difficult or impossible.

While some engines have deficiencies that can be corrected with aftermarket products, the more common problem is that the engine may be suffering from premature fatigue, although it's not ready for overhaul. Most of us are aware of basic preventive-maintenance procedures; we change our oil every 3,000 miles, get a tune-up every 10,000 miles, and then take it for granted that the engine should last for 100,000 miles. However, as we approach the halfway mark on the odometer, we may already begin to notice subtle signs of tiredness—lack of throttle response, more tendency to spark-knock, and an increase in oil consumption.

This chapter will use two approaches to analyze fuel economy and performance:

1. How to make the best of what you have by making sure the engine meets its full potential

2. How to correct an engine's factory deficiencies with cost-effective modifications, if available

First, let's have a look at causes of engine efficiency losses, and discuss how to measure such losses.

EVALUATING ENGINE CONDITION

The Timing Chain

Figure 2.1
The wear of the timing chain retards cam timing, reducing fuel economy and performance.

Many engines begin to show signs of fatigue when odometer mileage approaches 50,000 miles; others show it even earlier. Engine-fatigue signals usually include reduction in fuel mileage, a change in cranking compression (variance between cylinders of more than 10%), a reduction in acceleration and hill-climbing ability, an increase in the engine's tendency to spark-knock, and/or a tendency to run hotter. Oil consumption may increase.

The primary cause of mileage and performance deterioration early in an engine's life cycle is wear of the **timing chain** (Figure 2.1). Its role is to drive the camshaft. As the chain lengthens, camshaft timing is retarded, thereby reducing performance and mileage. Continued timing-chain wear will eventually result in the failure of the timing-chain assembly. This could leave you stranded, as well as damage valves and pistons.

In most cases, timing-chain wear is within acceptable limits until about 40,000 miles. By the time 60,000 miles have accumulated, most timing-chain assemblies should be replaced. The Dodge 360 and Ford 460 engines don't usually make it that far; it is not uncommon for the timing-chain assemblies of these engines to reach their wear limit by 30,000 miles.

The 460 camshaft is factory-retarded by 8½ degrees. This can be corrected when replacing the chain assembly, which theoretically is in violation of emissions rules. The use of a pre-1973 crankshaft sprocket will properly position the camshaft, resulting in an increase of throttle response and low-speed torque. Many timing-chain sprocket manufacturers have replaced the pre-1973 Ford 460 crankshaft sprocket with 1973 and later versions under the same part number. A visual comparison will show that the index mark on the sprocket is one-half tooth off, due to relocation of the crankshaft keyway position. The only reliable way to make sure the gear actually is a pre-1973 one that corrects cam timing is by visually comparing your old sprocket with the one you are considering.

Double-row timing-chain assemblies should be used in all applications except the Ford 460; the use of a double-row chain assembly on the 460 engine will not permit correction of the cam retardation.

Timing-chain wear can be checked by using this simple procedure:

1. Remove the spark plugs and distributor cap, and rotate the engine by using a wrench on the crankshaft nut.
2. Turn the engine in the opposite direction of the spark-timing scale until you reach top dead center.
3. Ask an assistant to observe the distributor rotor. Rotate the engine, and watch the timing mark as it moves up the scale. When the assistant notices that the distributor rotor is beginning to move, stop turning the crankshaft and note the number of degrees of crankshaft rotation.

This number of degrees relative to movement of the rotor is a measure of timing-chain lash. Lash in excess of 4 degrees will begin to affect performance. At 8 degrees, the loss in performance will become evident, and at 12 degrees the timing-chain assembly is nearing failure and should be replaced. Failure of a timing chain often causes major engine damage when pistons strike valves.

Oil Consumption

It's a good procedure to keep a record of mileage points at which oil is added and a list of oil changes by date and odometer mileage so you can have an accurate reading of the engine's oil consumption. Oil consumption usually occurs due to oil

Figure 2.2
Spraying lubricant on the intake manifold at its contact point with the cylinder head can help identify vacuum leaks.

leakage through valve seals and past intake-manifold gaskets, unless the engine is worn sufficiently that piston rings allow passage of oil into combustion chambers. Leakage past intake-manifold gaskets is particularly common. It can be checked while idling the engine. Spray WD-40 or a similar product on the intake manifold where it meets the cylinder heads (Figure 2.2). If engine RPM changes, or if you can see visible signs of the spray being sucked into the engine, the gasket is leaking.

There are two simple methods to determine if oil is passing through the valve guides or past the intake manifold. After shutting down a hot engine and allowing it to sit for thirty minutes, restart the engine without engaging the throttle. Observe the tail pipe, and if oil smoke is emitted upon startup, the oil is passing through the valve seals or leaking past an intake-manifold gasket.

Another method is to check for oil smoke after coasting down a long grade and applying throttle at the bottom. Oil smoke will appear immediately upon applying throttle and will disappear in a few seconds if continued throttle is applied.

If uncorrected, excessive oil consumption can create carbon buildup in the combustion chambers, resulting in the formation of varnish on the cylinder walls, which in turn can cause piston rings to lose their seal.

Figure 2.3
Compression readings
should not vary more
than 10%, comparing
one cylinder with another.

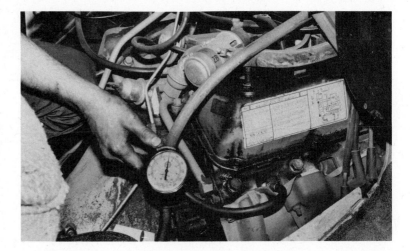

Cylinder Pressure

Compression testing should be performed with every tune-up,
or about every 10,000 miles, so you can maintain a continual
record. Always perform compression tests with the throttle held
open, and allow three or four strokes of each piston being
tested. Compression readings should not vary more than about
10% between cylinders (Figure 2.3). If a higher variance is
noted, inject a few squirts of motor oil into the low cylinder and
into the one adjacent to it, then retest both. If the retest figures
show that the cylinders are closer in compression, this indicates ring sealing is a problem. If cylinder balance remains
about the same as the first test, a valve problem is indicated.
When a piston-ring problem is indicated, recheck the compression after driving for about 100 miles. In many cases, a cylinder
wall may be washed down due to excessive fuel activated from
a cold start.

Crankcase Pressure

When engine fatigue is noticed, it's advisable to check for excessive crankcase pressure, which indicates combustion leakage
past the piston rings. The best method of doing this is to bring

the engine to normal operating temperature, remove the oil-fill cap, place the automatic transmission in drive, and with application of the foot and emergency brakes (block the wheels), have an assistant run the engine at approximately 2,500 RPM. (Take care not to stand in front of the vehicle in case the assistant's braking technique leaves something to be desired.) If a visible flow of oil smoke appears from the oil-fill opening, the rings are not seating properly. If the oil smoke is light and mileage on the odometer is 40,000 or less, chances are that the rings will reseal after correction of the valve seals or intake-manifold gasket leakage that was causing the excessive oil consumption.

Excessive Oil Use

Some vehicle manufacturers define excessive oil consumption as anything more than 400 miles per quart. Granted, RV engines work harder than typical automotive engines and generally have numerically higher axle ratios, resulting in higher engine RPM. Therefore, slightly higher oil use is acceptable. However, oil consumption in excess of one quart in 800 miles may indicate a problem; use of a quart in 500 miles requires diagnosis and correction; and consumption higher than 500 miles per quart indicates a definite problem that needs to be corrected.

Cylinder-Wall Taper

When visible oil smoke is seen at the oil-fill opening during the test, and when the engine has 50,000 miles or more on the odometer, cylinder-wall taper should be checked, which requires removal of the cylinder heads. If less than .004 inch of taper (wear) is found, and cranking compression does not indicate a radical cylinder imbalance (the test during which oil is added to cylinders that show abnormally low compression), chances are still good that rings may reseal. If wear is above that level but not greater than .009 inch, ring replacement is necessary. Proper honing of the cylinders and installation of moly piston rings will extend engine life.

Rod bearings should be inspected and may need to be re-placed; piston-pin fit and connecting-rod alignment should also be checked. The main bearings should be inspected, but they seldom need replacement. Valve lifters should be removed (keep them in proper order for replacement in their original positions) to permit visual inspection of the camshaft. The engine should be rotated so all cam lobes can be inspected for pitting and wear. The bottom of each lifter should also be inspected for wear and pitting.

Manifold Inspection

During the process of checking cylinder-wall taper, also inspect the intake manifold. Observe the gasket surface at the lower side of each intake port for signs of oil leakage past the gasket. Improper sealing compounds and/or improper torquing are common causes of this problem.

Engines that are equipped with exhaust-gas recirculation (EGR) systems also should be checked for manifold warpage. The best procedure is to thoroughly clean the manifold and place a light coat of oil on the surface contact areas. Cover the contact areas with a piece of glass. The coat of oil will contact the glass, and any warped areas will be evident because the oil will not adhere evenly to the glass. A warped manifold must be replaced.

Having the mani-fold professionally cleaned and mag-nifluxed is good practice.

The manifold must also be inspected for cracks. Having the manifold professionally cleaned and magnifluxed is good prac-tice. If oil leakage past the intake gaskets is discovered, use a gasket sealer such as Hi-Tack over the cylinder-head surfaces after these surfaces have been thoroughly cleaned. Put the gas-ket in place, then coat the gasket surface with sealant. Prior to installation of the intake manifold, apply a light coat of silicone sealer around each port and in each corner of the gasket. Im-mediately install the manifold, and torque to factory specifi-cations. After two weeks, retighten the intake manifold while the engine is cold. Tighten bolts in progression starting at the center.

If the valve seals must be replaced, the heads should be disassembled and the guides should be remachined to accept a

Teflon-type free-floating seal. The Pioneer brand is a good choice; Perfect Circle makes a similar seal. Both are available at auto-parts stores. These seals are to be used with the standard seal. With the heads off the engine and all of the carbon removed, it's logical to perform a valve job. At this point, installation of new nickel-alloy-hardened exhaust seats should be considered. Installation of nickel-alloy valve seats will eliminate the premature valve failure associated with the reduction of lead in today's gasoline. Engines supposedly designed for use with unleaded fuel also will benefit from the addition of nickel-alloy-hardened valve seats. Nickel-alloy seats are preferred over the more common stellite seats because the expansion and contraction rates of the cast-iron head and the nickel-alloy seats are more uniform.

Distributor Function

Fully electronic ignition and spark-advance systems have eliminated the distributor on many engines, but malfunction of the distributor is among the many causes of premature engine fatigue on vehicles with distributors. This is particularly the case with General Motors vehicles, which use a distributor with an inner shaft that binds, causing the automatic spark-advance system to stick.

Figure 2.4
After twisting the distributor rotor, spring tension should return rotor to its original position.

On all vehicles, the automatic spark-advance system is easy to check. To do so, just remove the distributor cap and twist the rotor against spring tension (Figure 2.4). Spring tension on the centrifugal advance weights should return the rotor fully to the rest position. If it does not, the distributor must be disassembled, cleaned with solvent and fine emery paper, relubricated, and reinstalled.

To check for proper operation of the vacuum spark-advance diaphragm, idle the engine and temporarily make and break the vacuum-line connection (using a source of **manifold vacuum**—vacuum evident at idle). You should be able to easily notice a difference in engine RPM as the vacuum advance affects spark timing.

Inspect the distributor rotor and the cap for evidence of **carbon tracking** (leakage of electrical current). Don't be concerned that the tip of the rotor or the electrical contacts inside the cap appear to be burned; it's not advisable to clean the carbon from those surfaces. Use a light coat of electrical silicone compound on these surfaces. Although silicone is an insulator, it does not impair the distributor's function, and it prevents burning of the contact surfaces.

Take the vehicle to a local auto-repair shop equipped with an oscilloscope and have a mechanic check the secondary ignition system (spark plugs and spark-plug cables). These components are a common source of engine problems. Make sure the mechanic loads the engine (running engine in gear, foot on brake, and hand brake set) while checking for secondary electrical ignition breakdown. This checkup will show bad spark-plug cables, spark plugs, or other ignition components. Primary voltage should be checked, especially on Chrysler vehicles. Resistors in the primary circuits of the ignition system often fail. They should be checked to determine if they meet factory specifications. Progressive failure of a resistor will affect voltage to the spark plugs.

Carburetor Function

Carburetors of almost all of vehicles of the mid-1980s and most earlier ones utilize nitrophyl (plastic) fuel-bowl floats. Since they all gradually become saturated with fuel, which raises the fuel level, they should be replaced every two years. Indication of float saturation is an increase in weight compared to a new float. The saturation causes excessive fuel use, stalling on corners and on abrupt stops, and hard starts while the engine is running hot.

Holley carburetors use power valves for fuel enrichment. Internal-gasket failure, vacuum leaks, and backfiring of the engine through the carburetor can cause the valves to leak. To check for leakage, bring the engine to operating temperature, shut it down, and allow it to sit for thirty minutes. Without touching the accelerator pedal, have an assistant start the engine while you watch for excessive black smoke, indicating a faulty power valve. Excessive fuel consumption is another indication. Use of a Holley 6.5 power valve and new gaskets for the metering body and fuel bowl are advisable.

Improper operation of the choke can adversely affect engine performance, as well as reduce engine life. An overrich choke allows excessive fuel to wash cylinder walls, causing accelerated wear. It also loads spark plugs with carbon and soot.

Most carburetors on the newest vehicles that still are carburetor equipped have choke systems that utilize many components, including diaphragms that open the choke when the engine starts. These vacuum-operated diaphragms are fairly easy to check visually, although their adjustment is more complex and must follow factory specifications. The choke diaphragm is located on the outside of the carburetor and is connected via linkage to the choke butterfly. Before initial startup, remove the air cleaner and observe the linkage that partially opens the butterfly. Start the engine to repeatedly check that the linkage partially opens the choke. If the diaphragm is faulty, remove it and take it to a parts supplier for visual confirmation that the new part is the same as the old one. The choke should progressively open and be fully open when the engine is up to operating temperature.

Fuel Volume and Pressure

The fuel pump of a carbureted engine should produce a pint of fuel under free-flow conditions in 15 to 20 seconds.

Adequate fuel volume and pressure must be available at the carburetor to insure maximum performance and mileage. Check fuel filters: You should be able to blow freely through them. (Do not use compressed air.) Fuel starvation can exist, creating a lean condition under a sustained load, without clear indication to the driver. This is especially true of fuel-injected engines. Fuel pressure and volume specifications are listed in shop manuals, along with testing procedures.

Generally, with carbureted engines, if volume is okay, pressure is acceptable. The fuel pump of a carbureted engine should produce a pint of fuel under free-flow conditions in 15 to 20 seconds. Check the factory specifications for fuel-injected engines. Fuel-pressure specifications on many are in the 30-psi range; variations of more than 10% will affect fuel mixtures.

Figure 2.5
A drinking straw inserted in the fuel-bowl vent can be used as an indicator of metering-rod movement in the Quadrajet carburetor.

Metering-rod movement should be checked in carburetors so equipped. Rods are externally accessible on some Carter carburetor models and can be checked to make sure they are not sticking. In Quadrajet four-barrel carburetors, common on General Motors vehicles, a piece of drinking straw inserted into the fuel-bowl vent will come to rest on the top of the metering-rod piston (Figure 2.5). When the engine starts, the piston will be drawn down and less of the straw will be visible. When the engine is shut down, the straw will rise. Under load, the metering rods should begin to rise at about 6.5 inches of manifold vacuum, which will be indicated by the position of the straw. A vacuum gauge can be used to test this function while running the engine in gear against the foot and hand brakes.

Secondary metering tubes in Quadrajet carburetors tend to loosen and drop into the secondary fuel bowl, causing a lean condition and power loss during heavy throttle (Figure 2.6). Checking for this problem requires removal of the air horn (top) of the carburetor; the tubes are pressed into the air horn. If they have dropped out, reinsert them with a light coat of epoxy glue to hold them in place.

Figure 2.6
Secondary metering tubes in the Quadrajet carburetor sometimes fall out, causing lean air–fuel ratios.

Electronic Fuel Injection

Inadequate fuel pressure, restricted filters, and other problems usually will be identified by the computerized codes (see pages 119 and 121). Beyond those items, it's especially important to make sure the air filter is in good condition.

In fuel-injected engines, proper maintenance of the air filter is crucial, especially on engines where fresh-air ducting is used. Although carbureted engines are also affected by restricted air filters, filter maintenance is much more critical in fuel-injected engines because fuel flow is controlled mainly by throttle position rather than airflow through venturi of a carburetor. Therefore, any restrictions in the air filter will dramatically affect fuel mileage. The air-filter element should be inspected every 10,000 miles. Also, look for restrictions in the fresh-air inlet tube. Hoses sometimes collapse, and foreign matter can partially block the inlet.

Valves

General Motors V-8s have adjustable valve lash, and it should be checked about every 20,000 miles. (Valves of other popular V-8 RV engines are not adjustable.) After valves are initially adjusted, audible valve noise is an indication of valve-train problems. Set GM valve adjustment to one-quarter turn down from zero lash, rather than the one full turn recommended by the factory. The valves should be adjusted with the engine idling. Rocker-arm adjusting nuts on GM vehicles are friction type; be sure there is resistance to turning during the adjustment procedure. If no resistance is felt, replace the nut.

With valve covers off, visually compare the movement or lift of one valve stem with another. They should be uniform. If one is low, it indicates a worn cam lobe or a bad lifter. Worn lobes are especially common with small-block Chevy engines.

A valve job usually is not required until 40,000 to 60,000 miles, or even later. However, with today's higher operational temperatures and the reduction of lead in fuel, valve failure occurs relatively early. Compression checks performed with each tune-up will provide information about overall valve condition.

AFTERMARKET MODIFICATIONS

In choosing aftermarket modifications, the question is, what works? Futhermore, the probability of error in choosing aftermarket engine modifications is high. Generally, these precepts hold true:

Ignition

Modifications of a standard electronic-ignition system designed to increase spark output or character don't help RV engines noticeably. The OEM systems are good enough for moderate-RPM duty. A good spark-enhancing system applied to an older breaker-points ignition system can help, but the difference usually is difficult to measure. Although illegal for highway use,

Figure 2.7
The spark-control system allows the adjustment of the initial spark advance by the driver while traveling.

manual spark-control units are available in performance shops (Figure 2.7). They offer the driver the ability to control initial spark advance with a dash-mounted control while driving. The driver can adjust initial spark timing in response to changing road, fuel, or altitude conditions, which can affect performance and mileage.

The factory-recommended initial spark-advance setting may be somewhat conservative, depending on individual driving conditions, and two to four additional degrees may add a noticeable measure of throttle response. Factory specifications for spark advance found on stickers affixed under the hood are specific, but factories usually allow variance of plus or minus two degrees, unless spark-knock problems are caused by an additional two degrees.

Air Intake

The addition of air ducting to feed a carburetor's cool air from ahead of the radiator rather than the air preheated by the radiator can have an effect on efficiency in hot weather. And it's legal, providing the air function of the diverter valve inside the air cleaner is not eliminated and the air cleaner's function is not fundamentally altered. An engine will perform better on cool air, which is denser that hot air (Figure 2.8). Make sure the potential for improvement is not counterbalanced by a restriction in the air ducting; it should be at least 4 inches inside diameter, with no sharp bends.

Air-intake tracts of many engines are restricted, which causes performance and fuel economy losses while operating under heavy throttle. Restriction can be measured with a manifold vacuum gauge (Figure 2.9). The restriction may exist in the cool-air ducting, in the air-cleaner housing, or in both. It's possible to measure the restriction by accelerating or climbing a hill under full throttle at 3,000 to 3,500 RPM while monitoring vacuum at the intake manifold. Vacuum readings should not exceed 1 to 2 inches Hg (mercury). Test with the intake system intact, and retest with the cool-air ducting disconnected from the air-cleaner housing to determine the effect of the ducting.

Figure 2.8
Preheating can be avoided if the air intake is positioned ahead of the radiator.

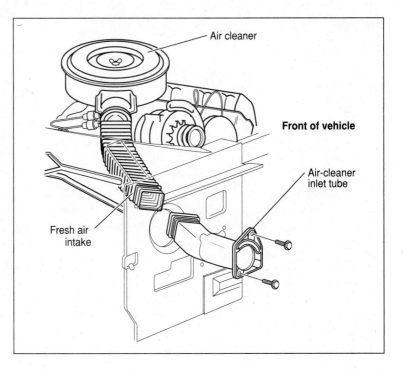

Many air-cleaner housings are inefficient and can be improved, as can the air filters themselves. Lids on air cleaners often can be shimmed to permit use of larger air filters, although this constitutes a modification to the emission system and is illegal in some states. A better arrangement is a nonrestrictive air cleaner connected to a cool-air induction tube. Effective aftermarket air-induction kits are available. On some air-cleaner housings, the air-intake snorkel is too small. On fuel-injected engines, air-intake tracts may have intake-air silencers to reduce noise; they often cause air-flow restriction.

While it may seem overly simple, neglect of air filters for carbureted engines can cause mileage and performance losses. Restrictions in the air filter will dramatically affect fuel mileage, therefore the air-filter element should be inspected every 10,000 miles. Also, look for restrictions in the fresh-air inlet tube. Hoses sometimes collapse, and foreign matter can partially block the inlet.

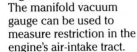

Figure 2.9
The manifold vacuum gauge can be used to measure restriction in the engine's air-intake tract.

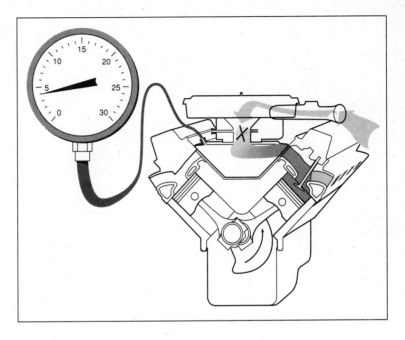

Exhaust

A variety of modifications can improve exhaust efficiency, although the effect on mileage and performance ranges from substantial to marginal. Thus, cost becomes factor. RV engines have varying degrees of restriction in their exhaust manifolds and in other components of the system (Figure 2.10), and improvements usually have some beneficial effect. However, modifications should not render any emissions-control equipment inoperative, even if you live in a state that does not currently conduct emission inspections; you may face inspections later. Steel tubing exhaust headers, per se, generally don't have a great effect on the fuel economy of the most popular V-8 engines. However, when included in a well-designed complete exhaust system that has been thoroughly tested, headers can be worthwhile primarily for performance, with mileage gains possible.

As a method of evaluating the need for exhaust improvements, exhaust backpressure can be measured at a point downstream from the exhaust manifolds. A fitting must be welded in

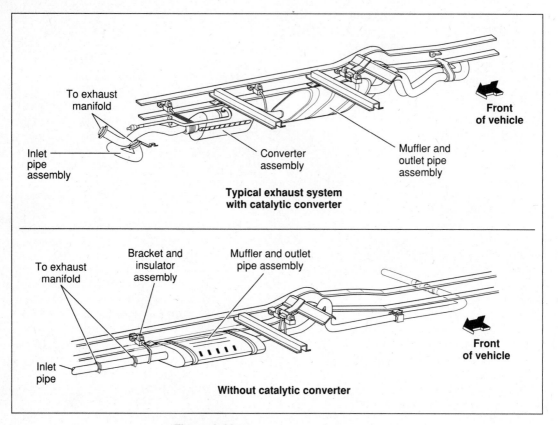

To exhaust manifold

Inlet pipe assembly

Converter assembly

Muffler and outlet pipe assembly

Front of vehicle

Typical exhaust system with catalytic converter

To exhaust manifold

Bracket and insulator assembly

Muffler and outlet pipe assembly

Inlet pipe

Front of vehicle

Without catalytic converter

Figure 2.10
Exhaust restriction can occur at any point from the exhaust manifolds to the tail pipes.

an exhaust pipe so a pressure-gauge sending unit can be attached (Figure 2.11). While accelerating or climbing a grade under full throttle at about 3,500 RPM, exhaust backpressure should not exceed 2 psi. Excessive backpressure in a noncatalyst vehicle usually can be corrected by converting from a single-exhaust system to dual exhausts and low-restriction mufflers. Or, a noncatalyst single-exhaust system can be converted to a single low-restriction muffler and larger pipe with mandrel bends that don't reduce the pipe size. Modifications of catalytic-converter-equipped exhaust systems are very limited in some states.

Figure 2.11
If exhaust backpressure is
more than about 2 psi,
improvements are needed.

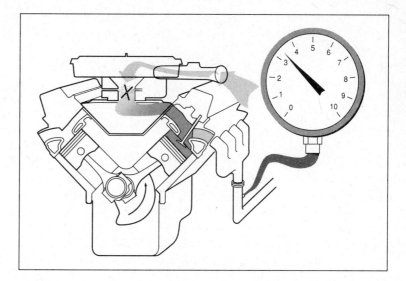

Measurement of pressure in an exhaust system with a catalytic converter should be taken immediately behind the converter, assuming the system is to remain intact from the converter forward. Smog-legal exhaust headers that make provisions for all the engine's original smog equipment can be used, although performance gains from headers alone in such a system may be very limited. Gains from modifications made downstream of a converter (reducing tail-pipe and muffler restrictions) may be worthwhile on some vehicles. Again, the pressure gauge will help you determine if changes are worthwhile.

If substantial improvement of intake and exhaust systems improves airflow into the engine, it may lean out air–fuel ratios. If the engine tends to spark-knock after alterations are made, reduction in spark advance may be needed.

The Cam

Since the cam determines how long each valve is open and closed—and the timing in relation to piston movement—a cam change can improve some engines. Changing the cam is illegal for highway use in California and in violation of federal laws, although there is no enforcement at the federal level, per se. Since there is no external evidence of a change in cam profile, the only possible measurement is a change in emissions measured at the tail pipe.

Of greater risk to the purchaser than illegality is the possibility that the cam will not do what its manufacturer claims. Many cams advertised specifically for RV use state that low-RPM power is improved, when in fact if there may be little, if any, improvement. Improvement may occur in the higher RPM ranges. Thus, a labor-intensive cam replacement can be counterproductive, especially on motorhomes, in which cams are more difficult to replace.

Carburetor/Manifold Change

While emissions regulations legally restrict what can be done with carburetors and intake manifolds, enforcement is limited to a few states, including California. In the 1970s, a large number of popular RV engines were fitted at the factory with two-barrel carburetors. Conversion to 600-cfm four-barrel carburetors on aluminum intake manifolds created very noticeable gains in throttle response and mid- to high-RPM performance when accompanied by exhaust-system improvements. The 1980s saw most of the problem engines at least partially corrected. Not only did a carburetor/manifold change become more expensive, it became more difficult to make the conversion while retaining all of the emissions equipment.

For most of the engines of the 1980s, a carburetor change is of marginal value for performance and does not usually improve fuel economy. A manifold change alone does not make a perceptible change in performance with most RVs.

Retuning

Likewise, distributor- and carburetor-tuning kits, popular in the 1970s, were effective on many engines. While some of those 1970s engines can benefit from retuning—as can some later models—owners nowadays must deal more specifically with legality and passing emissions inspections. In an engine that can benefit from distributor retuning, setting initial spark advance ahead two to four degrees usually provides much of the benefit that would be obtained by altering the automatic spark-advance mechanism

The Ford 460 is an example of an engine with a conservative spark-advance curve that can benefit from retuning or more initial spark advance. In contrast, the GM 454 V-8 is more aggressively calibrated and usually won't tolerate much additional initial spark advance without spark-knock. The hazard of increasing spark advance in any engine is spark-knock, which, in severe cases, can damage valves and break piston rings.

The hazard of increasing spark advance in any engine is spark-knock, which, in severe cases, can damage valves and break piston rings.

An engine's tolerance for additional spark advance increases with altitude, which is to say that all engines can benefit from more spark advance when gaining altitude. The reason is that an engine's efficiency is reduced by the lower atmospheric pressure that occurs in high altitudes. Usually it's inconvenient to change spark-advance settings by readjusting the distributor, and the spark-control system described on page 51 that allows manual timing control by the driver is the convenient way to handle it.

Changes in carburetor calibration via tuning kits, also popular in the 1970s, were effective on specific engines. But the situation is more complex on 1980s engines, both from the standpoint of installation and legality. Legality aside, carburetor recalibration should be performed by a competent shop equipped with a chassis dynomometer. The vehicle can be run on the dyno for a very specific evaluation of air–fuel ratios.

Computer Chips

Replacement computer chips designed to recalibrate electronic fuel-injection systems have created considerable interest among RV owners, and some of the devices appear capable of improving performance. However, they're relatively expensive, and furthermore, they're illegal.

Late-model cars, trucks, and vans are equipped with computerized ignition systems and electronic fuel injection that are controlled by a computer. Functions such as air–fuel ratios, spark-advance characteristics, and exhaust-gas recirculation are programmed by the computer, which relies on a chip for its instructions.

Because emissions play a significant role in the programming of engine fuel and spark-advance characteristics, it's possible to achieve significant performance gains by reprogramming fuel and spark characteristics, although it violates emissions rules. Replacement computer chips and modules are available at many performance shops.

DRIVING ECONOMICALLY

There are many ways to reduce fuel consumption if vehicle modifications are not feasible. The addition of a couple of relatively inexpensive driving aids usually is worthwhile for the RV owner who wants to make the best of each gallon of increasingly expensive gasoline. The two devices are the **manifold vacuum gauge** and the **tachometer.** Found in most auto-supply stores, both are helpful in making the best use of an engine's specific characteristics.

Engine Power Curves

Every engine has a power curve (Figure 2.12). The graphs include separate curves for torque and horsepower. **Horsepower** is a measurement of the engine's available power, while **torque** is defined as rotational force, measured in pounds-feet. Relating each of them to actual driving conditions is difficult. Suffice it to say that torque moves us along the highway in high gear or overdrive under cruise conditions, and that our engines are most efficient at their torque peaks. Horsepower, what we feel while climbing a hill, is torque times engine RPM, so the two are always related.

The torque peak is often given much too important a role in selecting an engine and axle ratio for RV use. For example, the torque peak of the late-model GM 454 V-8 occurs at 1,600 RPM. A 3:1 ratio would be needed to produce engine RPM of 1,600 at 60 MPH cruising speed in a typical GM pickup truck with the 454 engine and three-speed automatic transmission. General

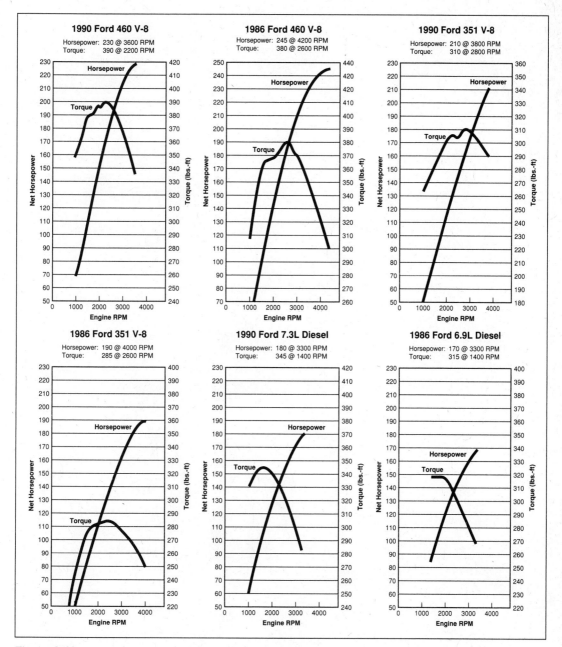

Figure 2.12
Engine power curves published by manufacturers in data books supplied to dealers indicate RPM ranges in which best torque and best horsepower occur. Curves shown here are a sampling of popular V-8 engines built during the mid- and late 1980s (*continued overleaf*).

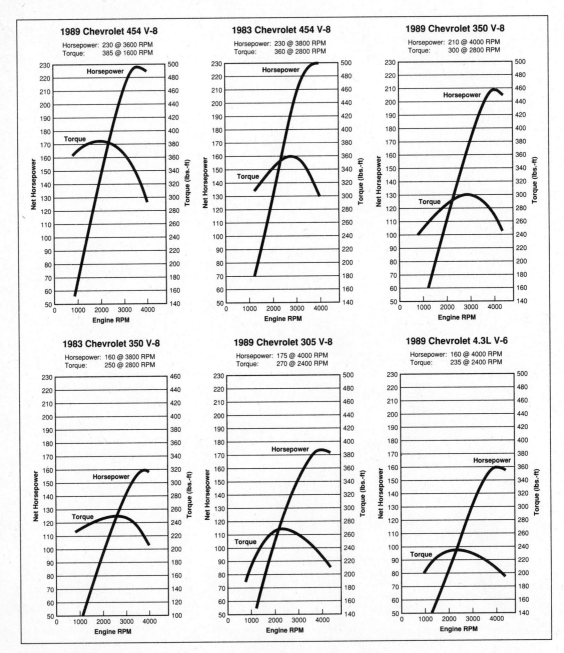

Figure 2.12, *continued*

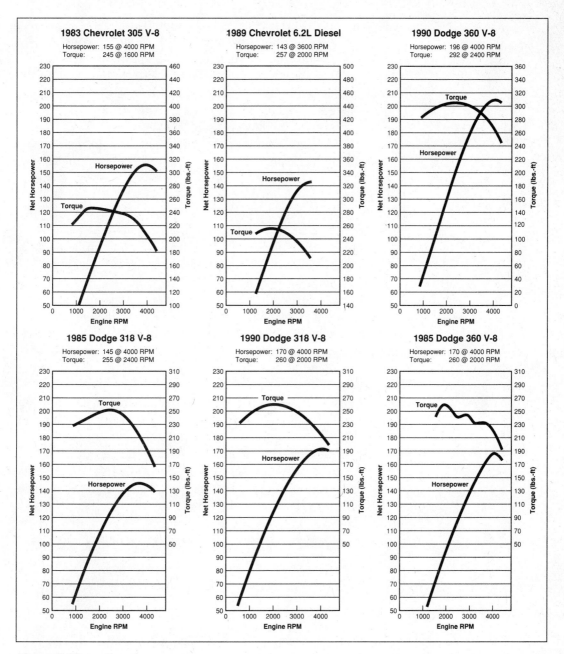

Figure 2.12, *continued*

The best operational range for gasoline engines is between the torque and horsepower peaks, assuming they are accurate.

Motors doesn't even offer that axle ratio with the 454 because it is suitable for minimal weight; it's a high-speed cruising gear ratio for a lightly loaded vehicle. The solution is the use of four-speed automatic transmissions with overdrive top gears, so the trailerist can cruise in overdrive gear while not towing, and drive in third gear (direct) while towing. With lightweight trailers, overdrive gear sometimes is usable while towing.

The important factor here is that sufficient gear reduction (torque multiplication) is required to move heavy vehicles. The recommended axle ratio for the example situation is 3.73:1, which will result in engine RPM of about 2,700 at 60 MPH (LT235/85R16 tires). The torque curve of the 454 shows that torque does not drop off substantially until about 2,400 RPM, so our cruising RPM is not as far off the maximum torque range as we might have assumed after having considered only the 1,600-RPM torque peak.

The best operational range for gasoline engines is between the torque and horsepower peaks, assuming they are accurate. With vehicles that are heavily loaded in proportion to the engine's power output, gear ratios must be numerically higher, raising engine RPM at cruising speeds farther above the torque peak.

The horsepower peak indicates maximum engine RPM. Although it's possible to twist the engine faster, horsepower usually drops substantially. Power output tends to drop with some engines before RPM reaches the horsepower peak, which means the factory numbers are not accurate. Using a tachometer while accelerating to the horsepower-peak RPM will indicate the realistic RPM peak for the engine.

Trailer Life's Towing Guide provide guidelines for selecting engine/axle ratios for varying RV weights and driving conditions.

When to Downshift

Beyond being entertaining to watch, a tachometer allows the driver to use the engine and transmission to their best advantage (Figure 2.13). Effecive downshifting can be accomplished even without a tachometer if the driver has a good feel for the

Figure 2.13
A tachometer helps the driver keep engine RPM in ranges where best performance occurs.

performance characteristics of the vehicle. RV engines usually are operated in the 2,500- to 3,500-RPM range, and that's where most of them perform best for hill climbs. Power output of some engines continues to climb up to 4,000 RPM.

Your engine's effective range can be defined during a road test. Under safe traffic conditions, reduce speed to about 35 MPH and apply full throttle, causing the transmission to downshift from third to second gear (assuming your transmission kickdown functions properly). Hold the accelerator pedal to the floor until the transmission upshifts automatically, which usually is about 4,000 RPM. During the acceleration trial, note the vehicle's ability to gain speed. It might be strong throughout the entire RPM range, or it may seem to lag before it reaches the upshift point. If the engine upshifts before 4,000 RPM, you either have an engine with an unusually low horsepower peak, or the downshift linkage or electrical circuit is not working properly.

In normal driving, your downshift should be timed so engine RPM does not rise above the point at which you noted best performance during the road test. In most cases that will be about 3,500 RPM. The engine may seem willing to go higher, but most of us are uncomfortable holding higher RPM levels for more than a few seconds because we envision pistons and connecting rods flying all over the place. Some engines don't handle high RPM well, and it's unrealistic to push them much beyond 3,000, which is the limit of their effectiveness, in spite of the fact that their advertised horsepower peaks may be higher.

Even though we recognize that an engine's peak torque may spread over a range of several hundred engine RPM, rather than occurring at one specific magical point, the downshifting method previously described de-emphasizes the significance of torque output when attempting to climb mountain grades or accelerate for passing. It's necessary to shift down and get RPM up. Waiting too long to downshift may allow RPM to drop into the maximum torque range, but too much loss of vehicle momentum occurs. In Figure 2.12 examples show that high torque occurs over an RPM range of about 1,000.

If you choose not to install a tachometer, it's possible to determine corresponding RPM for various road speeds and transmission gears by using this formula:

$$RPM = \frac{R \times M \times MPH}{60}$$

R = Transmission gear ratio multiplied by axle ratio.
M = Tire revolutions per mile (see pages 144–145 for a method of calculating tire RPM).
MPH = Road speed
60 = A constant

A list of engine RPM/road speed figures can be posted near the driver's field of vision.

Manifold Vacuum Gauge

Figure 2.14
The manifold vacuum gauge serves as a monitor for throttle position and is a valuable tool for boosting mileage.

The manifold vacuum gauge monitors partial vacuum in inches of mercury (Figure 2.14). The gauge is connected to the intake manifold of a gasoline engine so it can monitor the varying levels of partial vacuum inside the manifold. These levels change in relation to throttle position. Thus, the vacuum gauge is a relative indicator of throttle position for carbureted as well as fuel-injected engines.

By positioning the gauge on top of the instrument panel where it's easy to see, the driver has a constant reminder of throttle position and is prone to drive with a lighter foot on the accelerator pedal. Because fuel-injection systems gradually enrich fuel mixtures in response to heavier throttle, there is no single important point in the vacuum-gauge readings where a significant change occurs. However, there is a definite important change point with carburetors.

All carburetors have fuel-enrichment systems that allow lean mixtures to be used for light- to medium-throttle conditions and richer mixtures for heavy throttle. Four-barrel carburetors have three such systems: cruise, primary power, and secondary power. Two-barrel carburetors have two: cruise and power (Figure 2.15).

The four-barrel carburetor of an engine propelling an RV on relatively level highways in low altitude operates in the cruise range at light to medium throttle, producing vacuum readings between 8 and 12 inches. The readings are affected by the

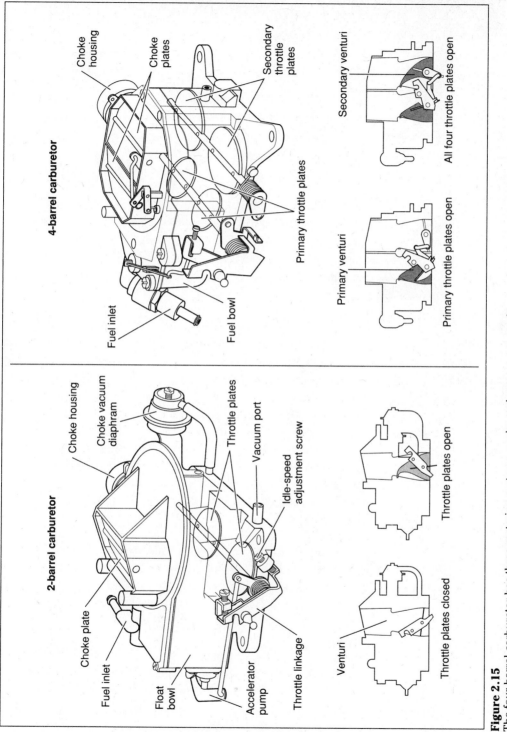

2-barrel carburetor

Choke housing
Choke vacuum diaphram
Choke plate
Fuel inlet
Float bowl
Accelerator pump
Throttle linkage
Throttle plates
Vacuum port
Idle-speed adjustment screw
Venturi
Throttle plates closed
Throttle plates open

4-barrel carburetor

Choke housing
Choke plates
Secondary throttle plates
Fuel inlet
Fuel bowl
Primary throttle plates
Primary venturi
Primary throttle plates open
Secondary venturi
All four throttle plates open

Figure 2.15
The four-barrel carburetor has three metering systems, cruise, primary power, and secondary power, in addition to the idle system (not shown). The two-barrel carburetor has two metering systems, cruise and power, in addition to the idle system (not shown).

weight of the vehicle, efficiency of the engine, and the axle ratio. When moderate hills are encountered, vacuum readings may drop into the 4- to 8-inch range. Therein lies the opportunity for fuel-economy improvement. The transition in most carburetors between the cruise fuel-metering system and the primary power-enrichment system occurs at 6 to 7 inches of manifold vacuum, and with some carburetors, it may occur as low as 4 to 5 inches. It's possible for the driver to maintain vacuum readings above 6 inches rather than slightly below that level, for a difference in fuel flow that ranges as high as 24%.

Although it might follow logically that downshifting early to maintain vacuum levels above 6 inches would also improve fuel consumption, that's not usually true because the engine uses additional fuel at higher RPM. It's simply best to hold vacuum above 6 inches as long as possible, then use heavier throttle until speed drops to a comfortable downshift point.

The secondary metering system of a carburetor further enriches air–fuel ratios, but the vacuum gauge is less useful in monitoring its action, which occurs near full throttle.

With two-barrel carburetors, fuel enrichment occurs at a single point, usually around 6 inches of vacuum. Below that level, the carburetor flows additional fuel.

Fuel-injection systems gradually enrich mixtures by electrically increasing the time during which the injector is open, spraying fuel into the engine, so the vacuum gauge will not be useful in singling out any particular important transition point in fuel metering. However, it's useful as a reminder of throttle position.

Vacuum readings are adversely affected by altitude at the rate of about 1 inch Hg per 1,000 feet of change in elevation. The gauge readings still are valid relative to the operation of a carburetor's fuel-enrichment system, but when driving in high altitudes, it's difficult or impossible to maintain high vacuum readings when vehicle weight is high.

Improvement of fuel economy can be elusive, but with the suggestions included in this chapter, it should be possible for you to make noticeable gains.

Troubleshooting Gasoline and Diesel Engines

A vehicle breakdown can be more than frustrating and expensive, it can be frightening. The best prevention is a regular maintenance program, which can save you countless hours of worry and many dollars. With even the best maintenance program, the possibility still exists that your RV may balk at the most inconvenient time.

This chapter, with its accompanying troubleshooting procedures, cover the most common vehicle failures, whether the rig is powered by diesel or gasoline. It will give you some hints designed to get you going again. Certainly there are a thousand things that could go wrong on the road, but the systems covered here—fuel, ignition, and cooling—are absolutely essential for mobility. Failures in these systems account for most on-the-road troubles.

BE PREPARED

In order to make the troubleshooting procedures work for you, a basic set of tools should be on board. It doesn't have to be a full-blown set weighing hundreds of pounds and costing thousands of dollars, just the basics. A good set for travel should consist of:

1. Wrenches, both open and box end from ⅜ to 1 inch
2. Several sizes each of flat and Phillips screwdrivers
3. A ⅜-inch-drive socket set from ⅜ inch to ¾ inch
4. A ½-inch-drive socket set from ½ inch to 1 inch
5. Needle-nose and regular pliers, plus slip-joint pliers
6. Spark-plug socket (check your engine's size, either ⅝ inch or ¹³⁄₁₆ inch)
7. A good set of jumper cables
8. An electrical test light or multimeter (volt-ohm meter)
9. Lengths of spare electrical wire in several gauge sizes, a wire crimper, butt connectors, and wire splicers
10. A flashlight with spare batteries.

Every RVer should carry along a few spare parts as well, including:

1. Spare engine drive belts. Whether your rig is a $250,000 diesel coach or a $10,000 gasoline-powered tow car, it can't function without a simple $10 belt.
2. A spare fuel filter. This is especially important with diesels, since one tank of dirty or water-contaminated fuel can render the rig helpless.
3. Extra top and bottom radiator hoses and about four feet of spare heater hose
4. A can of radiator stop-leak
5. A new set of distributor points and condenser (if you have a conventional ignition system)
6. A roll of heat duct tape and a few clean rags
7. And, last but not least, several spare fuses that not only fit the 12-volt RV accessories, but will fit any engine or chassis circuitry.

This is a basic "bare-bones" spare-parts assortment that will probably get you going in event of emergency. These supplies and tools can be absolutely invaluable, even if you are not the mechanical type.

TROUBLESHOOTING THE GASOLINE ENGINE

If Engine Fails to Start

When your RV's engine fails to start, it's important to remember that three systems must operate in harmony. First, the starting system must be able to crank the engine; second, the fuel system must supply the proper amount of fuel to the engine; and third, the ignition system (gas engines only) must supply sufficient voltage to the spark plugs to initiate combustion. The troubleshooting procedures in Figure 3.1 take you through each of these areas and give you points to check in order to single out the culprit.

Since many more problems occur than can be listed here, the procedures cover only the most common problems—those that that lend themselves to possible roadside repair.

Check the Battery

If an engine won't start, we must systematically eliminate possible causes. If the engine simply fails to crank, check the battery terminals for corrosion and/or looseness. If the terminal connections are heavily corroded, they should be removed and scraped clean with a knife. Or, purchase a battery brush/ terminal cleaner and keep it in the toolbox.

Caution: When working around the battery, acid can cause burns to your skin and eyes. Be very careful not to get any on you. If you do, immediately flush the area with water and, if it has affected your eyes, seek medical attention.

To insure that the failure to start is not caused by dirty battery components, thoroughly clean the battery and terminals:

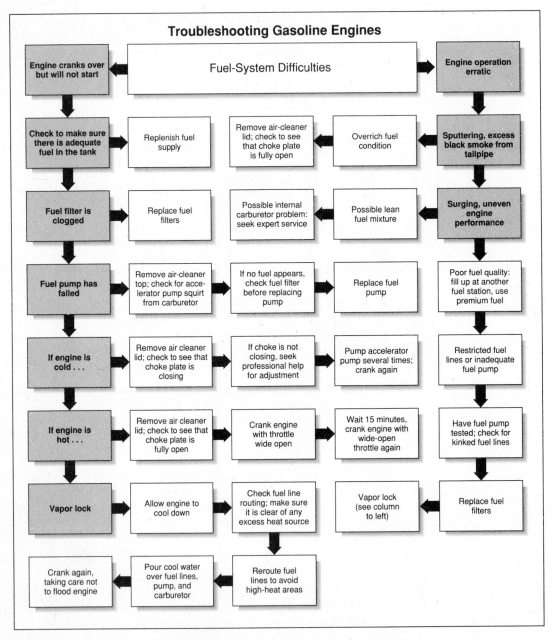

Figure 3.1
The use of gasoline-engine troubleshooting procedures in logical progression simplifies diagnosis of problems.

1. Mix a quarter-cup of baking soda in a quart of water.
2. Remove the battery terminals from the posts and dip the ends in the solution for a few minutes.
3. Then, pour the rest of the mixture over the battery top. The baking soda will neutralize the acid and remove corrosion.
4. Dry the battery and replace the terminals on the correct posts (positive to positive, negative to negative).
5. Finally, there are several commercial protectants that will prevent or slow terminal corrosion, or you can simply wipe some petroleum jelly or a white lithium grease on the terminals.

Next, try to start the engine. If there is still no activity from the engine's starter, turn on the headlights and check them for brightness. If they are dim or weak, the battery charge is low and will require a jump-start, battery recharge, or battery replacement. Some RVs, mainly large motorhomes, have battery-boost circuits that allow you to bring the vehicle's auxiliary battery(ies) into parallel with the starting battery by pushing a switch. This is invaluable, especially if you have forgotten to turn off chassis accessories like headlights. If you don't have a battery booster switch circuit, carry a set of top-quality jumper cables so that if the engine battery is dead, you can use them to connect the auxiliary battery to the engine battery.

If, after cleaning the terminals and attempting a jump-start, the engine still fails to crank, the problem is probably in the starter itself or its circuitry. Troubleshooting beyond this point will probably require the assistance of a professional mechanic with specialized test equipment.

Check the Ignition and Fuel System

If terminal cleaning and jump-starting bring the starter to life, but the engine still fails to start, new tactics are needed. When the engine is gasoline powered, the trouble can be narrowed to the ignition system or fuel system. If the engine is diesel, the fuel system is the only place you'll need to look since diesels don't have ignition systems.

First things first. Check the fuel gauge! This may seem obvious, but many professional mechanics have spent time troubleshooting a vehicle that fails to start or run without first
checking the simplest things.

Checking for Fuel Delivery   If the fuel tank appears to contain enough fuel, check to see if the fuel is getting to the engine.
In gasoline-carbureted engines it's easy, but in diesel or fuel-
injected gasoline engines it's more difficult and may require
professional help.

1. First, remove the air-cleaner cover to expose the air horn
   of the carburetor or throttle body of an electronic fuel-
   injection system (this procedure not applicable to port-
   type fuel-injection systems).
2. If the engine is carbureted, use a flashlight to look down
   the carburetor, and have an assistant slowly depress the
   throttle; check for fuel squirting into the carburetor bores
   (Figure 3.2). Squirting fuel is the result of the action of
   the accelerator pump. If there is no fuel present when
   the throttle is depressed, the fuel bowl of the carburetor
   is probably empty, or the accelerator pump may be
   defective.

Figure 3.2
Rotate the throttle lever and
check for fuel squirting into
carburetor bores.

3. In the case of a throttle-body fuel-injected engine, have the assistant turn the ignition key on and off a couple of times while you look into the throttle body. If no fuel is present, crank the engine for two or three seconds, and repeat the check for fuel at the carburetor or throttle body. If still no fuel is present, the fuel pump may be defective, the fuel filter may be clogged, or vapor lock may be the culprit if ambient temperature is particularly high.

4. If your RV has an electric tank-mounted pump for either a throttle-body or port-type EFI system, check the owner's manual for the fuse location and inspect the fuse. Have an assistant turn the ignition key on for a few seconds and off (but not to the start position) while you listen for the sound of the pump running. If the pump runs and the fuse is okay, but fuel still is not present at the carburetor or throttle body, have a professional mechanic check the fuel system.

5. If the fuel filter is suspected, it is usually easily changed. Many carburetors have inlet filters that can be removed, while other vehicles may have in-line filters between the pump and carburetor or between the tank and pump. In any case, hot engine, hot weather, and dripping fuel can spell disaster. Make sure that you take precautions to prevent fire when working with the fuel system. Let the engine cool, keep a fire extinguisher handy, and by all means, no smoking!

Checking for a Faulty Fuel Pump on a Carbureted Engine

Checking for a faulty fuel pump on a carbureted engine is relatively simple:

1. Disable the ignition system so the engine will not start. The best way to do this is to remove the 12-volt lead to the coil or the distributor.

2. Remove the fuel line from the carburetor. Hold a container at the end of the open line at the carburetor and have someone briefly crank the engine. Fuel should pulsate

from the line. If it does not, the pump is bad, the filter or fuel tank pickup is clogged, or the engine is still vapor locked. Again, be aware of fire danger.

Checking for Fuel Delivery to Electronic Fuel-Injection Engines

The fuel delivery to electronic fuel-injection (EFI) systems is more difficult to diagnose. Fuel pressure ranges from 9 to 45 psi depending on the model, versus 5 to 7 psi for carbureted engines. This creates the possibility that significant volumes of fuel can be sprayed in the engine compartment if you make an error. If your EFI-equipped engine has a fuel-delivery problem, see Chapter 5, "Understanding Electronic Fuel Injection," pages 110–111, for a method of checking pressure. Beyond that, contact your dealer or a professional mechanic who is proficient in the repair of EFI systems.

Incorrect Fuel-Tank Caps

Fuel-tank caps that are not the right design for your vehicle are another difficulty that can plague fuel-hungry RV engines. The wrong cap can cause the engine to starve for fuel, especially under high-demand situations like climbing steep grades. If the cap is not properly vented, air cannot enter the tank, and a partial vacuum forms, making it impossible for the fuel pump to do its job. If frequent fuel-starvation problems are noted, make sure that the gas cap is the right one. An easy way to test the wrong-cap theory is by loosening the cap and driving the vehicle under the same conditions that usually cause trouble. If the problem is solved, get the correct cap.

Vapor Lock

Hot weather can cause vapor lock by boiling the fuel before it can reach an engine-mounted pump or after it has passed the pump on the way to the carburetor. Pouring cool water over the fuel lines and pump will condense the fuel back into its liquid state. Vapor lock does not usually occur with fuel-injected systems because fuel in the entire system is under pressure, raising the vaporization point. If vapor lock is a persistent problem with a carbureted engine, it's likely that there's heat buildup in the engine compartment due to poor ventilation, or the fuel lines may be exposed to heat radiation from the engine (especially exhaust components), causing the fuel to vaporize in the line. Make sure fuel lines are routed well away from any excessive heat source and that they do not touch any metal component on the engine. Use procedures described earlier to check for fuel delivery to the carburetor.

Engine Flooding

The first sign that an engine is operating under a high fuel-to-air ratio (rich condition) is the presence of black smoke.

Well, so much for the lack of fuel, what about flooding of gasoline engines? The first sign that an engine is operating under a high fuel-to-air ratio (rich condition) is the presence of black smoke. Make sure that you don't confuse it with blue smoke, which is a sign the engine is burning oil. Black smoke is accompanied by sluggish performance and very poor fuel economy. This condition can occur with either gas or diesel engines. If your RV is equipped with a carburetor, a choke plate that is stuck closed or is not adjusted correctly is the most common cause of an overrich condition. Remove the air-cleaner lid and inspect the choke plate with the engine at full operating temperature. The plate should be in a vertical position to allow free flow of air through the carburetor. If the plate is closed on a warm engine, it partially blocks the airflow, causing the rich condition. The plate should be nearly closed when the engine is cold to enrich the fuel mixture. If the plate refuses to open when the engine is warmed, it may be possible to keep it open by temporarily wiring the choke linkage in the open position. This is a temporary fix that allows you to drive the vehicle, albeit with difficult cold starts. Make sure that the choke wiring cannot cause the throttle linkage to jam, which could cause engine overspeed and a dangerous situation. Other causes of an overrich condition cannot be easily corrected as they involve other internal circuits of the carburetor.

Incorrect Float Adjustment
and Other Causes of Flooding

Other fuel problems may be caused by incorrect float adjustment. This allows excess fuel to spill into the engine, causing an overrich mixture. If your carburetor is equipped with plastic floats, they can become saturated with fuel and raise fuel levels, allowing too much fuel into the engine. In addition to the float, a stuck or blown power valve can cause difficulties. Check with a mechanic if problems with these items are suspected.

An engine that is flooded may be difficult to start, especially in hot weather at high altitude. If it is possible to start a flooded engine, it will emit black smoke from the tail pipe. Make sure that you do not pump the gas pedal. This only floods the engine to a greater extent. Hold the throttle to the floor (wide open) to allow the maximum amount of air to enter the engine. This will tend to dilute the rich fuel mixture. Crank the engine with the throttle in this position for no more than 30 seconds at a time. Continual cranking may overheat and damage the starter motor and will deplete the battery in a short time. If there are no signs of life, wait 15 minutes and attempt to start again with the throttle held wide open. If results are negative, it may indicate ignition trouble.

Ignition Troubleshooting

EFI systems may also be plagued with an overrich mixture, but the causes are different. The electronic fuel-control system monitors oxygen content of the exhaust, engine temperature, incoming airflow, and throttle position, just to name a few. A problem with one of these sensing systems can feed the computer incorrect information. A defective temperature sensor may send the computer a signal that the engine is cold, even though it may not be. The computer's reaction is to tell the fuel-injection system to send more fuel, resulting in an unnecessary amount of fuel in the cylinders. There is little that can be done to analyze the situation since testing of these specific components requires sophisticated equipment and professional knowl-

Figure 3.3
Test ignition function by
holding the spark plug
against a metal engine
component while cranking
the engine.

An Ignition-System Check

When checking the ignition system of a gasoline engine, follow these steps:

1. Remove a spark-plug cable from a plug, or remove the center cable from the distributor cap. Some ignitions may not have a center cable to the distributor cap because the coil assembly is actually built into the distributor.

2. Turn on the ignition switch, and have someone crank the engine while you hold a spark-plug cable against a good ground (Figure 3.3) (which is any metal engine part). There should be an obvious spark every two engine revolutions. If there is a strong spark, the source of the problem apparently is in the fuel system. If no spark is present, remove the distributor cap and make sure there is no moisture inside. If you are near 120-volt-AC power, or if you have an AC generator, you can dry the distributor the easy way, with an electric hair dryer. If that's not possible, dry the cap and as many ignition components that you can with dry paper towels or a clean, absorbent rag.

3. Replace the dry cap and try the spark test again. If no spark is present, replace the spark-plug cable and determine whether your system is electronic or the old style with breaker points. The electronic system, a high-tech marvel of engineering, is very reliable and maintenance free. When it works, it works beautifully. When it fails, it fails so completely that only replacement of major components can get you rolling; roadside troubleshooting by the novice mechanic is nearly impossible.

edge of the particular EFI system. Difficulties in EFI systems are best handled by knowledgeable mechanics.

Diesel engines usually do not suffer from overrich conditions. If this does occur, diesel fuel injectors and pumps are calibrated to deliver a precise dose of fuel to the cylinder at just the right time. If excessive black smoke is evident, the pump and/or injectors may need adjustment. Professional help should be sought.

If an Engine Overheats

Overheating is one of summer's favorite tricks. There are many causes, some of which can be quite elusive. The following troubleshooting procedures cover the most common overheating causes, many of which can be handled at roadside. Diesel en-

---

Checking Breaker Points

Breaker points ignition systems lend themselves to troubleshooting quite well. Follow these simple steps:

1. If no spark is present at the coil wire, remove the distributor cap and locate the ignition points.
2. While an assistant cranks the engine, make sure that the points open and close. Maximum point gap should be about .020 inch (about the thickness of a matchbook cover). If the points open and close, there should be a spark from the coil wire.
3. If there is no spark, check to see that there is voltage present at the movable arm of the points. This can be done with a voltmeter or a test light. Bump the engine over until the points are in the open posi-

tion. With the ignition turned to the "on" position, set the voltmeter to the DC scale and touch the positive test lead to the point arm and the ground lead to a good ground on the engine. There should be about 10 volts present. Even if the voltage is near 8, the ignition should still function well enough to operate the vehicle.

4. If there is voltage present and it's still impossible to obtain a spark, the trouble may be in the points themselves, the condenser, or the coil may be defective. You should always carry a spare set of breaker points and a spare condenser.

gines seem to have less tendency to overheat compared to gasoline engines because combustion temperatures are usually lower, and most diesels are outfitted with huge, heavy-duty radiators.

First, let's define overheating. When is an engine too hot? Technically, an engine is not overheated until it continually boils out through the overflow. Typically, high temperature will cause an engine to operate poorly at temperatures well below the point at which boilout occurs. Accurate temperature gauges are needed for proper diagnosis of engine temperature. The gauges installed at the factory often are not precisely calibrated. If your RV has an "idiot light" rather than a gauge, or a gauge that is not calibrated in degrees Fahrenheit, install a top-quality gauge calibrated so you can read temperature accurately. By the time a hot-engine warning light is activated, overheating is in advanced stages, which may result in loss of a considerable volume of coolant or engine damage.

When overheating occurs, pull to the side of the road, shift the transmission to neutral, set the parking brake, open the hood, and operate the engine at a fast idle (1,500 to 2,000 RPM). If in two or three minutes the temperature has not dropped, it's best to shut the engine off and let it cool. Once the engine is shut down, coolant loss may be experienced due to afterboil (heat soak). When the engine is stopped, the coolant pump and airflow movement provided by engine operation cease, resulting in residual engine heat "soaking" into the stationary coolant, causing it to boil. This is normal if it occurs only in very high temperature conditions. If coolant is lost every time you shut off the engine, it may mean a defective radiator cap, a weak coolant solution, or an engine that typically runs hot, requiring repairs.

The troubleshooting procedure for overheating cites points in the engine compartment as possible culprits. Make sure the engine accessory drive belts are tight and in good condition. A loose belt can cause loss of coolant circulation and reduced radiator fan speed. The belts should be tightened so that moderate pressure with your thumb causes about a ½-inch deflection in the belt. Make sure all hoses and clamps are checked regularly. Carry spare hose and belts in your tool set.

When overheating occurs, pull to the side of the road, shift the transmission to neutral, set the parking brake, open the hood, and operate the engine at a fast idle (1,500 to 2,000 RPM).

Figure 3.4
The thermostatic fan clutch must function properly to prevent engine overheating.

A daily walkaround inspection of your RV should include the cooling system. Pop the hood and visually look at all hose connections and the hoses themselves for signs of leakage. Check the radiator for road debris. It's easy to pick up such things as plastic bags that can block most of the radiator's airflow. Continual neglect can lead to clogging with dirt, insects, and other debris.

Thermostatic fan clutches must function properly in hot weather (Figure 3.4). It's usually obvious when the clutch engages, as fan noise increases dramatically. If your RV is overheating and you have a fan clutch, it should engage as temperature rises and disengage as the temperature drops. If you don't hear the action of the fan, the clutch may be defective.

If you're trapped in stop-and-go traffic and the engine starts to overheat, it could be due to the idle speed being set too low. Slow idle speeds mean poor coolant circulation and slow airflow past the radiator. Turn off accessories, such as air conditioners, since they add heat load to the cooling system. Shift to the neutral position when stopped and run the engine at a fast idle speed (1,500 to 2,000 RPM).

Incorrect engine ignition timing can also contribute to overheating. If the ignition timing is excessively retarded, which may have been necessary to reduce the engine tendency to spark-knock, overheating at low speeds may result. The cure can be to use premium fuel so the timing can be returned to the normal setting.

In a few instances, overheating may occur at 55 to 60 MPH. This is sometimes caused by the collapse of the lower radiator hose. At high pump speeds, there is a strong suction on the inlet to the water pump. If the hose is not equipped with a wire coil insert to prevent collapse, change to a hose that is fitted with the coil.

Radiator Caps

It's not commonly known, but a poor radiator cap can cause overheating. The boiling point of the coolant is raised 2.5 degrees for every pound of pressure added to the system. Most

Figure 3.5
The radiator cap should hold 15 psi to prevent a premature loss of coolant.

cooling systems use 15-psi caps. Under this pressure, a 50-50 mix of water and ethylene glycol coolant has a boiling point of 265°F. If the cap seal is defective, or if spring pressure is insufficient, the pressure is reduced, allowing coolant to boil at a lower temperature; have the cap tested (Figure 3.5).

Water Pumps

Water-pump failure can cause coolant to leak, reducing coolant flow through the engine and radiator. The first sign that the water pump is failing may be slight leakage or bearing noise. The noise is a grumbling sound that may be heard at all speeds and may be particularly noisy at idle. Loss of the water-pump bearings leads to the loss of the water-pump seal, hence subsequent leakage of coolant from around the water-pump shaft.

The water pump can also cause overheating. A corroded pump impeller may fail to circulate enough coolant to transfer heat from the engine to the radiator. The reduced ability of the water pump can be checked only by removing the pump and visually inspecting the impeller. With this much work involved, it's wise to install a new pump.

Other Causes of Overheating

Other not-so-obvious overheating causes can be more serious and may be difficult to detect. Blown head gaskets, cracked cylinder heads, cracked blocks, and coolant leaking into the intake system dictate professional attention. A simple check with a leak detector can spot the presence of exhaust gases in the coolant, which indicates a blown gasket or crack that allows the gases to infiltrate the system. The test will not tell exactly where the leak is occurring, but most often it's a blown head gasket or a crack in a valve seat in the cylinder head, either of which is an expensive item to repair.

The key to preventing overheating is maintenance. Neglect of the cooling system allows rust and scale to form on heat-transferring parts that rid the engine of heat buildup. Use a 50% mixture of ethylene glycol and distilled water. This solution should be changed at least every two years. At coolant change time it's also a good idea to backflush the cooling system to remove any accumulated sediment. The system-flushing procedure applies to gasoline as well as diesel engines. Diesel owners should check the coolant filter system if the engine is fitted with one. The filter collects any debris that may form between changes and backflushing of the system, and it should.

TROUBLESHOOTING THE DIESEL ENGINE

If a diesel engine fails to start, it can usually be traced to one of two reasons: Lack of fuel injected into the system, or faulty preheating of the ignition system either by glow plugs or an ether-injection system. See Figure 3.6 for diesel troubleshooting procedures.

Checking for Lack of Fuel

If the RV's powerplant is diesel, lack of fuel is almost always caused by a dirty filter. Diesel systems have two (sometimes more) filters (Figure 3.7). Primary and secondary filters are usu-

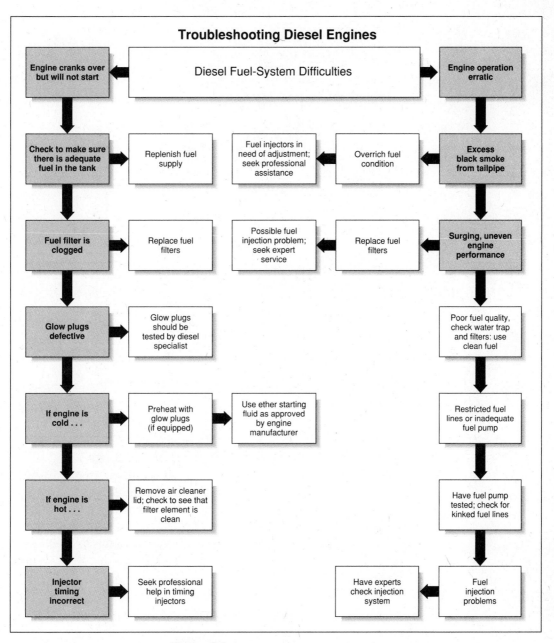

Figure 3.6
Diesel-engine troubleshooting procedures concentrate on problems with quality and delivery of fuel.

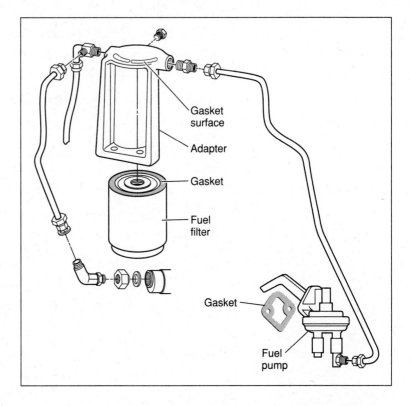

ally connected in series. Some systems use a special water trap just ahead of the primary filter to collect large amounts of water that sometimes find its way into a service station's supply tanks.

Lack of fuel is first evident in lack of performance. Diesel engine power output is directly proportional to the amount of fuel that is injected into the cylinder. Instead of controlling the airflow and fuel flow to the cylinders as a gasoline engine does, diesels control just the amount of fuel that is injected when the piston reaches the top of the compression stroke. A positive displacement pump that draws its supply from the filter housing supplies fuel to the fuel injectors. If fuel filters become clogged, they will pass only a fraction of what is necessary to keep the engine operating at peak performance. The engine may idle and run at low speed properly, but at full throttle, performance may drop off. The solution is to change both the primary and secondary fuel filters.

If Diesel Engine Fails to Run

As mentioned earlier, diesel engines do not require ignition systems to start. But many diesels require glow plugs to assist in starting. If the engine still fails to start or run, the next logical place to look is the electrical system. Some diesels have a starting circuit consisting of glow plugs.

Checking the Glow Plugs

A diesel's ignition method is the temperature of the air in the combustion chamber during compression. The high compression ratios associated with diesel operation heat the air in the chamber enough to ignite the fuel sprayed into the chambers by the injectors. When the engine is cold, glow plugs may be needed to add a enough heat to the combustion chamber to make for easier ignition of the fuel. With age, glow plugs become covered with carbon, and they require more battery energy to emit the same value of heat that a new plug produces.

A battery that must crank a high-compression diesel engine and the power-glow plugs must be in absolutely top condition. A weak battery will not be able to accomplish both tasks. Glow-plug circuits can be checked with special testing equipment to determine the condition of the plugs. A diesel-service shop should be able to do this. If the plugs check out poorly, they will not be able to generate enough heat to assist in starting and should be replaced.

Checking the Ether-Injection System

Some diesels use no glow plugs, but they may have an accessory that uses a canister of ether to assist in starting during severe cold weather. The canister, installed in a special holder device with an electrical solenoid, can shoot ether into the intake manifold of the engine when a dash-mounted button is depressed. If this system is disabled, starting the engine in very cold weather may be impossible. Ether is very flammable and should be used with care. If your diesel has such a device, it's best to leave service to the experts.

This chapter has covered basic on-the-road trouble situations and can help you diagnose malfunctions, which should be helpful whether you attempt to repair the problems yourself or ask for help from a professional mechanic. While most mechanics are honest, the motorist who is totally ignorant of the causes of a mechanical breakdown is a more likely target for overcharging. Many detailed automotive troubleshooting books are available in libraries and bookstores, if you are inclined to add to your knowledge of automotive troubleshooting.

Engine Replacement or Overhaul

O wners of tow vehicles and motorhomes that have accumulated many thousands of miles know they must soon decide whether to invest a sizable sum in a complete engine overhaul or to change vehicles. Many factors must be weighed, not the least of which are several that are purely personal:

1. Do you *like* your vehicle?
2. Does it serve your needs well (large enough, small enough, comfortable)?
3. Is its fuel economy acceptable? If not, will a new vehicle do measurably better? If yes, will it be sufficiently better to help justify the cost of the new vehicle?

Certainly, if you have some serious qualms about your present vehicle, sinking more money into it doesn't make sense. The wise move would be to buy a later model or a new vehicle.

Assuming, however, that you like the vehicle (in spite of the fact that its performance may have grown soggy and it may be using too much oil), the cost of repairs may be dramatically less than what you would have to spend on a later model or a new one. This is especially true if you're capable of doing some of the repair work on your present vehicle, which probably is relatively uncomplicated compared to later models that have more complex systems, including electronic fuel injection (EFI), computer-controlled ignition, and more complex emission controls.

Still another possibility is purchasing a vehicle that needs engine work with the idea of correcting its faults—or even improving performance beyond what the vehicle offered when it was new. The factors involved are not complex; they require diagnosis of your present vehicle's ills and what they will cost to repair at local rates for parts and labor, and then comparing those figures with the cost of a new vehicle.

EVALUATING THE LIFESPAN OF A VEHICLE

First, evaluate how much longer you would keep your present vehicle and how far you would drive it if it were put into top shape. It's not wise to undertake extensive repairs if you are liable to come down with a case of the new-vehicle "itch" soon afterward. Compare your uses for your present vehicle, if rejuvenated, to those for a later model or a new vehicle. Keep these thoughts in mind as this chapter progresses.

WEIGHING PRIORITIES

As an engine approaches 100,000 miles, it's usually time to weigh priorities. The overhaul decision may even be needed earlier, depending on how the vehicle was used. Some engines need overhauling by 70,000 to 80,000 miles if they have not been maintained properly. Other engines may go well beyond 100,000 miles. Follow the procedures described in Chapter 2, "Improving Fuel Economy and Performance," pages 39–50, to evaluate the condition of your engine.

The time to consider overhaul has arrived when performance has dropped substantially and the engine has begun to use oil at the rate of a quart in 500 miles or less. But the decision is not based on these factors alone. Arrange for evaluation of cylinder compression and crankcase pressure to determine if valve repairs will suffice or if a complete overhaul is needed. If the results are bad, you must decide if you want to keep the vehicle or to move on to a newer one.

Engines having 350 cubic inches of displacement (cid) or less are not prone to sudden failure when their condition deteriorates, but the large-displacement motors sometimes fail catastrophically and may leave you stranded in a strange area. It's best to analyze engine condition and perform an overhaul, if one is deemed necessary, before you're forced to do so under undesirable conditions.

Vehicle Replacement or Engine Rebuild?

In making the choice between purchasing a new vehicle and keeping the old one, the parameters for rebuilt or remanufactured engines include:

- Type of use, such as towing
- Weight of the trailer or motorhome
- Percentage of towing miles if a tow vehicle is involved
- Areas of travel (mountainous terrain versus predominantly level terrain, and percentages for each)
- Your level of satisfaction with performance and mileage of your present vehicle

Making the Right Engine Choice

If you decide to keep the vehicle and rejuvenate the engine, you'll face three choices:

1. A rebuilt engine from a local shop
2. A remanufactured engine from the vehicle factory
3. A new engine from the vehicle factory

The quality of the engine, the price, and the warranty coverage are three important factors in choosing the right engine as well. Check rebuild prices at well-respected local shops, and find out what the local new-vehicle dealer charges for new as well as remanufactured engines.

If your choice is a new engine—basically a factory stock-production item that is dependable but expensive—it should provide the same service as the previous engine if it has the same specifications. Many original engines have, however, been superseded by others with slightly different specifications. Cam characteristics may be different and compression may have been reduced, which could reduce performance and efficiency. The engine may or may not include specially hardened valves and valve seats, which give the valves the durability needed when using unleaded gasoline.

While a factory-sponsored remanufactured engine may be lower in cost, even though the factories offer assurances of quality, use of low-quality components can compromise its effectiveness in the same manner as such components can compromise a rebuild at a local shop. The GM Targetmaster remanufactured engines, for example, did not have a reputation for good quality and performance. In any rebuild or remanufacture, there can be a wide range of component prices. Piston rings, for example, can range from $20 to $100 per set. Varying quality also occurs in bearings, pistons, and other engine components. Internal parts that should have been replaced may have been retained, such as camshafts that may have been reground rather than replaced with new components. Thus, quality is critical when choosing between the two types of rebuilt engines.

Local engine-overhaul prices will vary with location, primarily because labor rates may vary from a low of about $30 an hour to a high of about $50. Regardless of the source of the engine, the do-it-yourselfer might consider doing the removal and installation work. Price comparisons are always a good idea, but one must also compare the reputation of the company and of the parts used in the engine.

THE REBUILD

In evaluating the purchase of a rebuilt engine, the most important decision is your choice of a rebuilding shop. The advantages of a rebuild may include quality and the ability of the shop to correct faults in the original engine design. If you cannot select a rebuilder in whom you have confidence, the reliability advantage of a factory-remanufactured engine may be a very strong point. The factory engines—whether new or remanufactured—also have the advantage of nationwide warranty coverage, as do some engines rebuilt by shops that subscribe to nationwide warranty programs. Even in the absence of such a formal program, a responsible local shop will compensate the vehicle owner for warranty work done at other locations.

The Importance of Cleanliness in the Rebuild

Proper cleaning and magnetic inspection are critical to make sure dirty or defective components are not reinstalled. The cleaning is done in a solvent-filled hot tank and the engine must be protected thereafter (see Figure 4.1). It's critical that assem-

Figure 4.1
Engine overhaul must be performed in a clean environment, and the engine must be protected until it's fully assembled and installed.

Figure 4.2
When magnetic force is applied, colored metal particles are attracted to any cracks in the metal surface—a cylinder head in this case.

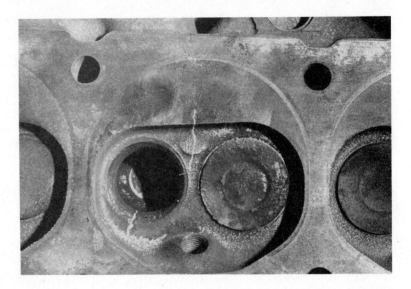

bly of an engine be performed in a clean environment because dirt and dust can cause serious abrasion during the high-friction conditions when an overhauled engine is started for the first time.

Components such as connecting rods and the crankshaft should be checked for cracks with the magnetic processes Magnaflux or Zyglo, in which fluorescent magnetic particles or a dye penetrant are spread over the part to be checked. When electricity is passed through the part, the magnetic particles gather around any crack (Figure 4.2), and the fluorescent material will stand out when viewed under a black light. When the dye is used, capillary attraction draws the dye into any existing cracks. A developer is then sprayed on the part, and it is viewed under a black light.

Boring is done when cylinder wear exceeds certain parameters, usually .009 inch. The number refers to **taper**—the amount of wear that occurs at the top of the piston's stroke (where maximum stress occurs), compared to the original bore, which is measured at the bottom of the cylinder. It's imperative that boring be done properly—that all cylinders are bored perfectly in alignment with the crankshaft throws (Figure 4.3).

Decking of the block is essential, but it is often ignored by some rebuilders, as well as by factory-sponsored remanufac-

Figure 4.3
Cylinders must be bored in proper alignment with crankshaft throws.

Figure 4.4
When one bank of a V-8 block is higher than the other, a special milling machine is used to create uniformity.

turers. The reason for decking is that the two cylinder banks of a V-8 engine are rarely uniform from the factory. Thus, the distance between the top of the piston at the top of its stroke and the top of the block may be different on one bank than the other, causing engine imbalance and greater stress under heavy throttle. The block should be milled to create uniform deck height (Figure 4.4).

Piston Choices

Only a few years ago we had a very limited number of piston-ring choices. Cast-iron rings that would almost guarantee immediate seating (wearing in) to cylinders were usually used. However, they did not provide extended service life, and they were highly susceptible to breakage due to preignition or detonation (engine "ping"). Chrome-plated steel rings also were available, and they were much stronger. However, they frequently did not seat, which required replacement.

The best piston-ring choice nowadays is ductile iron with chrome facing and moly inserts (Figure 4.5). These rings provide immediate seating and extended life.

The choice of pistons is controversial, with some shops choosing cast pistons to lower cost, while other shops insisting on the increased durability of forged pistons. A **cast piston** is created when molten (liquid) aluminum is poured into a mold. A **forged piston** is created when a hot aluminum ingot is forced under pressure into a mold, creating a denser structure that is capable of withstanding greater abuse, such as that which happens when an engine is under heavy load and preig-

Figure 4.5
The choice of piston rings determines the ease of seating, as well as durability.

nition or detonation occurs. The piston is subjected to intense shock that reverberates through the entire engine.

Many different pistons are available in the aftermarket, and prices vary widely. In cast pistons, use of the factory-original parts is advisable. The cost is greater, but well worth it. The factory pistons are of a conformatic design that allows closer piston-to-cylinder wall clearances. When these pistons expand with heat, they maintain their original cylinder-wall clearance, while also providing increased strength.

Forged pistons are considerably more expensive and are worthwhile when higher compression ratios are desired or the engine is used in extremely heavy service. They will provide additional protection against failure. The only negative aspect of forged pistons is that they require additional cylinder-wall clearance, resulting in a little more piston noise. The clearance factor, as well as their typically shorter skirts, may also reduce piston-ring life.

What to Expect in a Top-Quality Engine Rebuild

A top-quality engine rebuild or remanufacture should include:

- Cleaning and magnetic inspection of all parts
- Boring each cylinder to match the individual piston assembly
- Cylinder honing
- Moly-impregnated piston rings fitted precisely according to ring manufacturer's instructions
- Precision crankshaft grinding and polishing
- Connecting rods checked for trueness, pin-end roundness, cracks
- Cylinder heads, block, and intake manifold checked for warpage, cracks, excessive valve-guide wear
- High-volume oil pump

- Double-row timing-chain assembly (except Ford 460)
- New camshaft selected to provide maximum torque at moderate RPM levels to coordinate performance with personal driving requirements
- Deck heights (piston-to-top-of-block clearance) checked and corrected if necessary
- Engine components balanced
- Valves and valve seats resurfaced properly
- Use of spring-loaded Teflon valve seals
- Use of nickel-alloy valve seats and heavy-duty exhaust valves.
- New valve springs

Figure 4.6
Piston ring-end gaps should be staggered to prevent leakage of combustion gases into the block.

Fitting Components

Precision fit of piston rings to pistons is essential for proper durability, lubrication, and oil control (Figure 4.6). The ring manufacturer's specific instructions should be followed. The instructions specify how to stagger ring-end gaps so combustion gases will not be leaked into the lower engine block.

Clearance between crankshaft bearings and journals should be measured precisely for proper fit, including roundness, and Plastigage should be used during assembly to assure a proper fit. Most crankshafts are ground .010 inch smaller, which is called "10 under." Some are ground 20 (.020 inch) or 30 (.030 inch) under, which should be avoided. The reason is that bearings for 20-under and 30-under crankshafts usually are not as durable.

Excessive clearance between crankshaft and piston-rod bearings and their journals will reduce oil pressure and can result in excessive oil thrown into cylinders, thereby causing excessive oil consumption.

Valves and Seats

With the virtual disappearance of lead from gasoline, any engine replacement or overhaul should have specially hardened valves and valve seats. It's possible to go a step further on valve durability by installing nickel-alloy valve-seat inserts (Figure 4.7) and specially hardened valves. The special inserts are exceptionally hard and do not erode with the absence of lead in gasoline, as do valve seats of lesser durability.

Two methods are used to install the inserts. In both cases, pockets are precision-machined into the valve seats to accept the inserts. One method of installation involves heating the cylinder heads, which causes the machined recesses to expand, and reducing the temperature of the inserts, which causes them to contract. When temperatures equalize, a tight fit is created. In another method, slightly oversized inserts, coated with industrial-strength Loctite, are press fitted into the valve seat bores. In both cases, precise machining and exacting installation procedures are required.

Figure 4.7
With lead having virtually
disappeared from gasoline,
specially hardened valve
seats are a necessity.

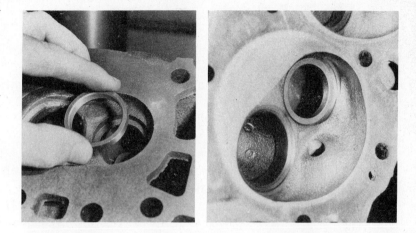

After the valve-seat inserts are installed, the inserts must be machined properly, which involves grinding them on three different surface angles for proper seal with the valve (Figure 4.8). The lower angle (deepest) is ground at a 70-degree angle, the middle at a 45-degree angle, and the top at 15 degrees. Only the middle surface contacts the valve face; the other two angles are designed to create proper flow characteristics. The width of the 45-degree surface should be about $1/16$ inch for intake-valve seats and $3/32$ inch for exhaust-valve seats. Valve faces are ground to 45 degrees to match the seats.

Figure 4.8
Valve seats must be
ground at three angles for
maximum durability.

Figure 4.9
Spring-loaded Teflon valve-guide seals help insure against oil leakage.

Valve-Guide Clearance

Valve guide-to-stem clearances should be precisely checked because excessive clearance can result, not only in reduced valve life, but in oil consumption, even when improved valve-guide seals are utilized (See Figure 4.9). Factory specs on valve guide-to-stem clearance should be used. Knurling should not be used take up excess valve guide-to-stem clearance if the clearance beyond specifications is in excess of .002 inch. **Knurling** is a method of scoring the inside of the valve guide, creating a ridge that reduces clearance between the guide and the valve stem and providing increased lubrication. However, when knurling is used to correct excessive valve-guide wear, the guide will soon return to its previous size.

Valve grinding also is critical to good engine durability. Valves should be ground at the three different angles commonly prescribed. Intake-valve seat width should be $\frac{1}{16}$ inch and exhaust seat width $\frac{3}{32}$ inch. The thickness of the valve head (edge of the valve) should be a minimum of $\frac{3}{64}$-inch exhaust and $\frac{1}{16}$-inch intake after grinding, or the valve should be replaced. The cylinder-head castings should be checked closely for cracks around valve seats.

Cam Selection

Few RV owners can resist the claims by aftermarket cam manufacturers of dramatic increases in power and mileage. In fact, cam design is a tradeoff. All too often, cams advertised as increasing low-RPM torque actually raise the powerband of the engine, reducing torque in the important 2,000- to 2,500-RPM range. Those that do improve low-end torque may do so by raising cylinder pressures, which can lead to preignition and the need for higher-octane fuel. When in doubt, stick with a factory-original cam or one that has similar or identical specifications. If the shop performing the work cannot offer specifics about characteristics of the aftermarket cam they propose to install, insist that they buy an OEM cam.

New-Engine Startup

Before starting a new engine or one that has been overhauled, it's best to turn the oil-pump drive to circulate oil. The oil pump is driven off the bottom of the distributor shaft. Wear should not be excessive if the shop has used assembly lube properly and the oil system is primed before starting.

Spark timing and air–fuel mixtures should be calibrated correctly for each mode of operation. A rebuild should be accompanied by an all-inclusive warranty of one year or 12,000 miles. A program should also be provided for retorquing and periodic engine inspection. Specific engine-oil and fuel-octane recommendations should be made.

Other Engine Components

Other engine-related components that should be checked, reconditioned, or replaced include the radiator, the alternator, the motor mounts, and the starter. A new transmission input-shaft seal should be installed while the engine is already removed, simplifying the seal installation.

THE CHASSIS

Transmission

The decision to keep one's present vehicle rather than trading for a later or new model may involve more than just the engine. Automatic transmissions typically will considerably outlast engines unless the transmission has been subjected to excessive heat. Use of an auxiliary cooler is necessary for most tow vehicles unless trailer weight is quite low. The transmission oil and filter should have been changed at least every 20,000 miles.

If the transmission shows signs of excessive wear, such as erratic shifting, slipping when cold, and excessive particles of metal and frictional materials in the pan, the cost of an overhaul must be included in the decision between repair or overhaul of the present vehicle and purchase of a new one.

Again, rates for transmission overhaul vary from one section of the United States to another, but it's important to choose a shop that has a good reputation for dependability and offers a nationwide warranty. Thus, if problems occur while traveling, the warranty will cover repairs made locally.

When considering a transmission overhaul, it's important to correct any factory defects or weaknesses. These are fairly well known to transmission-repair shops that do sizable volumes of work, and especially those that cater to performance-car enthusiasts.

Manual transmissions rarely are a durability factor until well after the 100,000-mile mark, and overhaul procedures usually are straightforward as dictated in factory-service manuals. Replacement of a clutch might be considered as part of a vehicle-rejuvenation program.

Other Components

The vehicle's front suspension and brakes should be evaluated for wear. Front-suspension repairs can be costly, as can brakes, if linings or pads have been allowed to wear down to metal, scoring drums or rotors. Also consider having shock absorbers replaced.

Rear axles that have been properly maintained seldom need work until well after 100,000 miles. The lubricant should be changed about every 30,000 miles.

Factory-Remanufactured Engines

General Motors, Ford, and Chrysler offer new as well as remanufactured engines. By checking with the various sources, you should have the prices, methods, and specifications for comparison. When evaluating a new or factory-remanufactured engine, keep in mind the deficiencies, if any, of your engine when it was new—especially performance and mileage. A new engine from the manufacturer probably will offer about the same levels of performance and mileage.

Chrysler

The corporation's remanufactured-engine program covers a variety of engines, specifically including the 318 and 360 V-8s commonly used in trucks and vans that tow trailers. A Chrysler spokesman said the remanufactured engines are "long blocks"—minus intake manifold, carburetor, and accessories—and are built to original new-engine specifications using parts from the same manufacturers who supply parts used on new-engine assembly lines. The remanufactured engines have applicability over several model years, depending on the emissions specifications Chrysler is attempting to meet. Model year availability varies. The engines are sold on a dealer-exhange basis, requiring that a core engine be turned in.

Warranty coverage is 12 months or 12,000 miles, and it does not cover motorhomes due to the labor costs of removal and reinstallation.

Ford

Ford remanufactured engines are built by twenty-five authorized, franchised shops through the nation, and the engines are sold through Ford and Lincoln/Mercury dealers. Pricing varies, but generally is 55% to 60% of the cost of a new engine through a Ford dealer.

Warranty for short blocks is 90 days or 4,000 miles, and for long blocks it's 12 months or 12,000 miles, including engines for mini-motorhome chassis but not Class A motorhomes. An extended service plan offers coverage for 24 months/24,000 miles or 36 months/36,000 miles.

Ford-authorized remanufacturing shops are required to adhere to specific standards. For example, cylinders cannot be bored beyond specific limits, and the shops are supplied a list of specific parts that *must* be replaced. About 90% of the parts used during the rebuild adhere to the specifications used for new engines, according to a Ford spokesman.

General Motors

Mr. Goodwrench remanufactured engines are built to the same specifications as new engines except for oversized pistons and reground crankshafts, according to a General Motors spokesman. Parts are of the same type as those used in new engines and are supplied by the same companies. New components for the 454 (Mark 4 engine), for example, include bearings, hard exhaust valve-seat inserts, intake valves, valve-stem oil seals, all gaskets, rear oil seals, connecting rod nuts, pistons, piston rings, oil-pump screen assembly, camshaft, cam sprocket, crankshaft sprocket, timing chain, valve lifters, rocker arms and nuts, main bearing bolts, head bolts, and cup plugs for water jackets and oil galleys.

Engines are updated with improvements that may have occurred in years subsequent to the year your original engine was built, according to the GM spokesman. Warranty coverage on light-duty engines is 36 months or 50,000 miles except motorhome engines. Check with Chevrolet or GMC dealers on warranty coverage for motorhome engines.

In the final analysis, the decision to buy a new vehicle or to renovate the old one will involve more than finances. There may be a definite reluctance to part with a trusty vehicle that has taken us many a mile and to many wonderful travel experiences. Few vehicles are so fraught with defects that they cannot be renovated at a fraction of the cost of a new one. So either decision—new or rebuilt—can be a satisfactory one.

CHAPTER 5

Understanding Electronic Fuel Injection

W hen you open the hood on a late-model vehicle, the engine is hidden by a maze of vacuum hoses, wires, cables, and a variety of unidentifiable components. And you know there is a black box somewhere that includes a computer to monitor and control fuel delivery, ignition timing, and a multitude of other engine and vehicle functions.

Initially, it would appear that diagnosis and repair must be left to experts who are trained and specially equipped to deal with such high-tech equipment. These procedures require expensive scan tools, scopes, and exhaust-gas analyzers. But all is not lost. The home mechanic can still do a considerable amount of troubleshooting and repair, given a little specific information and a few simple tools. Even if you don't intend ever to touch your electronic fuel-injection (EFI) system, knowledge of its principles and how the components work can be valuable in diagnosing on-the-road problems and finding help, not to mention improving your ability to assess the validity of a repair bill.

WHAT IS FUEL INJECTION?

Fuel injection, a system designed to meter the correct amounts of fuel into the engine during varying modes of operation, has been with us for a long time. In fact, airplanes have been equipped with it since the dawn of aviation with the Wright brothers in 1903. These early systems were rather crude, mechanically controlled devices. With the advent of solid-state electronics, electrons and transistors have taken over the job.

Electronically controlled fuel injection has gradually replaced carburetion and mechanical fuel injection as the system of choice because of its greater precision in providing the correct ratios of fuel and air under a wide variety of operating conditions. Engines will run on a wide range of air–fuel ratios, varying from about 8:1 to 20:1 by weight. However, the ideal (stoichiometric, for you chemistry buffs) mixture for low emissions is about 14.7 pounds of air for every pound of gasoline. Any more or less than this and emissions rise substantially.

The first electronic systems metered the fuel much like the current ones, but they didn't monitor the exhaust. Increasingly stringent emission and fuel-economy regulations have prompted the vehicle manufacturers to introduce **computer-controlled feedback** systems, first on cars (most 1980 models had them) and later on trucks and vans. These systems use oxygen sensors to sniff the exhaust and tell the computer whether the fuel-metering program has missed the mark and the engine needs more or less fuel for a certain amount of air.

HOW DOES IT WORK?

Carburetors rely on the small difference between atmospheric pressure and the partial vacuum inside the intake manifold to meter and atomize fuel. Fuel injection sprays (injects) fuel under higher pressure into the airstream entering the engine, hence its name.

Each major manufacturer has its own type of fuel injection, each of which uses a number of sensors to determine the

Think of an electronically controlled feedback fuel-injection system as a circle or loop.

amount of fuel needed to mix with the air going into the engine. A computer receives the signals from the various sensors and tells the fuel injectors how much fuel to spray.

Think of an electronically controlled feedback fuel-injection system as a circle or loop. When the engine is started, the oxygen sensor in the exhaust is cold and therefore unable to tell the computer what is happening. This condition is known as **open loop** because the circle is incomplete. When the engine warms up to normal temperature, the oxygen sensor starts working (at about 600°F), and the circle is completed. This is known as **closed loop**.

How does a typical system work? As the driver steps on the accelerator pedal, throttle plates in the throttle body open, allowing additional air to enter the intake manifold. As the air rushes into the manifold, the air pressure inside the manifold changes. Sensors detect this change and pass the information on to the computer. When the computer gets the signals, it orders the fuel injectors to spray more fuel. Then, downstream in the exhaust manifold, the oxygen sensor sniffs the exhaust. If it finds an overabundance of fuel, it tells the computer to cut back on the amount of fuel being sprayed into the engine. This monitoring occurs constantly. Each time the oxygen sensor detects a rich fuel mixture, it signals the computer to reduce the amount of fuel being injected. Corrections occur many times per second, allowing very accurate control of fuel flow. This precise metering is necessary to allow reduction-type catalytic converters to work efficiently in ridding the exhaust of nitrogen, carbon monoxide, and unburned hydrocarbon oxides.

THROTTLE-BODY VERSUS PORT-INJECTION SYSTEMS

There are two basic fuel-injection designs commonly used on domestic trucks and vans:

1. **Throttle-body** (or **single-point**) fuel injection (Figure 5.1)
2. **Port-type** (or **multi-point**) fuel injection (Figure 5.2)

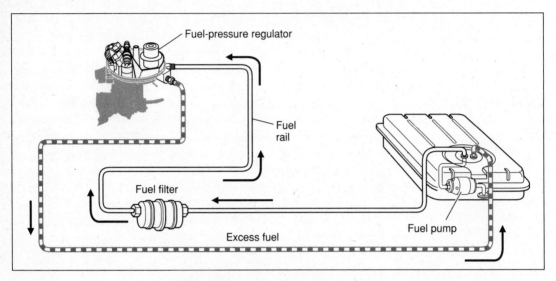

Figure 5.1
In a single-point electronic fuel-injection system, fuel is injected into the
engine at the throttle body, positioned on the intake manifold. Excess fuel
is returned to tank.

Both types work on the same basic principles. However,
throttle-body units more closely resemble carburetors in appearance and function, with the fuel being mixed with air in the
throttle bore.

With carburetors and throttle-body systems, the inner cylinders tend to get more fuel than the outer ones. This imbalance
results in lower fuel economy and higher exhaust emissions.
Engine designers try to compensate by supplying the inner cylinders with extra fuel so that the outer ones don't starve and
incur lean misfire.

Port-type fuel-injection systems also have throttle bodies;
however, the fuel is not mixed with the air at that point. Thottle-
body systems control the air–fuel mixture more accurately than
carburetors, are less prone to injector clogging, and cost less
initially than port-type injection.

On port-type fuel-injection systems, the fuel injectors spray
fuel into the intake ports just upstream of the intake valves,
making this system more efficient because each cylinder gets
the same amount of fuel.

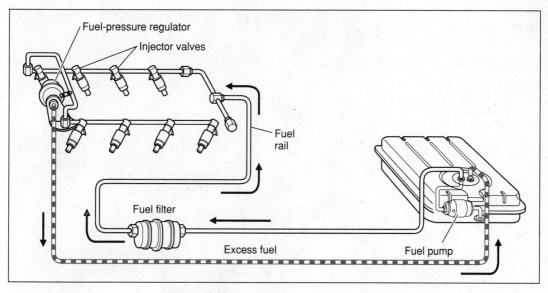

Figure 5.2
In a multi-point electronic fuel-injection system, fuel is injected at each cylinder, allowing precise metering.

Statistics show that if the computer lasts the first six months, it will probably outlast the vehicle.

The downside of port-type fuel injection is the higher initial cost and greater susceptibility to injector clogging. The smaller orifices (compared to throttle-body systems) may become partially clogged with fuel deposits, and the spray pattern slowly deteriorates, resulting in driveability problems.

Specially formulated fuel detergents have been added to most brands of gasoline to combat this problem, and nozzle designs have recently been changed to resist the tendency to clog. Several companies sell gasoline additives for your fuel tank that they claim will unclog injectors. If all else fails, many repair shops have special injector-cleaning devices that chemically clean the injection nozzles on the vehicle. If you suspect that your engine is running rough because the injectors are clogged, have them cleaned rather than replaced. Your wallet will thank you.

Computer control units don't fail very often. In fact, they are one of the least common causes of engine malfunction. Statistics show that if the computer lasts the first six months, it will probably outlast the vehicle.

Figure 5.3
A barometric-pressure
sensor monitors ambient
air pressure and allows the
system to compensate for
changes in air density.

THE FUEL-SYSTEM COMPONENTS

The Barometric-Pressure Sensor

Weather and altitude (air density) changes require alterations in
fuel mixture. The **barometric-pressure sensor** is used on
some systems to inform the computer of changes in ambient air
pressure so adjustments can be made to compensate for air
density (Figure 5.3).

The Check-Engine Light

Also known as the "service engine soon" or "power-loss" light,
the **check-engine** light is dash mounted to inform the driver
when the computer detects a malfunction in the circuits under
its control (Figure 5.4). The light should come on briefly as a
bulb check every time the engine is started.

The computer can only detect a short, ground, or opening in the specific circuit. It cannot pinpoint the problem to a certain wire or sensor. If a problem is detected, a trouble code is set in the computer's memory and the light will go on. If the problem goes away or is repaired, the computer is designed to shut off the lamp after a preset number of engine starts. See also pages 119 and 121 for a listing of trouble codes related to the check-engine light for various vehicle brands.

The Coolant-Temperature Sensor

The **coolant-temperature sensor** (**CTS**) is a temperature-sensing resistor (thermistor) (Figure 5.5). Cold engines need more fuel than warm ones. The CTS serves the same purpose as the choke on a carbureted engine, telling the computer how cold (or warm) the engine is by changing resistance as the engine-coolant temperature changes. As the temperature goes down, resistance goes up. The computer lengthens the "open" time of the injectors for a cold engine. The CTS, usually located in the intake manifold near the thermostat, is screwed into a coolant passage and has two wires connected to it.

Figure 5.5
Signals from the coolant-temperature sensor cause the control system to provide richer air–fuel mixtures when the engine is not up to normal operating temperature.

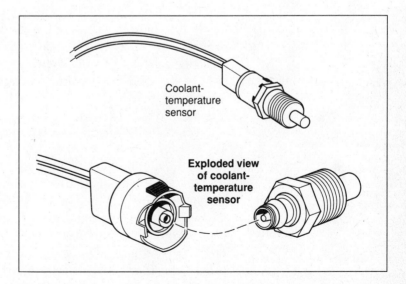

Coolant-temperature sensor

Exploded view of coolant-temperature sensor

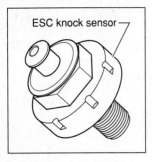

Figure 5.6
A detonation sensor monitors engine for spark-knock ("ping") and causes the computer to reduce spark advance.

The Detonation Sensor

The **detonation** (knock) **sensor** converts mechanical energy (vibration) into electrical signals (Figure 5.6). When the engine starts to knock or "ping," this block-mounted sensor generates a small voltage signal that tells the computer to retard the ignition timing and/or enrich the fuel mixture until the knock goes away. Then it will gradually return to the original setting until the sensor once again detects knock or pinging. To check its operation, connect a timing light and, with the engine running, tap on the engine block with a hammer. If the timing retards, the knock sensor is working.

The Electric Fuel Pump

Most electronically controlled systems have an **electric fuel pump** mounted inside the fuel tank, combined with the sending unit for the fuel gauge (Figure 5.7). Tank-mounting the fuel pump reduces vapor lock tendency by pressurizing the entire fuel system. Additional pressure raises the vaporization point of the fuel. Some vehicles have an additional pump mounted on the chassis between the tank and engine.

If the engine won't start and has good spark, check the sound of the fuel pump. Listen for the characteristic whirring noise near the fuel tank while an assistant operates the starter. Remove the gas-filler cap to hear better, if necessary.

If the fuel pump doesn't run, check for voltage at the pump's electrical terminals while the engine is cranking. Also check the fuse and the relay(s) before you replace the fuel pump.

If your vehicle seems to be starving for fuel (surging, bucking, backfiring, etc.) or seems to be getting too much fuel (black, sooty spark-plug tips and/or exhaust, poor fuel mileage, etc.), perform a fuel-pressure test. Always double-check the fuel level by thumping on the bottom of the tank(s)!

On Dodge and General Motors throttle-body systems, connect a T-fitting into the fuel line going to the throttle body (the one with the filter). Don't connect it to the return line; you'll get a false reading. On Ford systems, connect the gauge to the

Figure 5.7
An electric fuel pump creates fuel pressure ranging from 9 to 45 psi, depending on the design of the system.

pressure-checking port on the fuel-injector rail. These have "Shrader-type" valves with dust caps; you must have the right fittings for them! Use a gauge designed for fuel-pressure testing that has a rating higher than the maximum pressure specified for your engine. Dodge calls for 14.5 psi fuel pressure, Ford allows a range from 35 to 45 psi, and GM requires 9 to 13 psi.

If the pressure is too high, check for a restricted return line. If the return line is open, replace the fuel-pressure regulator.

If the pressure is too low, look for a restricted line, hose, pump, or fuel filter (don't forget the one in the tank). The fuel-pressure regulator could also be at fault. Momentarily pinch the fuel-return hose where it runs between the engine and frame. If the pressure rises rapidly, the regulator is probably bad.

The Electronic Control Module

The **electronic control module** (**ECM**) is commonly called the **computer** (Figure 5.8). (Dodge calls it a **Single Module Engine Control** [**SMEC**]). The computer is the brain of the fuel-injection system and uses input from all the sensors to determine how long the injectors must spray fuel. It is usually contained in a metal box located within the dash, behind a kick panel, under the driver's seat, or in a protected location in the engine compartment.

The ECM may go into a "limp-in" mode if the signals from certain critical sensors are outside of preset design parameters. The computer will substitute fixed average values and disregard the out-of-range information the faulty sensor provides. The "check engine" light will come on, and power may be reduced. Problems of this nature should be corrected as soon as possible.

Most intermittent problems are caused by loose or corroded connections or damaged wiring. The only way to locate such problems is to duplicate the conditions that caused the problem. Note any recent repairs or maintenance which may have disturbed connections. Since the computer rarely fails, if you suspect it has, get a professional to check it before you buy a new one.

Figure 5.8
An electronic control module includes a computer that collects input from various sensors and controls the amount of fuel injected.

Figure 5.9
A fuel injector sprays fuel into intake passages; the amount is controlled by the length of time the computer keeps the injector open.

Fuel Injectors

Fuel injectors are basically spray nozzles with electric-solenoid-operated pintle valves (Figure 5.9). When the computer sends a voltage signal to the fuel injector, the solenoid opens a path for the pressurized fuel to spray into the engine. When the voltage is shut off, the fuel flow is shut off.

Throttle-body injectors can be checked quickly by removing the air cleaner and looking at the injectors while an assistant turns the ignition key to "on" and cranks the engine. Fuel should spray out. If it doesn't, disconnect the wiring harness from the injectors and connect a common 12-volt DC test light (or special "noid-light" tester) to the terminals. The light should pulse when the key is turned on. This means the electrical portion of the system is working. A steady light or no light indicates electrical malfunctions.

Port-type fuel injectors can be electrically checked in a similar manner. However, you can't view the fuel spraying out as you can on a throttle body. Instead, remove a spark plug to see if it is dry or wet with fuel.

The Fuel Filter

On fuel-injected vehicles, the **fuel filter** is important because the system is so sensitive to dirt and water (Figure 5.10). The slightest speck of dirt can plug an injector nozzle. The fuel filter is usually located under the vehicle along the inside of a frame rail near the fuel tank. Most manufacturers recommend filter replacement at least every 30,000 miles; however, many mechanics suggest more frequent replacement.

Warning: The fuel system is under pressure, even when the engine is not running! Read the precautions in this chapter, and follow the procedure for relieving fuel pressure before loosening any lines. Always use the exact replacement filter; don't risk a fire by using a substitute.

When loosening the fuel lines at either end of the filter, use the proper line wrenches to avoid rounding off the hex shapes

Figure 5.10
A highly effective fuel filter keeps dirt out of delicate parts in an EFI system.

at the ends of the filter and use a backup wrench to prevent twisting the fuel line.

Pour the contents of the old filter from the filter inlet into a clean container (not glass) and check for water and other contamination. Note the arrow on the filter, which indicates the direction of fuel flow, and always check for leaks after startup.

The Fuel-Pressure Regulator

The **fuel-pressure regulator** keeps the fuel at a preset constant pressure to prevent fluctuations in the fuel mixture that would change the mixture (Figure 5.11). The regulator maintains a constant pressure by returning the excess fuel to the fuel tank.

On Dodge and General Motors vehicles, the regulator is mounted in the throttle body; on Fords, the regulator is mounted at the downstream end of the fuel-injector rail.

Figure 5.11
A fuel-pressure regulator allows varying amounts of fuel to be returned to the tank, thereby maintaining proper pressure at fuel injectors.

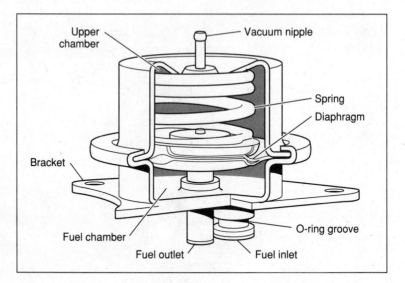

On port-injected vehicles, the fuel-pressure regulator has another function. Since fuel is sprayed into the intake manifold (or ports), a substantial difference between pressure at the ports and in the intake manifold must be maintained. This is accomplished with a vacuum line that connects the regulator to a source of intake manifold vacuum to compensate for the changes in manifold pressure due to engine load. This diaphragm may be checked with a hand-pump vacuum tester. Replace the unit if it won't hold vacuum.

The Idle Air-Control Valve

The **idle air-control valve** (IAC), a computer-controlled air bypass that maintains idle speed at a predetermined rate, consists of an electric motor connected to a variable orifice (Figure 5.12). The IAC increases the size of the air passage to raise the idle in response to signals from the computer. This occurs, for example, when the engine is cold, the automatic transmission is put in gear, or the air conditioning is switched on.

Idle speed is computer controlled and is not adjustable. If the

Figure 5.12
The idle air-control valve maintains idle speed at a predetermined RPM.

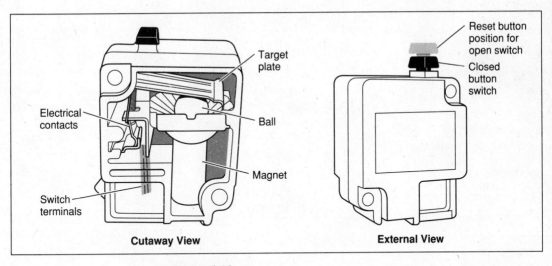

Figure 5.13
The inertia switch senses vehicle impact in an accident and shuts off the fuel pump to prevent a fire.

idle speed is too fast, check for vacuum leaks around the intake manifold, leaking hoses, and throttle-body base gaskets.

The Inertia Switch

The **inertia switch** shuts off the fuel pump in the event of an accident (Figure 5.13). Whenever the fuel pump is inoperative, the inertia switch should be checked and reset if necessary. See your owner's manual for procedure and switch location.

The Manifold Absolute-Pressure Sensor

Figure 5.14
The manifold absolute-pressure sensor monitors changes in the partial vacuum inside the intake manifold.

The **manifold absolute-pressure sensor** (**MAP**) keeps the computer informed of changes in intake manifold pressure (partial vacuum) by varying resistance in relation to changes in pressure in the manifold (Figure 5.14). As the engine load increases, the manifold pressure increases (or conversely, vacuum decreases).

Figure 5.15
Input from the manifold air-temperature sensor allows the computer to change air–fuel ratios in response to changes in air density.

The Manifold Air-Temperature Sensor

The **manifold air-temperature sensor** (**MAT**) sensor (also known as the air charge temperature sensor) monitors the temperature of the air coming into the intake manifold (Figure 5.15). Colder air is more dense and requires more fuel than hot air. Since the MAT sensor is a thermistor (resistance varies with temperature), it alters the voltage signal going to the computer in relation to the temperature of the incoming air.

The Oxygen Sensor

The **O² sensor** (Ford calls it an exhaust-gas oxygen sensor) is the component that allows the computer to know what is coming out the exhaust and to make corrections based on that information (Figure 5.16). Every feedback or closed-loop system must have one.

A zirconium element produces a small voltage in the presence of oxygen in the exhaust. This voltage, which will vary from 0 to 0.9 volts, with .450 volts indicating an ideal fuel mixture of 14.7:1, can be measured with a digital voltmeter probe inserted into the back of the oxygen-sensor connector. The voltage should constantly vary with the engine running; if it doesn't, replace the sensor.

Oxygen sensors are readily identified; they have a base similar in appearance to a spark plug and screw into the exhaust manifold or the exhaust pipe just downstream of the manifolds. Earlier sensors have only one wire coming from them; later models have additional wires for a heating element that gets them working sooner.

Most oxygen sensors require replacement every 30,000 to 50,000 miles. They are easily replaced, and you can save a considerable amount of money by doing it yourself. Be sure the threads are coated with an anti-seize compound (Loctite 771-64 or equivalent); new sensors should have some on already. Refer to your owner's manual for the replacement interval recommended by the manufacturer of your vehicle.

Figure 5.16
Input to the computer from the oxygen sensor is among data used to control combustion.

Note: Oxygen sensors may be ruined by the use of certain automotive silicone sealers; read the label to determine if it is compatible with oxygen sensors.

The Throttle-Position Sensor

The **throttle-position sensor** (**TPS**), which tells the computer the rate of throttle opening and how far the throttle is open, works by changing resistance as the throttle opens and closes (Figure 5.17). This allows the computer to enrich the fuel mixture when the throttle is opened suddenly, preventing hesitation.

The most common symptom of a faulty TPS is hesitation when the throttle is opened quickly. Two quick checks may be made with a digital voltmeter. With the ignition on:

1. Test for a reference voltage at the TPS (usually 5 volts). If voltage isn't present, trace and repair the wiring.
2. Check for a smooth voltage change as the throttle is opened and closed. If the voltage changes abruptly and unevenly, the TPS is probably faulty.

The initial (or base) setting of the TPS is also critical for good performance. Normally the TPS doesn't require adjustment. However, whenever it is replaced or when diagnosis indicates a problem, an adjustment should be performed following the factory-recommended procedure exactly. Since special tools are needed that are beyond the scope of the home mechanic, have this work done by a dealer or fuel-injection specialist.

The Vane Airflow Meter

The **vane airflow meter** (**VAF**), used on port-type systems (Ford trucks) only, measures the flow of air into the engine with an internal flap connected to a potentiometer (or variable resistor) (Figure 5.18). Air temperature is also monitored by a built-in sensor.

Figure 5.17
A computer monitors the position of the throttle and its rate of change in position via the throttle-position sensor.

Figure 5.18
The amount of airflow into the engine is measured by the vane airflow meter.

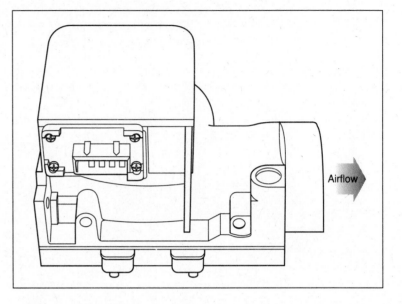

The VAF meter is mounted between the throttle-control valve (or throttle body) and the air cleaner. A reference voltage is sent through the potentiometer and back to the computer. When the driver depresses the accelerator pedal, the increased volume of air entering the engine forces the flap to open wider, thus changing the resistance. The computer uses this information in determining how much fuel the engine needs.

The Vehicle-Speed Sensor

Some vehicles are equipped with a **vehicle-speed sensor** (Dodge calls it a distance sensor) that tells the computer how fast the vehicle is going (Figure 5.19). These sensors are usually mounted somewhere on the speedometer cable or on the back of the speedometer. When the vehicle is moving, a pulsing signal is generated. The computer uses the information provided by the speed sensor to control functions such as exhaust-gas recirculation and torque-converter lockup (on automatic-transmission-equipped vehicles).

Figure 5.19
Road speed is monitored by the vehicle-speed sensor for input to the computer that affects emissions and transmission torque converter lockup.

DODGE TROUBLESHOOTING

Dodge trucks and vans use a throttle-body fuel-injection system. The computer (or SMEC) is usually located in the engine compartment adjacent to the left fender. Whenever the SMEC detects a problem, the "check engine" or "reduced power" light on the dash is activated. This light may also be used as a diagnostic tool. By turning the ignition key on-off-on-off within five seconds (with the engine not running—do not activate the starter), electronically stored trouble codes may be accessed. The lamp should light for three seconds as a bulb check before displaying the trouble codes.

These codes are displayed as flashes of light. For example, Code 11 would appear as one blink, a short pause, another blink, then a long pause before the next code.

Dodge Trouble Codes

Code 88	Start of test	Code 32	Exhaust-gas recirculation valve circuit
Code 11	Engine not cranked since battery was disconnected	Code 33	A/C cutout-relay circuit
Code 12	Memory standby power lost	Code 35	Idle switch circuit
Code 13	MAP sensor pneumatic circuit	Code 36	Air switching solenoid circuit
Code 14	MAP sensor electrical circuit	Code 37	Part throttle unlock solenoid driver circuit (automatic transmission only)
Code 15	Faulty vehicle distance sensor circuit (California only)		
Code 16	Loss of battery voltage	Code 41	Alternator field current
Code 17	Engine temperature too low	Code 42	Auto shutdown relay driver circuit
Code 21	Oxygen-sensor circuit	Code 43	Ignition coil-control circuit
Code 22	Coolant-temperature circuit	Code 44	Loss of FJ2 to logic board
Code 23	Throttle-body temperature sensor circuit	Code 46	High battery voltage
Code 24	Throttle-position sensor	Code 47	Low battery voltage
Code 25	Idle speed-control circuit	Code 51	Lean oxygen-sensor signal
Code 26	High resistance in injector circuit	Code 52	Rich oxygen-sensor signal
Code 27	Fuel-injector control problem	Code 53	Internal module problem
Code 31	Vapor canister purge solenoid circuit	Code 55	End of message

The computer will flash all codes stored in memory and then repeat them until the key is turned off. These codes represent problems detected by the computer in the last 50 (or so) engine starts. **Note:** Missing code numbers are intentional by the manufacturer.

After repairs are made, disconnect the negative battery cable from the battery for five minutes to clear all stored codes. Reconnect the battery and drive the vehicle for about 10 miles to allow the computer to relearn the engine's characteristics. The engine may run rough at first.

FORD EEC IV

Ford trouble codes may be accessed with a special tester or an analog voltmeter. The procedures vary considerably with each engine option and model and are so complex that we recommend you take the vehicle to a qualified technician for these checks.

Before you throw in the towel, check all the usual problem areas we have listed. In addition, check the inertia switch, as this seems to be a common problem on Fords. Simply push the reset button as described in the owner's manual. The inertia switch on F-series trucks is beneath the dash behind the left kick panel. On E-series vans, the switch is located under the right side of the dash under the heater blower.

GENERAL MOTORS THROTTLE-BODY INJECTION

General Motors computer trouble codes are displayed by the "check engine" light in the instrument cluster. They may be accessed by switching the ignition on with the engine not running. The "check engine" lamp should light as a bulb check. Then locate the 12-pin Assembly Line Diagnostic Link (ALDL) under the driver's side of the dash. Bridge the "A" and "B" terminals together with a special key or, in a pinch, use a bent paper clip or a short piece of wire.

These codes are displayed as flashes of light. For example, Code 12 would appear as one blink, a short pause, two blinks, then a long pause before the next code. (Missing code numbers are intentional by the manufacturer.) The computer will flash all codes stored in memory three times each and then repeat them until the tool is removed from the ALDL. After repairs are made, disconnect the negative battery cable from the battery for five minutes to clear all stored codes. Reconnect the battery and drive the vehicle for about 10 miles to allow the computer to relearn the engine's characteristics. The engine may run rough at first. After testing, remove the bridging device from ALDL to exit code display mode.

General Motors Trouble Codes

Code 12	Ready for self-test	Code 34	High MAP sensor vacuum (low or no sensor output)
Code 13	Open oxygen-sensor circuit	Code 42	ECM detected open or grounded electronic spark timing or bypass circuit
Code 14	High coolant-sensor temperature indication (grounded)		
Code 15	Low coolant-temperature indication (open circuit)	Code 43	ECM detected faulty electronic spark control signal
Code 21	Excessive TPS voltage (open or shorted to ground)	Code 44	Lean exhaust condition (oxygen-sensor signal)
Code 22	Low TPS voltage (open or shorted to ground)	Code 45	Rich exhaust condition (oxygen-sensor signal)
Code 23	Low MAT temperature indication (open circuit)	Code 51	Faulty ECM components (see dealer)
Code 24	No VSS speed indication (open circuit)	Code 52	Fuel CALPAK missing or faulty (see dealer)
Code 25	High MAT temperature indication (grounded circuit)	Code 53	Excessive charging system voltage (voltage regulator)
Code 32	Faulty exhaust-gas recirculation (EGR) valve circuit	Code 54	Low fuel-pump voltage
Code 33	Low MAP sensor vacuum (bad sensor or open circuit)	Code 55	Faulty ECM (see dealer)

A BASIC FUEL-SYSTEM CHECKLIST

Before you condemn any of the newfangled systems, check the basics! Most driveability problems are caused by the same old gremlins we've had for decades:

- Clogged fuel filters
- Dirty air filters
- Poor electrical connections
- Incorrect voltage—weak battery and/or faulty charging systems
- Vacuum leaks—hoses and manifold gaskets
- Plugged exhaust system (or catalyst)
- Fouled or worn-out spark plugs
- Faulty ignition components such as wires, caps, and rotors
- Low compression due to burned valves or worn engine parts

VEHICLE EMISSION CONTROL INFORMATION LABELS

The Vehicle Emission Control Information (VECI) label is required by federal law to be affixed to every emission-controlled vehicle sold in the United States and Canada. This sticker can usually be found on the radiator support, underside of the hood, fan shroud, or rocker-arm cover.

VECI labels provide important information on the specific vehicle you are working on, such as vacuum-hose routing diagrams and tune-up and emission specifications. If any discrepancy exists between the specifications shown in a service manual and the VECI label, trust the label.

TEST EQUIPMENT

To thoroughly test a computer-equipped vehicle, one would need thousands of dollars in special equipment, including an oscilloscope, exhaust-gas analyzer, scan tools, and breakout boxes. However, with standard hand tools, a 10-megohm impedance digital volt-ohm meter, vacuum gauge and tester, fuel-pressure gauge, and a little persistence, many maladies can be detected.

For specific information on wiring, component specifications, etc., refer to the manufacturer's shop manuals.

Fuel-System Precautions in Relieving Fuel Pressure

The fuel system is pressurized at all times. Be sure to read the following list before opening the fuel system:

- Remove the fuel-filler caps. With the engine idling, remove the fuel-pump fuse (on Fords, disconnect the wires at the fuel pump), and allow the engine to stall. Wrap a rag around the fittings to soak up any remaining fuel when you open them and *always wear eye protection!*
- When working on fuel systems, always have a fire extinguisher rated for gasoline and electrical fires at hand. Read the instructions!
- Never smoke or allow open flames or unprotected light bulbs anywhere near the work place.
- Never work in a closed garage or one with a gas-operated water heater or clothes dryer; the pilot light could ignite fuel vapors.
- Keep children and pets away from the work area.
- Remember to always wear eye protection when testing or disconnecting fuel-system components.
- Do not allow anyone near the driver's controls except a trusted assistant and only when needed during testing.
- Remove the keys from the ignition when they are not required for testing.
- Always relieve fuel pressure before disconnecting fuel lines and/or fittings.
- Never connect or disconnect jumper cables to the battery with the ignition key on.
- Before checking compression, disable the fuel-pump circuit by removing the fuse or relay.
- Never apply full battery voltage directly to any electronic component unless service manual specifically directs you to.
- Never work under a vehicle supported only by a jack.
- Cover all open fittings to avoid contamination from dirt or moisture.
- Handle components with care; avoid heat and liquids. Never weld near electronic parts.
- Never touch the computer input or ouput terminals; static discharge could destroy the ECM in an instant!

EMISSION SYSTEM COMPONENT WARRANTIES

Electronic engine-control systems are made up of large numbers of components. Knowing the functions of the various parts helps one understand how the entire system works and where to look when a problem arises.

Most of the emission-control components are covered by a 5-year/50,000-mile (whichever comes first) warranty against defects in materials and workmanship. Many people overlook this coverage, which is available at any franchised dealer of the brand. Federal regulations require the vehicle manufacturer (for example, Chrysler, Ford, General Motors, etc.) to provide this warranty to the original and subsequent owners of the vehicle.

These warranties generally include all of the major (read expensive) parts of the fuel-injection and emission-control systems. Limited diagnostic time may also be included. Certain items, such as filters, are considered owner-maintenance items and are not covered. Components damaged due to modification, abuse, or improper service procedures are also not covered. Refer to your vehicle owner's manual or your dealer for specific details.

Electronic engine-control systems are made up of large numbers of components. Knowing the functions of the various parts helps one understand how the entire system works and where to look when a problem arises. We have listed the major components used in domestic light-truck electronic-fuel systems. The descriptions in this chapter are necessarily generic in nature since not all fuel systems use all of the items listed here. However, they are representative of the majority of the systems used on domestic trucks and vans.

CHAPTER 6

Tires—and How to Care for Them

T ires are like any other component of a vehicle: they'll cause trouble if attention isn't given to their requirements. It's obvious that oil must be added to the engine or transmission when necessary, or their failure is assured. Some motorists appear to believe that tires are different—that they're immune to neglect—judging from their lackadaisical attitude toward tire maintenance.

Poor tire maintenance is liable to cause more trauma than allowing an engine to run out of oil, although neither is a good idea. A ruined engine may merely be expensive; a tire blowout can (and often does) cause serious accidents with injuries or fatalities, as well as being expensive. Proper tire maintenance should include:

- Regular checking of inflation pressure
- Evaluation of tire loading
- Regular rotation, to assure proper wear
- Periodic wheel alignment, to assure proper wear
- Good shock absorbers

Beyond actual hazards, proper tire maintenance can dramatically affect tire life. The combination of improper inflation and infrequent tire rotation *can cut tire life in half.* This chapter will deal with these factors, as well as tire design, radials versus bias-ply, wheel suitability, mixing of tires, and matching of dual rear tires.

LOAD VERSUS INFLATION PRESSURE

A tire can be inflated properly only if it is not overloaded, so it is impossible to discuss one topic without including the other. Simplified maintenance of inflation pressure merely requires that the tire owner read the numbers on the tire sidewall (Figure 6.1) and make sure the tires are continually maintained at the prescribed level. Although it would be nice if all tires were inflated this way, RVs are special vehicles that need more understanding and analysis because they often need special inflation procedures for the best possible wear and traction.

One of the first steps is to recognize that passenger-car tires and light-truck tires are different. When passenger-car tires are used on light trucks (some half-ton models), they are still regarded as passenger-car tires. Trailer tires are labeled "ST" (special trailer), and they may be in either the car or light-truck category for load and inflation, according to specifications published by the Tire and Rim Association. These specifications are used by all tire manufacturers (with only minor exceptions) for the purpose of creating commonality of load ratings and infla-

Figure 6.1
At tire maintenance's most basic level, proper attention must be paid to load and inflation data molded on the tire sidewall.

tion pressures among various brands. In the case of ST tires, the size designation identifies the category—automobile or light truck—to which the tire belongs.

Passenger-Car Tires

Most present-day car tires are designated with the letter *P* in front of a set of numbers (for example, P225/75R15), known as the **P-metric system.**

How to Read a P-Metric Tire

Example: **P225/75R15**

    P = passenger-car tire
  225 = cross-section width in millimeters
   75 = aspect ratio
    R = radial
   15 = rim diameter in inches

The **aspect ratio** is the proportion of a tire's cross-section height (from the tread to the bead seat) compared to the cross-section width (side to side). The height is 75% of the width of a tire that has an aspect ratio of 75 (Figure 6.2).

Figure 6.2
Height is 75% of width in a tire that has an aspect ratio of 75.

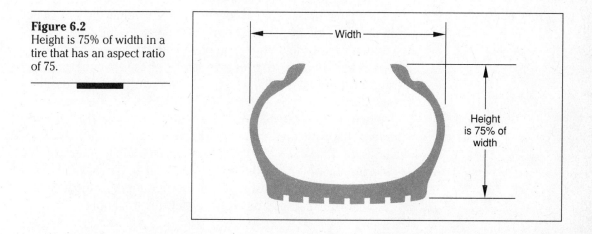

Any tire with the letter *P* in front of a series of numbers is a passenger-car tire. The P-metric system has replaced the previous alphanumeric system (still in limited use) that designated passenger-car tires on the basis of their load capacity.

How to Read an Alphanumeric Tire

Example: **GR78-15**
    G = load capacity
    R = radial
    78 = aspect ratio
    15 = rim diameter in inches

Inflation pressures stamped on all passenger-car tires are the *maximum pressures for the maximum loads listed on the tire and should not be exceeded.* For example, the P225/75R15 is rated for 1,874 pounds maximum load at 35 psi, cold. Pressure should not exceed 35 psi, cold, under any circumstances because the tire was not designed for higher pressures. Inflation maximums for passenger-car tires are:

- Load range B, 32 psi
- Load range C, 36 psi
- Load range D, 40 psi

The pressure ratings are intended for use when the tires are cold; higher pressures will occur while traveling due to heat buildup, and the pressure increase should not be bled off.

When a car or light truck equipped with passenger-car tires is used to tow a trailer, it's best to inflate all tires to the maximums listed on their sidewalls, which will produce the best possible towing stability.

When passenger-car tires are used on light trucks and trailers, the Tire and Rim Association recommends that load ratings be downrated to 91%. For example, if the tire must carry a maximum of 1,600 pounds, a tire rated for a maximum of 1,760 pounds (or thereabouts) is appropriate. Maximum inflation pressures stamped on the tire sidewalls still apply.

Special-trailer (ST) tires that have passenger-car size designations are the same in design, except that special rubber compounds usually are used to reduce deterioration due to sunlight and ozone.

Light-Truck Tires

Light-truck (LT) tires may have either the traditional numeric (for example, 7.50-16LT) or metric (LT235/75R15) identification:

How to Read a Metric Light-Truck Tire

Example: **LT235/75R16**
   LT = light truck
   235 = section width in millimeters
   75 = aspect ratio
   R = radial
   16 = rim diameter in inches

How to Read a Standard Light-Truck Tire

Example: **7.50R16LT**
   7.50 = section width in inches
   R = radial
   16 = rim diameter (bead seat) in inches
   LT = light truck

While graduated load/inflation tables exist for passenger-car as well as light-truck tires (including motorhome) tires, their most significant use is for light-truck tires. The reason is that passenger-car tire-inflation maximums—usually 32 or 36 psi—are relatively low compared to the maximum pressures for light-truck tires, which can range up to 100 psi.

It seems apparent that a tire loaded to only a fraction of its maximum capacity should be inflated accordingly. Tire companies differ on that, however. Goodyear recommends maximum inflation pressures even though they may far exceed the necessary inflation for the load, based on the assumption that

In contrast with car tires, whose inflation-pressure maximums should not be exceeded, adding 10 psi to the minimum recommended pressure is appropriate with light-truck tires.

an overinflated tire usually will not let the owner down, whereas an underinflated tire may fail catastrophically. In contrast, Michelin recommends inflating for the actual load, assigning the responsibility of determining the load to the vehicle owner.

Both recommendations appear to be valid for different types of vehicle owners; those who don't weigh their vehicles should use the cold-inflation pressure listed on tire sidewalls; more dedicated owners who go to the trouble of weighing their rigs can get the best tire performance and wear by inflating to the actual load.

Load-inflation ratings for light-truck and motorhome tires are included on pages 132–133.

Ratings for light-truck tires also are molded on the sidewalls. However, they are different from passenger cars. The inflation pressure listed on the tire sidewall is the *minimum* for the *maximum* load. In contrast with car tires, whose inflation-pressure maximums should not be exceeded, adding 10 psi to the minimum recommended pressure is appropriate with light-truck tires. To emphasize the point: The inflation pressure stamped on a light-truck sidewall tire (either bias-ply or radial) *can be increased 10 psi.* The additional pressure should not violate the maximum inflation capacity of the wheel (rim); *it does not increase the load-carrying capacity of the tire.* The recommendation also applies to bias-ply tires, but additional pressure beyond the minimum for the specific load may lead to accelerated wear in the center of the tread.

The additional 10 psi above minimum pressures for specific loads for light-truck tires stiffens the tire sidewall slightly, which may improve vehicle handling without a tendency to wear out the center of the tread. More important, it's insurance against underinflation that can occur from the slight pressure loss that gradually occurs with all tires—loss that should be detected and corrected with frequent pressure checking but often is not.

Manufacturers of light trucks typically recommend specific pressures for the maximum load the truck is designed to carry. The ratings (required by law since the 1970s) usually are listed in identification plates attached to the driver's side-door frame. However, light trucks usually are driven empty much of the time, and the actual load being carried by the truck is dramatically lower than the maximum load rating of the tire. Using maximum inflation when the tire is loaded *far below* the maximum degrades ride quality, lowers impact resistance, and reduces the size of the tire footprint. It usually will also cause accelerated wear in the center of the tread, although radial tires are minimally affected, compared with bias-ply tires. Using the graduated load-inflation tables on pages 132–133 will allow you to inflate specifically to your load.

For example, an LT215/85R16 tire in D load range is rated for 2,335 pounds load at a minimum of 65 psi. In a typical situation with a pickup truck used occasionally to tow a trailer, the tire may actually be carrying about 1,200 pounds while the truck is empty. The minimum inflation pressure for this load is 35 psi (see the load/inflation tables on page 132). Adding the recommended extra 10 psi for truck tires brings the correct pressure for this light-load situation to 45 psi.

Front tires of this same truck may be loaded to about 1,500 pounds. The same inflation pressure, 45 psi, would be appropriate for front tires.

If a load of firewood were added to this truck while it also tows a trailer, the load on the rear tires might increase to 2,000 pounds per tire. Minimum inflation pressure for 2,000 pounds per tire is 55 psi; adding 10 psi brings the recommended pressure to 65 psi. If the tires were loaded to their maximums, correct pressure would be 75 psi, established by adding 10 psi to the 65 psi cold-inflation pressure rating listed on the tire's sidewall.

Weighing a motorhome is a very important safety consideration.

Motorhome weights do not fluctuate widely and are usually high enough that maximum tire pressures usually can be presumed appropriate if accurate weight figures are not available for the loaded motorhome. The exception may be front tires, especially on mini motorhomes. Thus, it's necessary to weigh the vehicle to determine correct tire pressures for the actual load.

If a trip to the scales seems too much trouble, and you're prone to simply assume that inflating to the pressure listed on the tire sidewall is okay, hazards still exist because the tires may be overloaded (a common occurrence). *Weighing a motorhome is a very important safety consideration* (see Chapter 7, "RV Handling, Safety, and Weight Ratings," pages 165–167). Individual

Table 6.1 Tire and Rim Association Ratings
Tire Load Limits (Lbs) at Various Minimum Cold-Inflation Pressures (PSI)

Top section — column headers are Radial Ply PSI; Diagonal (Bias) Ply PSI = Radial value − 5 (i.e., 30, 35, 40, 45, 50, 55, 60, 65, 70, 75).

TIRE SIZE	S=Single / D=Dual	35	40	45	50	55	60	65	70	75	80
LT215/85*16	D	1360	1490	1625	1765(C)	1865	1985	2150(D)	2210	2320	2470(E)
LT215/85*16	S	1495	1640	1785	1940(C)	2050	2180	2335(D)	2430	2550	2680(E)
LT235/85*16	D	1545	1700	1845	2006(C)	2125	2260	2381(D)	2515	2645	2778(E)
LT235/85*16	S	1700	1870	2030	2205(C)	2335	2485	2623(D)	2765	2905	3042(E)
LT255/85*16	D	1745	1920	2085	2270(C)	2400	2550	2755(D)			
LT255/85*16	S	1920	2110	2290	2470(C)	2635	2800	3000(D)			
7.00*15LT	D	1190	1310	1420	1520(C)	1620	1715	1800(D)	1870	1960	2040(E)
7.00*15LT	S	1350	1480	1610	1720(C)	1830	1940	2040(D)	2130	2220	2320(E)
7.50*16LT	D	1430	1565	1690	1815(C)	1930	2040	2140(D)	2245	2345	2440(E)
7.50*16LT	S	1620	1770	1930	2060(C)	2190	2310	2440(D)	2560	2670	2780(E)

Bottom section — column headers are Radial Ply PSI; Diagonal (Bias) Ply PSI = Radial value − 5.

TIRE SIZE	S/D	55	60	65	70	75	80	85	90	95	100	105	110	115	120
8*19.5	D			2230	2350	2460	2570	2680	2780(E)	2880	2980	3070(F)			
8*19.5	S	2270	2410	2540	2680	2800(D)	2930	3060	3170(E)	3280	3400	3500(F)			
8*22.5	D			2490	2620	2750(D)	2870	2990	3100(E)	3210	3320	3430(F)			
8*22.5	S	2530	2680	2840	2990	3140(D)	3270	3410	3530(E)	3660	3780	3810(F)			
9*22.5	D				2960	3120	3270	3410	3550(E)	3690	3820	3950(F)	4070	4200	4320(G)
9*22.5	S		3010	3190	3370	3560	3730	3890	4050(E)	4210	4350	4500(F)	4640	4790	4920(G)
10*22.5	D				3510	3690	3870	4040(E)	4200	4360	4520(F)	4670	4820	4970(G)	
10*22.5	S		3560	3770	4000	4210	4410	4610(E)	4790	4970	5150(F)	5320	5490	5670(G)	
11*22.5	D				4380	4580	4760(F)	4950	5120	5300(G)	5470	5630	5800(H)		
11*22.5	S		4530	4770	4990	5220	5430(F)	5640	5840	6040(G)	6240	6430	6610(H)		
11*24.5	D				4660	4870	5070(F)	5260	5450	5640(G)	5820	6000	6170(H)		
11*24.5	S		4820	5070	5310	5550	5780(F)	6000	6210	6430(G)	6630	6840	7030(H)		
12*22.5	D				4780	4990	5190(F)	5390	5590	5780(G)	5960	6150	6320(H)		
12*22.5	S		4940	5200	5450	5690	5920(F)	6140	6370	6590(G)	6790	7010	7200(H)		
12*24.5	D				5080	5300	5520(F)	5730	5940	6140(G)	6330	6530	6720(H)		
12*24.5	S		5240	5520	5790	6040	6290(F)	6530	6770	7000(G)	7220	7440	7660(H)		

*Indicates position where R (radial-ply) or B (bias-ply) designation will appear—i.e., LT215/85R16.

Letters and **boldfaced** tire load values indicate tire load ranges C through H.

Table 6.1 Tire and Rim Association Ratings (continued)
Tire Load Limits (Lbs) at Various Minimum Cold-Inflation Pressures (PSI)

TIRE SIZE	S = Single / D = Dual	Radial Ply 35 / Diagonal 30	40 / 35	45 / 40	50 / 45	55 / 50	60 / 55	65 / 60	70 / 65	75 / 70	80 / 75	85 / 80	90 / 85	95 / 90
8.00*16.5LT	D	1195	1310	1415	1520(C)	1620	1710	1800(D)	1885	1970	2050(E)	2130	2200	2280(F)
	S	1360	1490	1610	1730(C)	1840	1945	2045(D)	2145	2240	2330(E)	2420	2500	2590(F)
8.75*16.5LT	D	1380	1515	1630	1750(C)	1855	1970	2070(D)	2175	2260	2360(E)	2450	2540	2620(F)
	S	1570	1720	1850	1990(C)	2110	2240	2350(D)	2470	2570	2680(E)	2780	2880	2980(F)
9.50*16.5LT	D	1635	1785	1925	2070(C)	2200	2330	2445(D)	2570	2685	2790(E)			
	S	1860	2030	2190	2350(C)	2500	2650	2780(D)	2920	3050	3170(E)			
10*16.5LT	D	1620(B)	1770	1910	2050(C)	2180	2310	2420(D)	2540	2650	2760(E)			
	S	1840(B)	2010	2170	2330(C)	2480	2620	2750(D)	2885	3010	3135(E)			
12*16.5LT	D	2090(C)	2280	2460	2640(D)	2810	2970	3120(E)	3275	3420	3560(F)			
	S	2370(C)	2590	2800	3000(D)	3190	3370	3550(E)	3720	3885	4045(F)			

TIRE SIZE	Radial Ply 25 / Diagonal 20	30 / 25	35 / 30	40 / 35	45 / 40	50 / 45
31×10.50*15LT	1400	1595	1775(B)	1945	2100	2250(C)
31×11.50*15LT	1455	1660	1845(B)	2020	2185	2340(C)
32×11.50*15LT	1575	1795	1995(B)	2185	2360	2530(C)
33×12.50*15LT	1755(B)	2000	2225(C)			

TIRE SIZE	S = Single / D = Dual	Radial Ply 35 / Diagonal 30	40 / 35	45 / 40	50 / 45	55 / 50	60 / 55	65 / 60	70 / 65	75 / 70	80 / 75
8*19.5	D	1445	1575	1700	1820(C)	1935	2050	2155(D)	2260	2360	2460(E)
	S	1640	1790	1940	2075(C)	2205	2335	2455(D)	2575	2685	2795(E)

Michelin Tire Load Limits
(Michelin ratings differ from Tire and Rim Association values for indicated tire size)
2 Tires: S = Single; 4 Tires: D = Dual

Tire Size	Tread Designs		50	55	60	65	70	75	80	85	90
8R19.5, PR8-LRD, PR10-LRE,	XZA, XM+S4,	S		4710	5035	5365	5600(D)	5950	6340(E)	6650	7000(F)
PR12-LRF (Tubeless)	XZY	D	9150	9770	10,390	10,800	11,475	12,200	12,825	13,500	

wheel scales often are unavailable, but it's possible to weigh a motorhome's axles individually on a platform scale.

Again, if the motorhome's tires are loaded to their maximums, 10 psi can be added to the inflation pressure stamped on the tire sidewall. For example, 8R19.5 tires in load range D are rated for 5,600 pounds maximum weight per axle as singles, and 9,840 pounds per axle as duals, at 70 psi. Adding the prescribed 10 psi brings the inflation pressure to 80 psi, and the extra pressure does not increase the load-carrying capacity of the tire.

A common situation in which the additional 10 psi may be desirable is when the vehicle tends to wander. Some vehicles wander more with tires that are inflated to the minimum pressure for the actual load than when higher pressures are used. Correction of a wander problem should start by weighing the vehicle. Begin with minimum inflation pressures for the actual load and adjust pressures upward in stages (not exceeding the cold-inflation pressure molded on the tire sidewall, plus 10 psi for light-truck tires) to determine the ideal pressure for minimum vehicle wander. Wheel alignment (caster) usually has the most significant effect on the tendency of the vehicle to wander.

Tire inflation should be checked prior to each trip, and at least once a week during trips. *Always check pressures when tires are cold.* A visual check of tires should be included in a routine walkaround inspection that occurs every time you take a break from driving. Tires build pressure while the vehicle is moving, and the pressure increase is taken into account in the manufacturer's (cold) inflation-pressure recommendation. Thus, if you begin the day with tires at 45 psi and find them at 55 psi later, don't reduce the pressure. When the temperature drops, the tires will return to the original 45 psi.

Finally, make sure your pressure gauge is accurate! Ask your tire dealer to verify it.

Flotation Tires

Flotation-type tires have their own special category under the light-truck classification, and they're distinguished by a set of numbers beginning with the tire's overall diameter in inches.

How to Read a Flotation-type Tire

Example: **31x11.50R15LT**

31	=	overall diameter
11.50	=	section width
R	=	radial
15	=	rim (bead seat) diameter
LT	=	light truck

TIRE DAMAGE YOU CAN'T SEE

The significance of proper inflation and loading is not appreciated by most drivers because the results of underinflation and/or overloading often don't show up immediately. An underinflated/overloaded tire may not fail immediately, but it may fail later, depending on driving conditions, long after the underinflation has been corrected. The usual cause of such failures is tread separation.

Heat is a tire's worst enemy, and excessive heat is the result of underinflation/overloading, as well as the cause of tread separation (Figure 6.3). When the temperature of the tire's core

Figure 6.3
Heat created by under-inflation or overloading can cause delamination and result in tire failure.

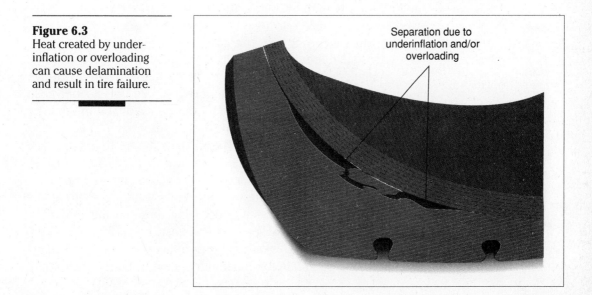

Separation due to underinflation and/or overloading

compound exceeds 250°F, cords lose strength; the bond is loosened between the cords and the surrounding rubber compound, making the tire more susceptible to failure. If the owner escapes a failure and is not even aware of the underinflation until later, the underinflation incident then appears to have had no consequence. To the contrary, an overheated tire does not cool to its original strength; it is permanently weakened, and a blowout or tread separation probably will occur later, after the underinflation incident is long forgotten. When the tire eventually fails, the owner may blame it on manufacturing defects or poor quality when in fact the tire was damaged by negligence.

When is a tire overheated? It's not practical to measure tire temperature with a thermometer, so the primary defenses against excessive heat are proper loading and adequate inflation. The worst condition is traveling superheated highways, so it's best to avoid the heat of the day in summer if possible.

HOW TO MAKE TIRES LAST LONGER

In addition to proper inflation and loading, routine tire rotation can be important to tire longevity. Even though we attempt to maintain ideal inflation pressures to maximize the tire's footprint, it may be impossible to avoid at least limited overinflation when loads vary. Accelerated tire wear may be inevitable with bias-ply, but proper tire rotation can hold it to a minimum. Radial tires are minimally affected by overinflation.

Again, tire companies differ. At least one major truck-tire manufacturer says it's not necessary to rotate unless abnormal wear is noticed, although rotation in absence of abnormal wear does no harm. But others assert that an important aspect of tire rotation escapes most RV owners: Tires should be rotated *before improper wear characteristics are visible.* They suggest rotation every 7,000 miles or earlier if an abnormal wear pattern becomes visible. If you notice abnormal wear, have the alignment checked immediately. According to some tire manufacturers, *the first two rotations are the most critical.*

If abnormal tread wear becomes noticeable, some manufacturers say it's too late for maximum tire life because a pattern of uneven wear, once established, may be impossible to reverse.

The cost of rotating tires varies with the type of vehicle and can be somewhat expensive with motorhomes. Owners who are reluctant to rotate tires regularly should inspect closely, and measure tread depth with a gauge (available in auto-supply stores). When rotation is deemed necessary, use the pattern recommended by the manufacturer of your vehicle, or use one of the patterns featured in Figure 6.4. *The original rolling direction of tires does not need to be maintained unless tread design dictates a specific direction!* The rolling direction can be reversed by moving the tire to the opposite side of the vehicle (as indicated), except when using mud/snow tires that are clearly designed for best traction in a specific rolling direction.

Summarizing, the keys to extended tire life are:

- Proper inflation for the specific load
- Proper loading
- Proper tire rotation
- Proper wheel alignment and use of effective shock absorbers.

Some Causes of Improper Tire Wear

Some causes of improper tire wear may be apparent, while others are more difficult to diagnose. The apparent causes of improper tire wear include:

- **Irregular wear:** (Also called heel/toe wear) Tread blocks wear more on one end (longitudinally) than the other. May indicate worn suspension parts, but in many flotation and mud/snow treads it's a characteristic of the tire design. Minimize problem with frequent rotation of tires from driving to nondriving positions.

- **Improper camber:** One shoulder of front tire will wear more quickly than the other.

- **Excessive toe-in/toe-out:** Rapid, uneven wear on front tires, often feathering the edges of tread serrations.

- **Overinflation:** Center of tread will wear more quickly than shoulders (primarily with bias-ply tires).

- **Underinflation:** Shoulders will wear faster than center of tread, and tread may tend to ripple.

Figure 6.4
Tire rotation is important for the best possible wear, particularly when abnormal tread wear becomes evident. Tires need not remain in their original direction of rotation.

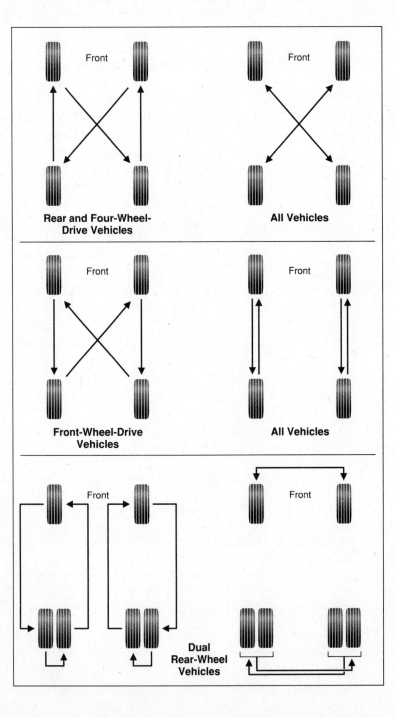

Rear and Four-Wheel-Drive Vehicles

All Vehicles

Front-Wheel-Drive Vehicles

All Vehicles

Dual Rear-Wheel Vehicles

Tire Selection

Tires vary widely in design as well as materials. We usually think of tires as made of rubber, but in fact natural rubber is a relatively minor ingredient. The basic building blocks of the rubber compound are **polymers,** combinations of natural rubber and two types of synthetic rubber. These combinations vary with the intended use. Another important building block is **carbon black,** a reinforcing material that provides strength in the rubber compounds. Actually glorified soot, its use in conjunction with rubber provides the matrix structure that gives strength. Then there are **oils,** used as softeners to provide traction within the compound. A high-performance tire will have more oils, helping the tire conform to the road. Next, **sulfur** is used as a cross-linking agent or network to keep the carbon black and rubber together for strength and flexibility. **Accelerators** control the rate of reaction in the rubber compound. Finally, **antioxidants** and **antiozodants** are used for protection.

Radial-ply tires are by far the most common type sold today (Figure 6.5). They are available with steel belts or a combination of fabric and steel. All-steel-belted tires are preferred in the trucking industry for their performance as well as retreadability.

Figure 6.5
Radial-ply tires are preferred for their extended wear capability, reduced rolling resistance, and improved traction.

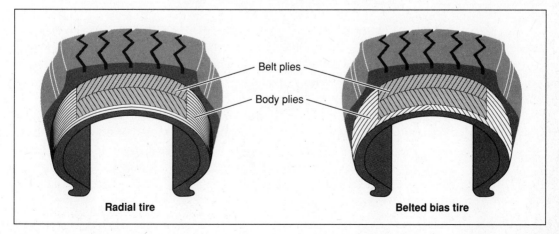

Belt plies

Body plies

Radial tire   **Belted bias tire**

Bias-ply tires still are widely available, but generally have more rolling resistance, wear faster, and offer less traction on slippery surfaces. In their favor, they have more sidewall stiffness and do not tend to follow grooves in road surfaces, as radials oftentimes do.

Tire buyers nowadays focus their attention on radial-ply tires. Most new vehicles, with the exception of some motorhomes, are equipped with radials when they're built. Trailers are the exception (bias-ply tires are still widely used), although radials are suitable on newer models.

When choosing replacement tires for a vehicle, the replacements usually can duplicate the original tire size and type. Exceptions include overload situations and stability problems that may require wider tires.

Weighing the vehicle by axle or, preferably, by each wheel is very important when abnormal tire wear suggests overloading has occurred.

If a tire has worn abnormally fast, with accelerated wear on the shoulders of the tread, the tire probably has been overloaded and/or underinflated. The vehicle should be weighed (loaded) before purchasing new tires to make sure the tire-load capacity is adequate. Don't rely on the vehicle's load ratings for tire selection because an overloaded vehicle may exceed the GAWR on either or both axles. Weighing the vehicle by axle or, preferably, by each wheel is very important when abnormal tire wear suggests overloading has occurred.

TRAILER TIRES

When choosing trailer tires, any of three types (car, light truck, or special trailer) can be used, providing the load range is adequate for the weight, and the wheels are suitable. Special-trailer (ST) tires are compounded for extra resistance to deterioration (cracking) from the effects of the sun and ozone in the air and are preferred if you take several years to wear out a set of tires. When using passenger-car tires on trailers, the Tire and Rim Association recommends reducing their load ratings by 9%. The reason is not that a trailer, by nature, is harder on tires, but that it is capable of being overloaded more dramatically than a passenger car.

Radials on Trailers

Radials are suitable on trailers and should not have an adverse effect on towing stability. Usually it's difficult to determine officially if the wheels on your trailer are designed for use of radial tires, but it's worthwhile to check with the trailer manufacturer or the wheel manufacturer (whose name the trailer manufacturer should be able to supply).

Choose tires with a load capacity high enough to insure that they are not loaded to their maximums; allow at least 10% weight margin under the load maximums. If the trailer originally was equipped with passenger-car-type tires rated for 32 or 35 psi, don't assume that the wheels are suitable for truck-type tires rated for 40 psi or higher; the wheels probably were not designed for the higher pressures. If your trailer load requires tires with considerably higher ratings than you can find in passenger-car tires, and you decide to use tires that require higher inflation pressure, new wheels with higher load and inflation-pressure ratings may be necessary.

TIRE QUALITY

Aside from the design differences between radial-ply and bias-ply tires, there are many differences in tire design and compounds. Unfortunately there are few reliable ways to compare tire quality other than by the manufacturer's reputation. Tires that look the same are not necessarily the same because the quality of the materials—particularly the rubber compound—can vary widely. Poor-quality tires shed tread rubber rapidly, while those of good quality have high resistance to tread wear. All-purpose and mud/snow tires generally wear faster than tires with highway tread. Tire compounding is a compromise, with cost an important factor.

Passenger-car tires display government-mandated quality grades that indicate relative tread wear among various brands. The ratings with numerically higher numbers indicate better wear characteristics.

Figure 6.6
The proper spacing of dual tires is important to prevent damage.

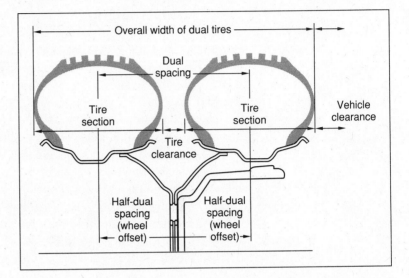

Dual-Tire Spacing

When choosing tires that are a different size than the originals for a motorhome or truck with dual rear tires, pay close attention to wheel size and to spacing of the rear tires. Dual-wheel spacing is measured from the center line of one tire to the center line of the other (Figure 6.6). Insufficient dual spacing causes the insides of the tires to touch at the point where the tread meets the road, which results in excessive heat and sidewall wear. In addition, rocks or debris can be trapped more easily between the tires, causing punctures. Tire chains cannot be used when dual spacing is inadequate.

Tire Matching

Tires used as sets on a dual-wheel axle must be properly matched. The tires should have the same size designation, be of the same type, and have the same or nearly the same outside diameters. Mismatched dual sets cause friction and heat because one tire is larger than the other, which means it attempts to travel farther than the other with each revolution. The smaller tire has less contact with the road and must scrub off most of the difference between the two tire diameters, causing excessive heat and wear in both tires. Tire diameter should not vary more than ¼ inch (tires inflated equally). A truck-tire dealer can measure diameters. Diameter can be calculated by measuring circumference with a steel tape measure that conforms properly to the tire. Divide the circumference measurement by 3.1416 to get diameter. If tires are new, wait at least twenty-four hours after initial inflation to check diameters.

When replacement tires exceed the load rating of the original tires, wheel suitability becomes an important factor. For example, original motorhome 8R19.5 load-range D tires may be due for replacement, and the owner may assume that moving up to the E-load range would offer an extra margin of safety. Unfortunately, the reverse may be true with many chassis, particularly Chevrolet. The original wheels are rated for 2,780 pounds maximum load and 95 psi maximum inflation pressure—suitable for 8R19.5D tires rated for 2,800 pounds at 80 psi in load range D. When moving up to load range E, the tire is rated for 3,170 pounds at 95 psi; in load range F, the tire is rated for 3,500 at 110 psi.

The problem is that the load limits as well as inflation limits of the 8R19.5 load-range E or F tires are beyond the load-carrying capacity of the wheels. Load-range E or F tires should not be used on wheels designed for maximum load/inflation of load-range D tires because their sidewall markings will encourage wheel overloading and overinflation.

Tire Mixing

If radial and bias-ply tires must be mixed, the radials should be used on the rear to prevent oversteer.

When changing tire sizes, more than one rim width usually is specified as suitable. For example, rim widths of 5½ to 7 inches may be specified for a 15-inch tire. The wider rims offer better road stability, but are more easily damaged when striking curbs or other obstacles.

Figure 6.7
Tires of differing design
require specific rim
contours. Incorrect tire/rim
combinations are
dangerous.

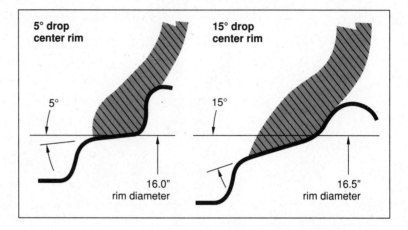

Figure 6.7
Tires of differing design
require specific rim
contours. Incorrect tire/rim
combinations are
dangerous.

Make sure replacement tires are of the correct size and con-
tour for the rims. **Warning:** It's possible to fit a 16-inch tire on a
16½-inch rim, but the tire cannot be safely inflated or used. In
addition to the size error, rim contours are not correct. The 16-
inch tire requires a 5-degree drop-center rim while the 16½-inch
tire requires a 15-degree drop-center rim (Figure 6.7).

Calculating Effect on Performance

When purchasing replacement tires of a different size than the
originals, it's wise to estimate the effect on performance. Tires
that are larger in diameter than the originals will have the effect
of lowering the numerical axle ratio. The opposite is true of
smaller-than-original tires. A formula can be used to calculate
the difference (RPM is revolutions per mile):

$$\frac{\text{New Tire RPM}}{\text{Original Tire RPM}} \times \frac{\text{Original}}{\text{Axle Ratio}} = \frac{\text{Effective}}{\text{Axle Ratio}}$$

The actual axle ratio does not change, but the relationship
between engine RPM and road speed is altered as if the axle
ratio had been changed. The reason is that the larger replacement tires will travel farther in one revolution than will the

original tires. The reverse is true for smaller tires. Speedometer error caused by a change in tire size also can be calculated:

$$\frac{\text{Original Tire RPM}}{\text{New Tire RPM}} \times \begin{array}{c}\text{Indicated} \\ \text{Speed}\end{array} = \text{Actual Speed}$$

Tire RPM can be calculated from measurement of circumference. Measure the tire's circumference with a steel tape measure or a string that can be measured with a tape. Divide the tire's circumference (inches) into 63,360 (the number of inches in a mile), and the result is approximate revolutions per mile.

A speedometer shop can recalibrate if the error created by a tire change is excessive—more than 3 or 4 MPH.

Time for Replacement

The Rubber Manufacturers Association recommends that tires on vehicles of more than 10,000 pounds gross weight be replaced when less than ⅛ inch of tread depth remains (not including tread-wear indicators). On vehicles less than 10,000 pounds gross weight, front tires should be replaced when worn to tread-wear indicators, or when 1/16 inch or less of tread remains. At least one major tire company recommends that tires be replaced if they are more than seven years old, regardless of the amount of tread remaining.

ABOUT WHEELS

A **wheel** is composed of a rim and a disc. The tire is mounted on the rim and the disc is used to attach the wheel to the vehicle. The assembly will vary widely in design, depending on tire size, type, and vehicle application. Wheels are tested by their manufacturers to withstand specific maximum weights and air pressures. All wheels are rated for maximum load and inflation pressures, although the ratings are not usually marked on the wheels. It's necessary to check with the wheel manufacturer for wheel ratings and radial-tire suitability.

Many errors are made in wheel selection when replacement tires are purchased. Errors are common even at the RV-factory level, especially when styled wheels are used. Most styled wheels are rated for less than 2,000 pounds, and some are not suitable for radial tires. Few tire dealers pay much attention to the fact that the wheel has limits and that the tires and wheels must be compatible. It is dangerous to mount a tire rated at 3,000 pounds on a wheel rated at 2,000, although it happens every day. Few wheels break, but when they do, it is with explosive force, possibly resulting in an accident.

Suitability for Radials

A decision to replace bias-ply tires with radials on an older vehicle, especially a motorhome, should be preceded by an inspection of the wheels for the word *radial* or by a circled *R* stamped on the rims that will indicate suitability for use of radial tires. If the wheel does not have these markings, it may not be designed for radials, and radials should not be used. Few trailer wheels have these markings, although many are suitable for radials.

Precarious radial-tire/nonradial-wheel matchups include 17.5 × 5.25-inch wheels used on Dodge M-400 motorhomes of the 1970s, supplied with 8-17.5 bias-ply tires, and 16.5 × 6-inch wheels supplied on many motorhomes produced prior to 1976. A 17.5 × 5.25-inch wheel suitable for use with radial tires does not exist. Original wheels used on pre-1976 General Motors light trucks, vans, Class C motorhomes, and on the GMC motorhome were not suitable for use with radial tires, although replacement wheels suitable for use with radials are available.

Trailer Wheels

Wheels used on trailers may be passenger-car type, light-truck type, or they may be specifically designed for use on trailers. Late-model wheels usually are suitable for use with radial tires. Wheels on earlier trailers probably weren't specifically designed for radials, but are not typically prone to break unless tires are loaded to their maximums. When in doubt about wheel suitability, contact the wheel manufacturer on the wheel's suitability for radials and load- and inflation-pressure maximums.

Wheel Dimensions

Styled replacement wheels have become very popular during the last decade, and it's helpful to know how to check dimensions when choosing replacement wheels, especially when attempting to widen a vehicle's track (width between center lines of tires) to improve handling.

When buying new wheels, make sure they are approved for the tires that will be used. (See also the tire data on pages 132–133). Your tire dealer has additional listings. It's wise to measure wheel offset when comparing new wheels with the originals. **Offset** is the difference in distance between the center line of the rim and the mounting surface (surface of the bolt pad that contacts the hub). A wheel with **negative** offset positions the tire farther from the vehicle's frame, widening the vehicle's track. **Positive** offset moves the tire inward, reducing the vehicle's track. When offset is zero, the disc is positioned in the center of the rim.

To calculate offset it's necessary to measure wheel spacing. Divide the total wheel width (B) by 2 and subtract the result from rear spacing (A) (Figure 6.8) to get offset in positive or

Figure 6.8
The measurement of offset is important for proper clearance between the tire and the vehicle frame when changing wheels.

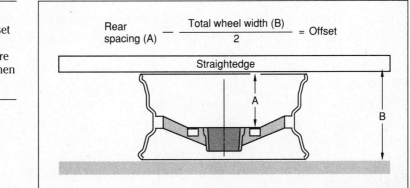

Figure 6.9
Offset can be calculated even though the tire is mounted on the wheel.

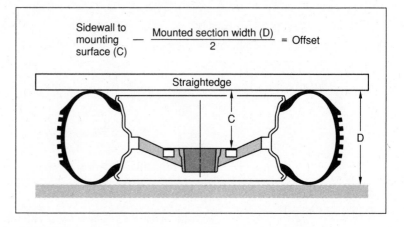

negative. Use the same formula to calculate offset with a tire mounted on the wheel (Figure 6.9). Divide section width (D) by 2 and subtract that figure from rear spacing (C) to get offset. Figures for the wheel alone and for the wheel with a tire mounted on it are valid for comparison.

TIRE STORAGE

RVs normally are not driven as far each year as family or business vehicles. Thus, tires last longer and are more subject to deterioration from ozone in the air and the effects of sunlight. **Protectants** typically bleed to the surface of the tire to provide some protection. Eventually, all the protectants are bled off and the tire sidewall begins to crack.

Surface cracks, called **crazing,** usually are not a problem. But when the cracks extend into the tire compound, durability is affected.

When the vehicle is out of service, cover all tires and maintain normal inflation pressure. It's not necessary to elevate the vehicle because the tires are designed for much greater stress than that which occurs when the vehicle is parked.

Tires are a critically valuable component of any vehicle. When proper care is taken, they should provide the performance and safety of which they're capable.

RV Handling, Safety, and Weight Ratings

N o one expects recreational vehicles to handle like sports cars. But they can be expected to handle safely and offer pleasurable driving. When a trailer is hitched to a tow vehicle, the two become an articulated vehicle and involve a whole new dimension in vehicle dynamics. In itself, a motorhome is not an articulated vehicle, but the majority of motorhome owners tow small cars or trucks.

New criteria and some adjustments in driving habits are necessary to graduate from a car or truck to an articulated vehicle or a motorhome. It isn't difficult, and few problems occur unless a driver fails to realize that tow vehicles and motorhomes aren't as agile or as powerful as cars and light trucks alone. Violation of their weight limits can have serious consequences.

The factors that must be considered for safe RVing include:

- Visibility—forward and via side- and rear-view mirrors
- The vehicle's length, width, and height
- Turning circle
- How the vehicle tracks while turning
- Braking ability
- Stability during emergency maneuvers
- Stability on curves
- Stability in crosswinds
- Acceleration for passing
- Load ratings
- Weight distribution

VISIBILITY

Obviously, good forward and side visibility are needed in any motor vehicle, particularly in one that is larger and more difficult to handle than a typical car or truck alone. The levels of visibility we tend to accept as adequate may not be very good; visibility often can be improved.

Few vehicles have poor forward visibility even though some may have relatively small windshields that restrict the upward scenic view. In motorhomes, side vision often is restricted by excessively large corner posts between the windshield and the side windows and by mirrors that are positioned too high. Little can be done about corner posts after the fact, but it's a point of consideration while shopping for a new rig. Side visibility in motorhomes may be restricted by window frames—particularly those that block the view through mirrors (Fig 7.1). The solution is either to move the mirror to a more advantageous position or to modify the side window. Moving the mirror usually is the easiest solution.

Mirrors themselves are an area of poor visiblity, which can lead to accidents. Fortunately, RVing accidents are few, not necessarily because we're better drivers (no reliable statistics are available to prove the point one way or the other), but because

Figure 7.1
The side mirror may have to be repositioned if visibility is partially blocked by a window frame.

we are conservative drivers and our vehicles are quite large, making them easier for other motorists to see.

Mirrors on a towing vehicle or motorhome should be at least 10 × 7 inches to offer an adequate field of vision. On tow vehicles, door-mount positions are far better than fender mounts, although most passenger cars are not easily fitted with permanent door-mounted mirrors. Fender-mounted mirrors don't offer a good rear view due to their size and their distance from the driver. Also, a convex right-side mirror, which helps the driver monitor his or her "blind spot," cannot be used as a fender mount. Passenger cars have standard door-mounted convex right-side mirrors, which in most cases must suffice even though their angle of view is restricted. The solution for cars is a set of good door-mounted mirrors, with a convex mirror added on the right side. On trucks and vans, extensions may be used to move some mirror heads outward, or a replacement set of extended mirrors may be purchased. Extensions and replacement mirrors are available at RV-supply stores.

While trucks, vans, and motorhomes usually have larger mirror heads, the owner still must make sure visibility is not restricted by window frames or by insecure mirror mounting that

Figure 7.2
A large convex mirror,
mounted immediately
below or above the primary
mirror, can improve visibility by limiting blind spots.

causes excessive vibration, blurring the reflected images. Some
right-side mirrors are about two-third conventional view and
one-third wide angle. This combination tends to restrict the
driver's ability to see the area around the rear tires, which is
helpful to keep from running over curbs while making tight
turns, as well as checking for exhaust smoke or an errant wheel
cover. The preferred arrangement is a large convex mirror, available at RV-supply stores and other stores that sell equipment to
truckers, positioned immediately below or above the primary
mirror (Figure 7.2). The preferred location is the one that offers
maximum visibility.

PHYSICAL SIZE

The best defense against problems associated with the vehicle's size is practice.

The majority of us drive passenger cars or light trucks most of the time and graduate to our RVs only occasionally. Thus, it's always necessary to make a mental transition and keep the size and handling characteristics of the larger rig in mind. Failing to do so may result in a tendency to make turns too tightly, run over curbs, hit stationary objects, or crowd other traffic. It may take some concentration for the novice RV owner, but acclimation happens fairly rapidly. The get-acquainted period may be difficult to get through without minor dings and scrapes, but traffic accidents are unusual, even though the new driver may not have fully adjusted to the particular characteristics of handling an RV.

The best defense against problems associated with the vehicle's size is practice. All too often, we encounter a tight turn into or out of a campground site or service station and are tentative about our ability to make the turn. Practicing tight maneuvers will improve our judgment, reducing the chance of embarrassingly tight situations. Practice also helps improve our judgment in making sure we don't hit overhanging tree limbs and other such obstacles. It's helpful to measure the actual height of the vehicle and list the height somewhere on the dash for reference when driving under structures that are marked for road clearance. If you're uncomfortable driving under unmarked overhangs, exit the vehicle and check clearance if the situation permits. Soon you'll have a clearer mental picture of your RV's height.

Tailswing is an RV handling characteristic that causes quite a number of dings and scrapes. It occurs during tight, slow-speed maneuvers when the rear of a trailer or motorhome swings opposite the direction you are steering (Figure 7.3). Tailswing can be monitored in the mirrors of a motorhome or truck-camper, allowing you to avoid costly conflicts with lampposts and other obstacles. But with a tow vehicle and trailer, you're blind on the right side during left turns. Also, while backing to the left, we can see where we're going on that side, but we can't see the right side of the trailer. Pulling forward sharply to the left and then straightening the wheel can swing the trailer's rear to

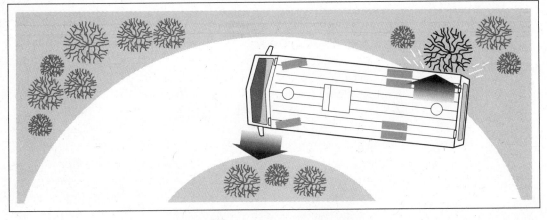

Figure 7.3
Tailswing occurs when the rear of the trailer or motorhome swings in the opposite direction of the turn.

the right—into a post, tree, or other obstacle if it happens to be your misfortune. The best defense is to practice in a parking lot and observe how the vehicle's rear changes position. With a tow vehicle and trailer, have someone else drive while you watch what happens in tight turns.

PASSING POWER

RVs are like most other vehicles that are larger and heavier than cars and light trucks in that they must be driven differently. We can't expect to pass other vehicles with the same authority in a 14,000-pound motorhome as we do a car. However, it is possible to pass. Drivers of 18-wheelers do it, but they wait for enough clear highway.

While passing, don't hesitate to use the full RPM potential of your engine when necessary. This means holding the accelerator pedal to the floor, causing the automatic transmission to downshift, and allowing the transmission to determine the upshift point. With V-8 engines, the transmission is programmed to upshift at about 4,000 RPM, a level that is not excessive in short bursts.

THE COURTESY FACTOR

RVs are heavier than cars, and they climb hills more slowly than other private passenger traffic, as do 18-wheelers. But fast traffic seems more tolerant of slow 18-wheelers than of slow recreational travelers, which makes courtesy a safety factor. It's best to frequently monitor rear-view mirrors and be aware of vehicles behind us. When a vehicle is tailgating and trying to pass, drive slightly to the right to give the other driver a better view of the road ahead. Use turnouts when possible, and don't follow another vehicle so closely that the vehicle passing you cannot return to your lane. Failure to display courtesy to other drivers can affect your own safety by causing angry reactions and poor judgment in other motorists who are trying to pass you.

TURNING

While all RV drivers must acclimate themselves to longer vehicles that require more care while maneuvering, some RVs track differently in turns than others. With the exception of very large motorhomes, all the self-propelled RVs are relatively easy to handle in turns. With the large ones, the driver must take extra care to swing as wide as possible in tight turns. The techniques are to keep the vehicle as far away from obstacles as possible, and proceed as far as possible into the area of a turn before beginning the turn.

Trailers require more practice and more visualizing because it's necessary to learn how the tow vehicle and trailer respond to steering input. Small- to medium-length travel trailers will follow closely in the tracks of the tow vehicle in turns, so the tow vehicle needn't be steered exceptionally wide in turns. A long travel trailer will track moderately on the inside of the turn, requiring more space. A fifth-wheel trailer tracks considerably farther to the inside of the turn (Figure 7.4), so a turn that seems rather wide will result in the trailer climbing a curb. The reason is that a fifth-wheel trailer's steering point is virtually above the rear axle, whereas the pivot point of a travel trailer is four to five feet behind the axle, behind the rear bumper. The tow vehicle's

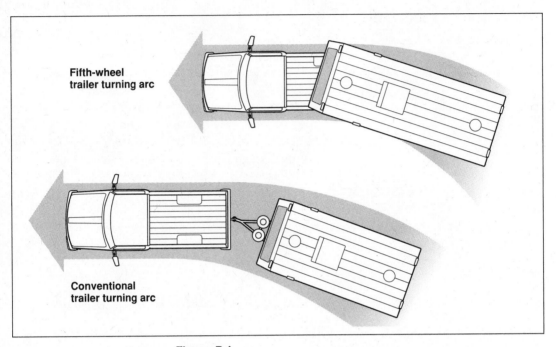

Figure 7.4
Travel trailers track moderately on the inside of a turn, while fifth-wheelers track farther to the inside, requiring even more turning space.

tailswing tends to make a travel trailer follow closely in the tow vehicle's tracks. But tow vehicle tailswing does not steer a fifth-wheel trailer, so it tracks farther to the inside of the turn. As fifth-wheel trailer length increases, more care must be taken during turns.

BACKING TRAILERS

With conventionally hitched trailers, ease of backing increases with size—the opposite of what most newcomers often assume. Fifth-wheel trailers are more difficult to back than conventional trailers, requiring more practice. Techniques for backing differ widely.

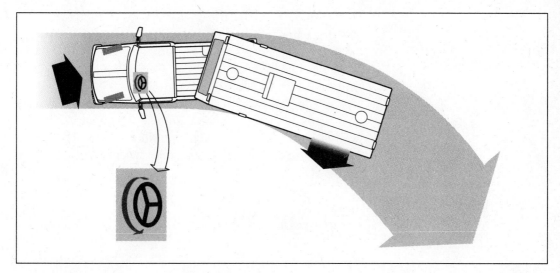

Figure 7.5
When backing fifth-wheelers, watch your outside mirrors and turn the
steering wheel in the direction you don't want the trailer to move.

Backing Fifth-Wheelers

Following are some tips that should help when backing a fifth-
wheeler. You'll develop others as you become accustomed to
the task:

- Watch your outside mirrors and when you see the trailer
  moving where you *don't* want it to go, turn the steering
  wheel in that direction. For example, while looking in the
  left mirror, if you see the trailer moving toward that side
  and you don't want it to go in that direction, turn the wheel
  to the left (Figure 7.5). Easy does it. Position someone near
  the rear of the trailer, in the driver's view, to watch for
  obstructions.
- Remember that you have no leverage to help you steer the
  fifth-wheeler while backing, as one has with a conventionally hitched trailer. Therefore, the tow vehicle must be
  at an angle to the trailer before any turning occurs. This

does not necessarily mean that extreme winding of the steering wheel is required, but it does mean that turns must be started before you get to the slot into which you're trying to move. The trick is figuring how much earlier. Each time you pull out of a slot, observe the path the trailer wheels make, and pay particular attention to the surprisingly long way you go before the trailer is aligned straight behind the tow vehicle. That is the magical point at which you should start to turn if you were to reverse the process and back into that slot.

Tips on Backing All Types of Trailers

Here are some general guidelines for backing all types of trailers:

- When you are ready to begin backing, place your hand at the bottom of the steering wheel. Then move it in the direction you want your trailer to go (Figure 7.6). (This is more effective with conventional trailers than with fifth-wheelers, which require more turning of the steering wheel.)
- Hand-held CB radios, available at low cost, can allow an assistant to relay backing instructions to the driver more effectively.

Figure 7.6
A good tip for backing trailers is to place your hand on the bottom of the steering wheel and turn in the direction you want the trailer to go.

• After arriving at a site, inspect it for the final position of the trailer and lay a length of white cord (clothesline) along the intended path. Begin laying the line a few inches to the left of where you want the left rear wheel of the trailer to be. Lay the line out to about where the left front of the tow vehicle will be when the trailer is in position, and continue with the line along the intended backing path so the line can be seen in the left rear-view mirror. Backing to the left is easiest, but this method can also help while backing to the right.

Backing All Types of RVs

Before backing an RV, be sure to inspect the site, decide where you want the wheels to be, and place "targets" on the ground—small rocks, pieces of wood, and such—along the path that the wheels must follow to end up where you want them (Figure 7.7). When the wheels are directly opposite the target, they serve as guides not to back up too far.

Figure 7.7
Placing "targets," such as wood or rocks, on the ground along the path you want the trailer to move will serve as guides while backing.

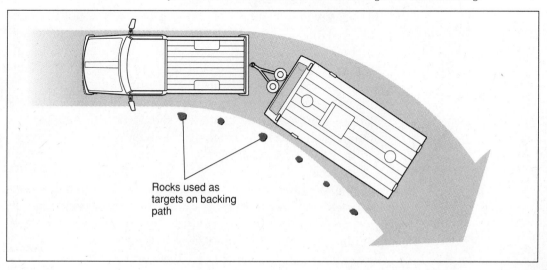

Rocks used as targets on backing path

No matter what the type of rig, practice is the answer. Regardless of the techniques the driver and his or her helper may use, there is no substitute for repetition of backing maneuvers until they become almost second nature.

BRAKING

While RV brakes are adequate for most situations, care is necessary to avoid overheating, which can lead to **brake fade.** When brakes fade, friction has increased the temperature of brake pads and linings to extremely high levels, resulting in temporary loss of friction between the pads and linings and the drums and rotors. The brake pedal is still firm, and its height is normal, but heavy foot pressure on the pedal produces little or no braking action. This is a frightening situation, caused by excessive use of brakes to retard downhill speeds on long, mountain grades. Beyond use of top-quality brake components, the cure is prevention—downshifting to a gear range that is low enough to retard speed sufficiently that brakes need not be used more than occasionally. This way, we reserve enough braking performance to make an emergency stop if it becomes necessary.

Many RVs have relatively high centers of gravity, which complicate the use of brakes while traveling curving roads.

If brakes fade prematurely—which means an emergency stop cannot be made effectively on level highway even though brakes have not been preheated—or if braking is not sufficient for more than moderate reduction of speed on a downhill grade, the brake system should be checked for glazed brake pads and linings. Top-quality semi-metallic brake pads and linings should be used. When a trailer is involved, action of the electric trailer brakes should be apparent to the driver and sufficient to take care of the trailer. The controller should be adjusted so maximum braking action does not cause trailer-wheel lockup.

Many RVs have relatively high centers of gravity, which complicate the use of brakes while traveling curving roads. By staging test situations, it should be possible to determine the vehicle's response to braking action on curves. Handling deficiencies such as a tendency toward excessive body roll (lean) can be exaggerated by the use of brakes. You should practice using brakes in situations other than straight-ahead driving so you will know what to expect. Handling deficiencies may be caused by weight imbalance, overloading, or poor shock absorbers. An RV whose handling is difficult to improve due to design deficiencies must be driven at slower speeds to allow reaction time in emergency situations.

LOAD RATINGS

All vehicles have load ratings, which determine how much weight (payload) we can add. We don't pay much attention to the ratings in cars because they are difficult to overload—there's not much space for cargo. Pickup trucks and vans have more cargo capacity, and overloading is possible, although unusual, in typical use.

When RVs are involved, the overloading potential rises sharply. Trailers are not usually overloaded because they don't have voluminous exterior storage capacity. Camping equipment, tools, and other supplies can be hauled in the tow vehicle. A pickup camper is the largest, highest, center-of-gravity load normally hauled by a pickup truck. Almost all the weight of

---

Manufacturers' Weight Ratings

Gross Vehicle Weight Rating (GVWR): the maximum weight of the vehicle and all its contents, including passengers—i.e., the maximum to which the vehicle can be loaded.

Gross Axle Weight Rating (GAWR): the maximum to which the axle can be loaded.

Vehicle Weight: the weight of a vehicle, such as a truck, van, or car, with full fuel tank(s) and all accessories but with no passengers or load.

Dry Weight: the manufacturer's weight of an RV, with no supplies, water, fuel, or passengers.

Actual Weight, Loaded: the weight of the vehicle loaded for a trip; the weight figure needed to compare with chassis-load and tire-load ratings.

Payload: the amount of load, including passengers, that can be added to the vehicle without exceeding the GVWR (dry weight plus water, fuel, passengers, and supplies).

Figure 7.8
The manufacturer's identification sticker or plate for cars or trucks will be on the driver's door pillar.

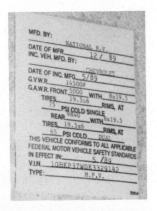

Figure 7.9
The motorhome identification sticker is usually affixed to an inside wall near the driver's seat.

the camper—which can range up to about 3,000 pounds—is carried by the truck's rear axle. For hauling large, heavy campers, rear tires must be rated to carry the amount of weight involved, and they must be inflated properly.

Motorhomes have greater amounts of storage capacity—especially the "basement" models with large subfloor storage areas—and they're rather heavy to begin with, which encourages overloading. Unfortunately few RV owners bother to weigh their vehicles, so they never discover overload situations that can lead to tire blowouts and, in severe cases, wheel breakage. Also, overloading usually causes spring sag, poor handling, and inadequate braking. An understanding of the manufacturer's weight ratings is necessary to avoid overloading and improve safety and handling.

With these terms in mind, perform a weight checkup on your rig, using these procedures.

1. Locate the manufacturer's identification sticker or plate for future reference. On cars and trucks it will be on the driver's door pillar (Figure 7.8); on motorhomes it usually is inside, near the driver's seat, or just inside the door (Figure 7.9); on trailers it's usually on the left front exterior (Figure 7.10).

2. Weigh the vehicle while loaded for a trip, using the procedures that follow. *If the vehicle is a motorhome, camping van, or truck camper,* weigh each wheel if you can find an axle scale or a wheel scale. In absence of such a scale, a platform scale will suffice, although it's not sufficiently accurate to measure individual wheel weights. If you must use a platform scale, weigh the vehicle five times: gross weight, front axle, rear axle, left side, right side. If the vehicle cannot be loaded for a trip, estimate the amount of weight to be added so you can determine if an overload condition might occur.

   If you are weighing a trailer, get two figures: trailer wheels only (hitched to the tow vehicle, with tow vehicle off scale) and gross trailer weight (trailer unhitched from tow vehicle). The gross weight is used to double-check the other weights; don't expect them to match precisely.

Figure 7.10
The travel trailer identification sticker can usually be found on the left front exterior sidewall.

3. Compare your weight figures with the manufacturer's load ratings and with the ratings stamped on the sidewalls of your tires. *The weight of your loaded vehicle should not exceed the GVWR, either of the GAWRs, or the individual ratings on your tires.* The reason multiple weight readings are necessary is that improper weight distribution may overload an individual tire or set of dual tires even though the GVWR has not been violated.

Weighing

Platform or wheel scales can be found at equipment-rental yards, moving companies, grain elevators, and other such establishments. Check the Yellow Pages of your phone book under Scales, Weighers, Weight, or Weighing. Using a scale is a simple procedure, but one very important procedure must be observed: *the vehicle being weighed must be level.* All platform scales are flat, but the aprons surrounding them may not be. When the aprons are not level, the RV must be positioned so it is level even though one side or one end may be off the scale.

Weighing a Trailer

Position the trailer wheels on the scale for a weight reading with the tow vehicle hitched to the trailer but off the scale (Figure 7.11). This is the figure you will use to determine if axle or tire load ratings are violated. Unhitch the trailer on the scale (vehicle off scale) to determine the trailer's gross weight.

Substantial lateral imbalance with trailers is unusual, which in most cases eliminates the need to weigh each side of the trailer. The exception would be a situation in which weighing the trailer's axle(s) indicates that weight is near or over the tire ratings. In that case, weighing each side of the trailer is advisable to make sure the heavy side is not above the tire maximum load ratings. If it is, reduction in weight is necessary.

Although it's not a necessary part of evaluating tire loading, you should also measure hitch weight, which will help in eval-

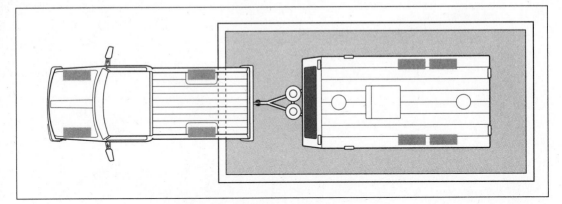

Figure 7.11
To determine axle weight, position the trailer wheels on the scale and the tow vehicle rear wheels immediately off the scale while hitched.

uating the trailer's stability (see Chapter 10, "Safe Towing," pages 210–211). **Hitch weight** is measured by positioning the trailer so the hitch support (tow vehicle or tongue jack) is off the scale. (Don't use spring bars, which will prevent an accurate hitch-weight measurement.) Weigh the trailer wheels; subtract that figure from the trailer's gross weight to determine hitch weight.

In Table 7.1, notice that the total actual trailer weight exceeds

Table 7.1
Weight Ratings Comparison of a 26-Foot Travel Trailer

Manufacturer's Weight Ratings (in pounds)	
GAWR, front axle	3,500
GAWR, rear axle	3,500
GVWR	7,000
Actual Vehicle Weight, Loaded	
Front axle*	2,800
Rear axle*	2,800
Hitch weight	700
Total trailer weight	6,050

*Weighed with trailer hitched to tow vehicle, utilizing a load-distributing hitch. Axle weights will differ when measured without use of load-distributing hitch.

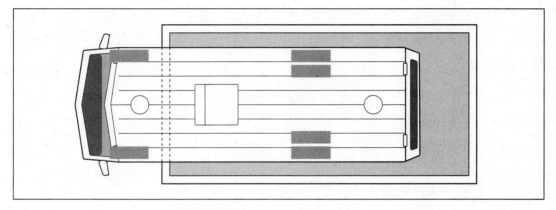

Figure 7.12
Motorhome or camper individual axle weights can be determined by
moving the opposite wheels immediately off the scale.

the combined weight on the two axles, but it does not equal the total of the axle weights plus the hitch weight. The reason is that the action of the load-distributing hitch transfers part of the hitch weight back to the trailer axles.

In this example, 205/75R15ST load range C tires rated at 1,820 pounds at 50 psi are used. Their rated carrying capacity is in excess of the actual load—a safe situation.

Weighing a Motorhome, Truck Camper, or Camping Van

If a wheel or axle scale is available, weigh each wheel individually. If the weights must be taken on a platform scale, weigh the entire vehicle first. Then move it fore and aft for front and rear axle weights (Figure 7.12). Move it left and right to weigh each side (Figure 7.13). If the aprons around the scale are not level, you will need to carefully position the vehicle so the off-scale tires are only an inch or so outside the perimeter of the scale—on a surface that is level with the scale.

The motorhome in Table 7.2 is obviously overloaded—in excess of its GVWR and its rear GAWR, as frequently is the case when basement-style motorhomes are loaded indiscriminately.

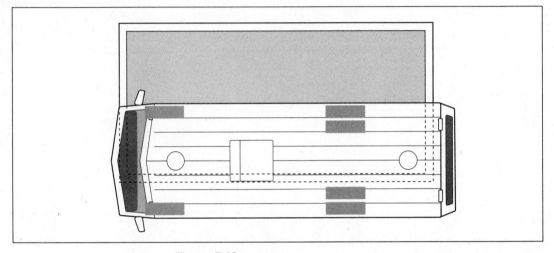

Figure 7.13
To determine the side weights of a motorhome or camper, the vehicle must be placed on the scale with front and rear wheels on opposite sides immediately off the scale.

The tires are 8R19.5E, rated to carry 2,780 pounds each at 80 psi—5,560 pounds per set of dual wheels, or 11,120 pounds total tire capacity on the rear axle. In this example, if the rear axle is loaded evenly (same weight on one side as the other), the tires are not overloaded. However, rear axles rarely are loaded evenly, which is why weights ideally should be mea-

Table 7.2
Weight Ratings Comparison of a 30-Foot Class A Motorhome

Manufacturer's Weight Ratings (in pounds)	
GAWR, front axle	5,000
GAWR, rear axle	9,840
GVWR	14,500
Actual Vehicle Weight, Loaded	
Front axle	4,400
Rear axle	10,300
Left side	7,000
Right side	7,700
Total	14,700

sured on an axle or wheel scale. Unfortunately, they're difficult to find. The solution is to assure enough margin of safety below the tire maximums to allow for uneven loading.

Some motorhomes have **tag** axles—an add-on rear nondrive axle with single tires. These axles are designed to boost the rear GAWR and allow the coach builder to assign the motorhome a higher GVWR. Use of a tag axle, which raises the number of rear tires to six, does not change the rear-drive axle's load rating or the tire ratings. However, by supporting some of the motorhome's rear weight, rear-axle and rear-tire overloading can be avoided. To determine weight on the tag axle, weigh the coach with the tag axle off the scale and subtract that number from the motorhome's gross weight figure. Compare the readings to the manufacturer's GAWR rating and to the individual tire ratings.

Correcting an Overload

If weight figures indicate overloading, correction is necessary to assure safety. Correction is particularly important if tires are overloaded because they are subject to overheating and blowout. If tire ratings are not violated, yet GVWR or GAWR ratings are exceeded, remedies are less urgent but still important. Tire-load ratings usually are matched fairly closely with GAWRs, so overloading of an axle usually means tire overloading is imminent.

Overloading adversely affects springs, wheel bearings, wheels, and other chassis components. but as mentioned pre-viously, the most vulnerable compo-
ing is combined with underinflatic
trous blowout (see pages 135–136

TOW VEHICLE/TRAILER MATCHING

When a prospective trailer buye
vehicle, knowledge of trailer we
the tow vehicle is rated for the

error by prospective buyers who don't know the meaning of the load ratings is to assume that the GVWR is the trailer-weight figure they must deal with in selecting a vehicle with the correct towing rating. As the definitions listed earlier explain, the GVWR is *not necessarily* the actual trailer weight. In fact, the actual trailer weight usually is considerably less than the GVWR. When selecting a new trailer, add the dry-weight figure to the estimated weight of water, propane, and all supplies for an estimated actual weight of the trailer, loaded for a trip.

The important factor in selecting a new self-propelled RV is to make sure there is enough load capacity. Again, this can be estimated by adding the manufacturer's listed dry weight to the weight of fuels, water, supplies, and passengers.

Proper attention paid to weights and weight ratings will pay large dividends in handling and safety, particularly as insurance against tire failure. A bonus is fewer mechanical problems and extended tire longevity.

8

How to Choose a Tow Vehicle

A proper amount of homework is necessary in preparation for nearly any major purchase, and it's particularly important for the prospective trailer buyer to make sure the tow vehicle/trailer marriage is correct.

Fortunately, this is not difficult if a new tow vehicle is to be purchased because most motor-vehicle manufacturers offer a considerable amount of specific information on vehicle types and how they should be equipped. Selecting a suitable used tow vehicle may involve quite a bit more guesswork, however. It's not always possible to find a used vehicle equipped with specialized towing options, even if the buyer knows which towing options were available when the vehicle was new—which has been rare. *Trailer Life's Towing Guide* contains ratings designed to solve that problem—ratings for passenger cars, light trucks, vans, and sport-utility vehicles, beginning with the most recent model year and dating back five years. The data, combined with the information provided in this chapter, offer you the ability to analyze a prospective purchase much more closely.

SELECTING YOUR VEHICLE TYPE

Consider the following points when selecting your vehicle type:

- Evaluate your needs and desires. How many people will accompany you, and where do you like to drive? Do you prefer a passenger car, truck, or van? If you prefer a car, is your trailer too large to be towed by the model that interests you?
- Make sure the vehicle's overall size and wheelbase are adequate for the trailer in question. *Trailer Life's Towing Guide* will help. Evaluate the drivetrain in view of the ratings. Engine performance and axle ratio must be appropriate to handle the weight of your trailer.
- Tires should have adequate capacity for the weight of passengers and supplies in the vehicle, as well as for that portion of hitch weight carried by the tow vehicle. (The **load-distributing hitch** distributes hitch weight to all axles of tow vehicle and trailer, with the tow vehicle carrying about two-thirds of the hitch weight, while the remaining hitch weight is carried by the trailer wheels.)
- Suspension components should also be adequate for the load. The vehicle should have a heavy-duty radiator, which usually is standard if the vehicle has factory air conditioning. If a new vehicle is being purchased, special heavy-duty cooling options should be ordered.
- Evaluate the mechanical condition of the vehicle if it is secondhand.

NEW TOW VEHICLES

Covering all the bases in selecting a new tow vehicle may sound like quite a project. And it would be, without the benefit of special information. Such information is available on all new cars in the form of trailer-towing brochures (Figure 8.1), and a purchase should not be made before you read the appropriate brochures for the vehicles you are considering.

Figure 8.1
Trailer-towing brochures published by vehicle manufacturers offer
equipment recommendations and weight ratings.

All domestic manufacturers and most foreign companies offer towing guides in one form or another. Some guides are
abbreviated, while others are quite extensive—educational even
beyond simply listing specifications for the brand in question.
Typically the best guides are published by Ford and Chevrolet.

These companies also have developed the most extensive
option packages for towing. Chrysler Corporation does a good
job in trucks and vans, but does not give passenger cars very
high towing ratings. Among Japanese manufacturers, Toyota is
the principle player, with aggressive ratings (5,000 pounds maximum, with selected options), while Nissan has become more

The reason that manufacturers' towing literature should be required reading for the prospective buyer is that many car and truck salesmen have not read the information.

aggressive in the recent past. Most Japanese cars are rated for maximums of 1,000 pounds, if they're rated at all. In the absence of a towing brochure, check the vehicle-owner's manual.

Most midsize or larger cars will tow 1,000 to 2,000 pounds without special options, and their manufacturers offer special packages for towing more than 2,000 pounds. More specific options are required or recommended for trailer weights above 3,500 pounds (which is the weight level separating the companies that are serious about towing from the companies that don't give it much consideration).

The reason that manufacturers' towing literature should be required reading for the prospective buyer is that many car and truck salesmen have not read the information, or they have merely skimmed it. Thus, their recommendations may be incorrect, or they may simply recommend the vehicles already on their sales lots, suitable or not.

When you visit a dealership, you should already know what the manufacturer recommends for the weight of your trailer with full water and propane tanks and all your supplies aboard. Determine that weight by adding the estimated weight of supplies, water, and propane to the trailer manufacturer's dry-weight listing in the company's brochure, unless you already own the trailer. (Water weighs 8.2 pounds per gallon, propane 4.25 pounds per gallon.) Also, add the weight of one or two batteries because trailer manufacturers generally don't include them in their dry-weight figures. (Batteries weigh 50 to 60 pounds each.) If you already own the trailer, take it to a commercial scale (see also pages 163–165).

While examining the literature, take particular note of weight ratings. In particular, the vehicle manufacturer will specify a maximum trailer weight rating, or that rating may be specified along with a gross combined weight rating (GCWR). These are the keys to safe towing and adequate performance, and they also have a bearing on fuel economy. (See also pages 163–164 on weighing and pages 210–211 on safe towing for more information on the importance of weight ratings.)

If you're buying a new or used travel trailer, pay particular attention to the portion of hitch weight versus gross weight because this will determine how well it handles (see also pages 163–165). As this section specifies, minimum hitch weight often means mediocre or poor handling. If you already own a trailer with minimum hitch weight or have found one with a floor plan you simply can't resist, you'll need to select a tow vehicle with as much inherent stability as possible. That means a truck or van with maximum wheelbase length and minimum rear overhang.

With a good understanding of the weight situation, you're ready to shop for the proper tow vehicle. The trailer-towing brochures will offer detailed information. The highest trailer-weight rating for new passenger cars typically is 5,000 pounds— a rather optimistic rating if a considerable amount of mountain driving is planned. Trucks and vans are more suitable tow vehicles for trailers over 4,000 pounds (loaded weight) because of their larger engines, numerically higher axle ratios (higher numbers mean better pulling power), improved engine cooling, heavier suspensions, and longer wheelbases (in some cases). However, a passenger car can do the job nicely if weight is not excessive and driving conditions are not too severe.

AXLE RATIOS

The choice of engine size versus axle ratio often is difficult for the tow-vehicle buyer. The axle ratio is the relationship between driveshaft revolutions and wheel revolutions (see Figure 8.2). For example, in a vehicle with a 3.50:1 axle ratio, the driveshaft revolves 3.5 times for each revolution of the wheels. As you can see, more driveshaft revolutions for each wheel revolution mean more torque multiplication. Ideal axle ratios for driving without the trailer are numerically high, such as 3.08:1. They keep engine RPM to minimum levels for best possible fuel economy. But they are not well suited to moving large amounts of weight. Typical axle ratios for passenger cars range from 2.50:1 to 3.08:1, while typical ratios for light trucks range from 3:1 to 4.56:1.

The choice of axle ratio for a tow vehicle is a compromise between fuel economy in solo driving and performance while towing. Fortunately, the wider use of four-speed-automatic and five-speed-manual transmissions in cars and light trucks has reduced the compromise somewhat. Four-speed automatics

Figure 8.2
The axle ratio is an important consideration when choosing equipment for a new tow vehicle.

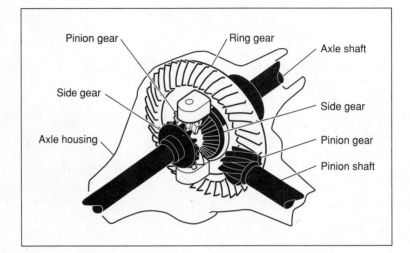

have overdrive top gears, which means the vehicle still can have a "tall" solo cruising-gear ratio even if a torquey axle ratio such as 3.73:1 or 4.10:1 is chosen in the interest of good towing performance in mountainous terrain.

CHOOSING AN ENGINE

The selection of an engine may seem very confusing because more than one may be suitable for your trailer weight. Indeed, generalized recommendations don't necessarily cover all specific situations.

It's necessary to second-guess the manufacturer's ratings when a marginal situation exists. The ratings are for typical driving conditions, which assume medium to low altitude. An engine loses about 3% of its horsepower for each 1,000 feet of rise in elevation. Thus, at 10,000 feet elevation, about 30% of the available horsepower has been lost (see Figure 8.3). When a considerable amount of travel at high altitudes is planned, the tow vehicle should have more horsepower or a numerically higher axle ratio than is indicated in *Trailer Life's Towing Guide*.

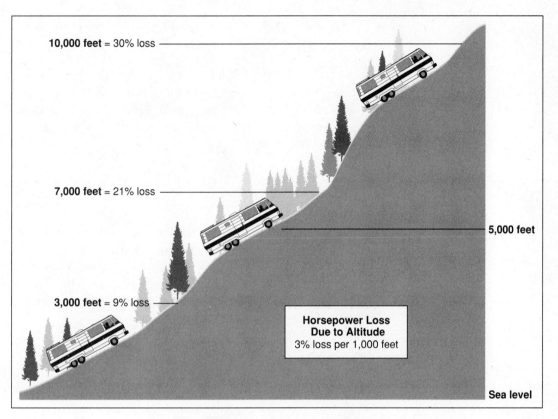

10,000 feet = 30% loss

7,000 feet = 21% loss

5,000 feet

3,000 feet = 9% loss

**Horsepower Loss
Due to Altitude**
3% loss per 1,000 feet

Sea level

Figure 8.3
Engine performance diminishes as altitude increases.

Typically, we're torn between the smaller engines for fuel economy and the larger engines for performance. When trailer weight is in the middle to upper middle of the weight-rating category for a given engine/vehicle combination, the engine is a valid choice for good performance. When trailer weight approaches the maximum, the prospective buyer must examine his or her travel habits and priorities very closely.

For example, a trailerist has a 32-foot fifth-wheel trailer that weighs 8,000 pounds, loaded for a trip. He is considering a Ford F-250, either with the 5.8- or 7.5-liter gasoline engines, and is having trouble deciding between the two. The differences: The 5.8 should get slightly better fuel economy but have noticeably less muscle for climbing grades than the 7.5. However, the 5.8 is a willing performer. The decision should favor the 5.8 if most towing is in low elevations and the buyer is not heavily performance oriented. The 7.5 would be preferred if considerable mountain travel is planned and/or if the buyer wants to maintain a relatively fast pace. One buyer's definition of "adequate" performance may be quite different from that of another, so personal preferences are important.

TOWING OPTIONS

Manufacturers of tow vehicles that receive serious attention by trailerists offer special trailer-towing-equipment packages, which usually are good values. The packages may range from very simple, possibly including only a wiring harness and a few other minor items, to a large package priced at several hundred dollars that includes a hitch receiver.

The prospective buyer should order the towing package and closely analyze the option list for other items that should be ordered, some of which are essential to towing performance and others that are merely for convenience and comfort. The list should include:

- Heavy-duty radiator
- Heavy-duty transmission-oil cooling
- Engine-oil cooler
- Hitch receiver
- Heavy-duty shock absorbers
- Stabilizer bar
- Heavy-duty springs
- High-output alternator
- High-capacity battery
- Cruise control
- Increased fuel capacity
- Positive-traction differential
- Wiring harness
- Extended mirrors

In vans and ¾- and 1-ton trucks, ordering heavy-duty springs usually results in an excessively stiff ride, although some of the motor companies specify heavy-duty springs in their towing packages.

External engine-oil cooling is available only on a few large V-8s in trucks and vans. Some companies offer factory-installed auxiliary transmission-oil coolers, while others increase the size of the transmission-oil cooler inside the radiator. In the latter situation, it's often wise to add an auxiliary transmission-oil cooler if the vehicle will be used for heavy towing in mountainous terrain.

The hitch receiver usually is an aftermarket item, but can be ordered from the factory on General Motors trucks and vans. It's wise to order heavy-duty springs in passenger cars and half-ton trucks and vans. In ¾- and 1-ton vans and trucks, ordering heavy-duty springs usually results in an excessively stiff ride, although some of the motor companies specify heavy-duty springs in their towing packages. The only situation in which heavy-duty springs are needed in a ¾- or 1-ton van or truck is when hauling substantial amounts of weight in the vehicle in addition to towing a trailer. Data books supplied to dealers can help you select the proper gross vehicle weight rating (GVWR), which dictates spring ratings, depending on your specific anticipated loading of the vehicle.

A high-capacity alternator is important only if your trailer is equipped with a refrigerator that is operated on 12-volt power while traveling. Otherwise, the standard alternator will suffice. Cruise control theoretically is a convenience item, albeit one that most of us feel we cannot do without. Increased fuel capacity is essential because of the adverse effect of towing on fuel consumption. A positive-traction differential is not necessary for towing; it's generally helpful, however, if the vehicle is to be driven often on slippery surfaces. Extended mirrors can be added later, but the ones that come from the factory may be of higher quality and usually are mounted more securely.

After you have followed the selection procedures described here, you should be assured that your new car, truck, or van meets your personal needs regarding passenger capacity and suitability for your intended uses. And if you've applied the data in the manufacturer's towing literature, you can be reasonably well assured that the vehicle will do at least an adequate job of towing your trailer.

SELECTING A USED VEHICLE

The manufacturer's recommendations serve as the primary guide in choosing vehicle type and drivetrain equipment for new vehicles. If a used vehicle appears to suit your needs, check the manufacturer's ratings provided in *Trailer Life's Towing Guide* to give you an idea of the engine sizes and axle ratios suitable for various trailer weights, along with the types of special equipment recommended or required by the manufacturer. The ratings reflect that power output of several engines

Used-Vehicle Evaluation Checklist

A thorough evaluation of any used vehicle should cover the following items:

Engine condition: Cylinder compression, spark-plug condition (look for evidence of oil consumption). Compression should not vary more than 10% from one cylinder to another (see Figure 8.4). Black, wet-looking soot on spark plugs indicates that the engine uses excessive oil. If possible, have a qualified shop perform a cylinder-leakdown test, which will give an even better indication of the condition of piston rings and valves.

Cooling-system condition: If the vehicle is not equipped with factory air, it probably does not have a heavy-duty radiator. Such a vehicle is more liable to overheat when used for towing, particularly if the trailer weighs over 3,000 pounds. Beyond the size of the radiator, the condition of the cooling system is critical. If the system has not been maintained, not only may the radiator be partially blocked by corrosion, but flow of coolant through the engine block may be restricted as well. A thorough check of the cooling system

should be performed by the mechanic, including inspection of the radiator tubes for partial blockage.

Transmission: While driving the vehicle, pay close attention to shifting characteristics. The transmission should shift smoothly and without delay. It should downshift automatically when the accelerator pedal is pressed to the floor. Remove the dipstick and check the color and odor of the transmission fluid. (New fluid is red and has clarity.) If the transmission has been overheated, the oil will be darker than new fluid and will not have clarity. It may also have an odor that is distinctively different than new fluid. Overheating causes transmission fluid to oxidize and lose lubricating ability.

Brakes: Inspection should include the condition of pads and shoes, as well as a check to see if the rotors or drums have been ground excessively to make up for damage,

Figure 8.4
Cylinder compression is an important indicator of engine condition.

changed some time ago. The most notable examples are the Ford 302 (5-liter) and 351 (5.8-liter) V-8 engines, whose power output was increased considerably in 1985 and 1986. If you're considering an early-1980 or late-1970 vehicle with one of these two engines, for example, you should make allowances either in axle ratio selection or trailer weight to account for the reduced performance of earlier engines.

Output of many other engines has remained basically the same during the past ten years, which allows you to use engine/axle ratio recommendations as guidelines. While this is not a guarantee of satisfaction, it will usually get you closer to a proper choice than mere guesswork. If you want specific information on engine horsepower and torque ratings, check automotive reference books such as the *Chilton Automotive Repair Manuals* in your local library.

---

meaning you may have to replace rotors or drums when the next brake work is needed.

Tires: Inspect closely for large repair plugs that would indicate the tire has been punctured by a large object. Check for bubbles or other irregularities that would indicate ply separation. Check for irregular wear, such as ripples in the tread. Once established, irregular wear is nearly impossible to correct.

Shocks and suspension components: A road test will provide an indication of the condition of the shock absorbers. However, worn-out shocks are the least expensive replacement item. Have a mechanic check the suspension components, such as ball joints and struts, for wear. Use high-quality gas-type replacement shocks if a change is needed.

Air-conditioning system: Conduct an air-conditioner performance test during your test drive, unless cool weather prevents it. If so,

you'll just have to trust the seller's appraisal of the situation. See if the selling party will guarantee the condition of the air conditioner on the bill of sale. If the system is defective, it doesn't mean the seller will come through on the guarantee, but it's better than nothing.

Fuel sensitivity: Operate the vehicle at full throttle for several seconds in a safe area, preferably while climbing a hill, to see how the engine handles heavy loads at medium to high RPM. Ask the owner what grade of fuel is being used. You should hear no rattle or knocking from metal parts or any spark-knock (ping). If the engine pings, either the initial spark advance setting is too high or the engine is sensitive to regular grades of fuel. If spark is too far advanced, you'll have to retard it for towing (to prevent ping), which will reduce performance. If the engine pings and the spark is set to manufacturer's specifications, it means you'll have to use more expensive grades of fuel to prevent knocking.

A MECHANICAL CHECKUP

If the vehicle is being purchased from a private owner who has used it for towing, the owner's assessment of its performance may be helpful, although it should be taken with a grain of salt, since an optimistic description of the vehicle's towing prowess may help make the sale.

A thorough mechanical evaluation of a used vehicle by a reliable mechanic can also be helpful, if the vehicle's current owner will permit it.

OIL COOLING

Unless your trailer is exceptionally light (below 2,000 pounds), and you know the vehicle is equipped with the optional factory-installed auxiliary or high-capacity transmission-oil cooling, it's usually wise to add an auxiliary oil cooler, available at any RV-supply store.

If the vehicle is equipped only with warning lights to monitor engine functions, you'll need to add a gauge for coolant temperature. You might consider adding a multi-function gauge that monitors a variety of engine functions, including coolant, engine, and transmission-oil temperatures. Such gauges are available in the auto sections of some department stores and from automotive specialty stores.

Whether your choice of tow vehicle is new or used, the time you spend on research can pay off in good performance and trouble-free towing.

CHAPTER 9

How to Choose
a Towed Vehicle

T en years ago, towing an extra set of wheels behind a motorhome was an oddity. Today, it has become so popular that traveling the highways without seeing a towed car, truck, or sport-utility vehicle is rare. The advantages are numerous. The convenience of being mobile wherever you go is probably the number one reason that towing has become commonplace.

Towing a "dinghy" vehicle adds convenience, mobility, and versatility to motorhome travel (Figure 9.1). The fact that you don't need to move your coach for sightseeing, shopping, and sidetrips allows the rig to be set up more permanently.

Another convenience that towing offers is that you are always traveling with a backup vehicle in the event of mechanical difficulty with the motorhome. It's especially important while traveling little-known byways where service facilities are few and far between.

There are a few disadvantages. One, of course, is cost. As you undoubtedly know, motorized vehicles are expensive to own, operate, and insure; towing a vehicle adds to the cost of owning and operating a motorhome. If you already own a vehicle that is suitable for towing, the initial cost is significantly less.

Figure 9.1
Towing a small car, truck, or sport-utility vehicle adds a great amount of convenience to motorhome travel. This "dinghy" vehicle is perfect for running errands and sightseeing.

Many RVers choose the motorhome mode of travel because they don't like to tow a trailer. However, connecting a vehicle to the rear of a motorhome creates a trailering situation, albeit one without the potential for sway that exists while towing travel trailers. Most motorhomes will pull small vehicles easily, without sway or stability problems, but the driver must be continually conscious of the tag-along vehicle in the rear. If you are considering a towed vehicle, make sure the total weight of the motorhome; vehicle; and necessary hardware, such as the dolly, trailer, or tow bar, does not exceed the motorhome manufacturer's gross combined weight rating (GCWR). (See *Trailer Life's Towing Guide* for a detailed listing of towed-vehicle ratings.)

TOWING SUITABILITY RATINGS

Controversy has surrounded dinghy towing for a number of years because, until recent years, most manufacturers of compact cars and trucks recommended against it. In particular, Japanese manufacturers issued blanket recommendations against towing their vehicles for long distances at highway speeds without disconnecting driveshafts, even though thousands of motorhome owners towed a variety of Japanese-made vehicles successfully throughout the late 1970s and 1980s.

The towing suitability ratings in *Trailer Life's Towing Guide* list the latest recommendations on dinghy towing by the various manufacturers. Fortunately, many of them have specifically addressed towing, and the number of approved vehicles is increasing. Following is additional information about specific brands listed in the towing suitability ratings.

Chrysler Motors

The Chrysler line (Chrysler, Dodge, Plymouth) includes a wide selection of approved tow cars. Many are low-priced, lightweight vehicles that are easy on the pocketbook and easy, weightwise, on the motorhome, too. The Dodge Caravan and Plymouth Voyager minivans are especially suitable, although somewhat heavy. Owners must keep a close eye on gross combined weight (GCWR) when towing these vehicles. (Gross combined weight ratings are listed on page 190.)

If you prefer the traction of a four-wheel-drive, but would rather have a car-type vehicle, the Colt Vista wagon is suitable. Popular pickups and sport utilities from Chrysler include the Dodge Ram 50 in two-wheel drive or 4×4 versions and the Raider.

Ford

The Ford Escort, one of the world's most popular cars, is lightweight and exhibits excellent tracking characteristics up through 1990 models, making it very attractive to motorhome owners. The 1991 model was redesigned, and Ford specified that the car should not be towed on all four wheels, even with a manual transmission, due to the possibility of transmission damage. *Trailer Life's Towing Guide* will indicate any change in Ford's attitude on towing the Escort. If you'd like a bit more luxury than the Escort provides, the Taurus (Ford) and Sable (Mercury) are capable of being towed, providing they are equipped with manual gearboxes.

A large number of the vehicles that Ford approves for towing are four-wheel-drive—the most versatile of the tag-alongs. Exploration of backroads and out-of-the-way locations that are inaccessible to two-wheel-drive trucks and passenger cars is the primary reason for selecting 4 × 4s, as well as the convenience of towing automatic-transmission vehicles without making modifications to the drivetrain. The Ranger pickup, for instance, in 4 × 4 configuration and fitted with a shell, makes an excellent transportation vehicle with go-anywhere traction and loads of storage space.

Four-wheel drives are equipped with **transfer cases** that can be placed in neutral, effectively stopping rotation of any components in the transmission, allowing certain 4 × 4s to be towed with either automatic or manual transmissions.

Ford's Explorer and its predecessor, the Bronco II, are fine towed vehicles, but they must be equipped with manual-shift transfer cases and manual-locking front hubs to be pulled on four wheels behind motorhomes. Vehicles with the optional electric-shift transfer box (pushbutton control) cannot be towed without a driveshaft disconnect.

Although it's been generally acknowledged that the Bronco II has been suitable for towing with an automatic transmission, an apparent error in the owner's manual has created some confusion. The owner's manual clearly states that there are no towing restrictions as long as the manual transfer case is placed in neutral. But the 1989 version limited speed to 50 MPH, making the sport-utility vehicle less desirable for towing. Manuals printed in September, 1988 (for 1989 model year), which are labeled *First Printing,* are incorrect, according to Ford. The correct speed should be 55 MPH.

General Motors

Long-distance towing of General Motors cars and trucks is not recommended by the manufacturer. Owners of GM vehicles who would like to tow them will need to use a dolly (small trailer that supports only one axle), a trailer, or install a driveshaft- or halfshaft-disconnect kit. For owners of automatic-transmission vehicles, use of an aftermarket oil-circulation kit will assure adequate transmission lubrication. However, GM will not authorize warranty work on driveline components if the car or truck has been towed with four wheels on the ground and the damage ap-

General Motors cites transmission lubrication with automatic as well as manual transmissions as its primary concern about towing.

pears to be related to towing. General Motors cites transmission lubrication with automatic as well as manual transmissions as its primary concern about towing.

Geo

Two models sold by GM dealers under the Geo nameplate are towable: the Prizm and the Tracker. The Geo Prizm is actually built on a Toyota Corolla frame and is suitable for towing without modifications. The Tracker, also known as the Suzuki Sidekick, has excellent towing manners.

Honda

Although Honda cars with automatic and manual transmissions have been successfully towed on all four wheels for many years, the company's literature specifically disclaims any responsibility for problems that result from towing. Honda cars have previously been listed as manufacturer-approved for towing in the first printing of this book and in *MotorHome* magazine, based on descriptions of trouble-free towing by owners and the Honda service department. But the consistent Honda disclaimer has prompted editors of this book and the magazine to reclassify Honda with the substantial number of other companies that do not offer warranty protection against problems connected with towing.

For owners who choose to tow Honda cars on all four wheels, the Honda service department specifies that 1991 Acura Legend cars should not be towed due to probable transmission and differential damage, whereas earlier models of the car had been successfully towed. On other 1989 and later Acuras and Hondas with automatic transmissions, it is mandatory prior to towing to shift the transmission to neutral after positioning the selector in drive while the engine is running. Failure to do so will result in severe transmission damage.

Pre-1989 Acuras and Hondas are towed on all four wheels by placing the transmission lever in neutral. For all models, the Honda service department recommends starting the engine and shifting the automatic transmission through the gears about good preventive maintenance to start the engine and run through the gears every 200 miles in order to provide periodic lubrication.

Hyundai

Hyundai Motor America produces the popular Excel and more luxurious Sonata; both of the manual-transmission models are towable. These cars are low priced, lightweight, and track well. Automatic models can be fitted with a halfshaft disconnect.

Isuzu

The popular Isuzu Trooper sport utility is not supported by the manufacturer as a tow-behind vehicle. Troopers are a bit heavy to tow, and their tracking is fair to marginal, but other Isuzu models tow well. Reports from tow-bar manufacturers state that the pickups and Amigo track beautifully.

Jeep

All Jeep models are towable in both automatic- and manual-transmission models. From the Wrangler (the descendant of the military Jeep) to the Grand Wagoneer, all are rated as having excellent tracking. If there is a disadvantage, it's probably weight. Most Jeep models are not especially lightweight, except the Wrangler and the Comanche pickup.

A word of caution when using the Selectrac or Commandtrac transfer-case systems: Jeep recommends that when towing, the transfer case be in neutral and the automatic transmission in park. The transfer-case lever may not move freely, making it difficult to place in the proper detent. Drivers should first put the transfer case in neutral and the transmission in drive, and gently accelerate to confirm that there is no power to the drive wheels, then shift the transmission to park. If the transfer case is placed inadvertently in one of the adjoining drive positions, it, or the transmission, can be damaged.

Mazda

Mazda Motors builds some fine cars and trucks that seem to have great towing potential, but they have not yet been officially approved for towing by the factory, which leads owners to drive-train modifications for protection against damage.

Mitsubishi

The Mitsubishi line represents a wide diversity, and all cars and trucks with manual transmissions are factory supported for towing. The multipurpose 4 × 4 Montero is the same as the Dodge Raider and tracks nicely behind motorhomes. The four-door may be a little heavy, so owners are advised to check the motorhome's GCWR carefully.

The Mighty Max mini-truck line includes two- and four-wheel-drive pickups, suitable for towing. Van fans can pull the Mitsubishi Van/Wagon that offers seating space for seven and loads of storage space, but weight may be a concern.

Nissan

The Nissan line is very popular and diverse, but alas, it's not approved by the factory for towing. If you've got a Nissan car or truck, you'll have to use a dolly, trailer, or driveline disconnect to get around warranty problems, even for vehicles with manual transmissions.

Subaru

Like Nissan, Subaru does not support towing. Many Subarus are towed behind motorhomes, even though some owners of older models have been plagued by poor tracking. Readers of *Trailer Life* and *MotorHome* magazines say that the Justy model is the best tracker. It's super lightweight at about 1,750 pounds and is also available in a 4 × 4 configuration.

Suzuki

Suzuki is supportive of recreational towing. In the automotive line, the Suzuki Swift is both lightweight and inexpensive. If 4 × 4s are your fancy, the Samurai and the Sidekick are available. Both are rated as excellent trackers. Suzuki requires owners of the 4 × 4 models to stop after towing 200 miles and operate the engine for a few minutes to circulate oil throughout the transmission.

Toyota

Toyota offers the widest line of cars and trucks with the corporate blessing for towing, although two that previously were included in the list have been dropped. The Land Cruiser no longer is towable without a driveshaft disconnect because Toyota is using a transfer case that does not have a neutral position. The pickup trucks have excellent tracking, but some also are equipped with the non-neutral transfer cases and are not towable. When the transfer case has a neutral position, the truck is towable on its own wheels. Apparently the only car in the Toyota line that has had tracking problems is the pre-1988 Corolla; front suspension geometry was changed in later models, improving tracking.

Volkswagen

Most VW models with standard transmissions, including the sporty Cabriolet convertible, are approved for towing. The Jetta is available in two- and four-door versions. The Vanagon wagon is not approved for towing.

Yugo

Yugo offers the lowest prices, but according to the factory, the vehicles are not designed to be towed on all four wheels. They received poor tracking ratings from users as well as tow-accessory manufacturers.

DINGHY TOWING EQUIPMENT AND PROCEDURES

A prerequisite for successful dinghy towing is a proper combination of vehicles, discussed earlier in this chapter. Other important aspects are proper equipment, installed and used properly, along with vigilance by the owner to make sure towing is safe.

Although even a relatively small motorhome may be able to tow a heavy car, the questions are how far, how well, and how safely. Weight limits prescribed by manufacturers of motorhome chassis are intended to insure adequate performance and braking for the motorhome. Applying those limits to one's personal situation requires knowledge of the motorhome's curb weight and the chassis manufacturer's gross combined weight rating (GCWR), the maximum total weight of the motorhome, towed vehicle, and all their contents. With knowledge of the motorhome's weight loaded for travel (including passengers), it's possible to calculate the weight allowance for a towed car or truck.

Analysis of the weight factors can save a lot of trouble down the line. Gross combined weight ratings of various motorhome chassis are shown in Table 9.1.

For example, a 31-foot motorhome's curb weight, including supplies and passengers, is 14,000 pounds. The allowance for weight of a towed vehicle by Chevrolet is 5,000 pounds—a rather generous figure but neverthless one that Chevrolet officially approves. As one might assume, less weight means better performance, better fuel economy, and improved braking.

Weight factors encourage motorhome owners to choose to tow compact or subcompact vehicles weighing about 3,000 pounds or less. Popular exceptions are compact four-wheel-drive vehicles such as the Ford Explorer, Bronco II, and Jeep Cherokee, which weigh 3,500 to 4,000 pounds. Even when the gross combined weight is within the manufacturer's limits, the ability to keep speed in check on steep downhill grades may require more braking than the motorhome can produce from the combined effect of downshifting the transmission (engine-compression braking) and application of service brakes. See pages 200–201 for more on braking.

Table 9.1
Motorhome Gross Combined Weight Ratings

Motorhome Chassis	GCWR (lbs)
Chevrolet P30	19,000
Chevrolet G30 w/5.7 engine	13,500
Ford E350	18,500
Ford F-Super Duty	25,000
Gillig	
MHF460	20,000
MHM	30,000
MHA3208	36,000
MHHD6V92	40,000
Oshkosh	
M line (gasoline	20,000
M line (diesel)	22,000
VC18R	20,000
VC20R	30,000
VC26R	30,000
Roadmaster	27,500 for gasoline-powered chassis; no limit for diesels
Spartan	
Standard chassis	19,000
Mountain Master	32,000
Vironex	13,500

Towing Equipment

Beyond maintaining a realistic weight situation, the choice of towing equipment is important to safety and convenience. Vehicles can be successfully and legally towed three ways: on their own four wheels utilizing a trailer (Figure 9.2), a tow bar (Figure 9.3), or with two wheels on a dolly (Figure 9.4).

Figure 9.2
Trailers can be used to legally tow a vehicle behind a motorhome, but the additional weight may limit the payload.

Figure 9.3
The most popular method of towing a small vehicle behind a motorhome is on all four wheels. Basic tow bars are usually attached to a baseplate bolted to the towed-car frame.

Many motorhome owners find that the extra weight of a dolly (310 to 600 pounds, depending on brand and model) or trailer (700 to 1,000 pounds) does not cause their gross combined weight to exceed the motorhome chassis manufacturer's gross combined weight rating, while others prefer "flat" towing with a tow bar. In either case, proper choice and installation of equipment is important—especially so with tow bars since they are mechanically attached to the towed vehicle, whereas a dolly or trailer is hitched to the motorhome and only requires that the towed vehicle be secured.

Figure 9.4
Tow dollies allow the drive wheels of a dinghy vehicle to be supported off the ground.

Hitch Platforms and Ball Height

Whether the towing method is a tow bar, dolly, or trailer, the height of the **hitch ball** is important to proper handling and safety. Ball height will vary with the road clearance of the vehicle or trailer, which means that there is no precise ideal ball height; however, the average will be around 18 inches. The proper ball height is one that places the tow bar or tongue of the dolly or trailer in a level attitude. When the ball position is too high, coupler damage is possible if the motorhome is driven into an unusually high or low position relative to the towed vehicle.

A proper hitch setup for a motorhome will include a **hitch platform** that does not reduce the motorhome's rear ground clearance any more than necessary. The receiver should be positioned flush with the bumper. If the ball is positioned at the level of the receiver, it may be too high or too low depending on the towed vehicle's height. Ball mounts of different configurations are used to create proper ball height regardless of the position of the receiver (Figure 9.5).

The hitch platform attached to the motorhome must be clearly rated for the total weight of the car and car/dolly or trailer to be towed. Ratings usually are stamped on hitch receivers and on ball mounts. Likewise, couplers must be clearly stamped with load ratings that are sufficient for the weight being towed.

Beyond the ratings, use a mechanic's creeper to get under the motorhome and check the integrity of the hitch attachment to the motorhome frame. The hitch platform should be bolted securely with Grade 5 bolts and lockwashers or locking nuts, or use Loctite thread sealant. Check all nuts for tightness. Welding is not recommended because the quality of the welds varies from one shop to another.

In their original length, most motorhome chassis are not long enough to extend fully to the bumper of the motorhome. Thus, coach builders typically add frame extensions. It is to these extensions, sometimes hastily welded to the chassis, that the hitch platform is attached. Obviously, periodic inspection of the quality of the welds is very important.

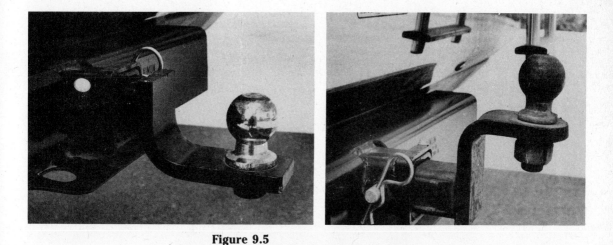

Figure 9.5
A number of ball mounts are available that allow the owner to attain the proper ball height regardless of the position of the receiver mounted to the motorhome.

Hitch-Ball Choices

Hitch balls are available in various quality levels and types. The ball should be stamped with a load rating equal to, or in excess of, the entire weight of your towed vehicle—and dolly or trailer if either is used. If the ball is not stamped with a rating, discard it and buy one that is. The ball should have a stem that allows the coupler full flexibility of movement. Don't use a ball without a stem because it restricts the coupler's range of movement, and when the motorhome and towed vehicle are at odd angles, the coupler could be forced off the ball.

Safety Chains

Federal law requires the use of safety chains or cables, regardless of the towing method (Figure 9.6). Two chains or cables should be attached in an X pattern under the ball mount, and they should be rated for the equipment involved, either Class 2 or Class 3 chain or cable rated for 3,500 or 5,000 pounds capacity, respectively.

Figure 9.6
Safety cables or chains
must be attached to the
motorhome and towed
vehicle using an X pattern
under the ball mount.

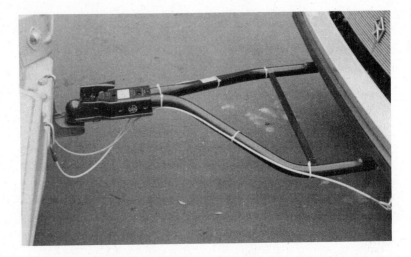

Installation of Tow Bars

Although rental yards offer tow bars that are designed for temporary installation using chains and partially relying on vehicle bumpers for support, we will deal only with tow bars that are bolted to the frames of towed vehicles, by far the safest arrangement and the one most commonly used by motorhome owners (Figure 9.7).

A variety of tow bars is available, ranging from universal units to late-model telescoping self-aligning bars that offer additional flexibility while positioning the car or truck for hitching (Figure 9.8). All tow bars should be identified with ratings for maximum vehicle weight. Make sure your vehicle's curb weight does not exceed the tow-bar rating.

Locking pins make many tow bars easily removable; they're stowed in the vehicle or with the motorhome until needed. Special tow bars are designed so they can be swung to vertical positions and locked while the vehicle is driven.

All tow bars utilize a triangular structure for rigidity, whether the structure is steel tubing, flat steel-bar stock, or two lengths of chain that form triangular support for a telescoping center bar. Rigidity is necessary because heavy stress can be exerted

Figure 9.7
A quality baseplate bolted to the front frame of the towed vehicle is the safest hardware for attaching a tow bar.

on a tow bar during sharp turns or when traversing uneven terrain.

Tow-bar lengths vary, but length apparently is not critical to towing stability. With the possible exception of some of the Jeep-style universal bars, most bars are long enough to prevent

Figure 9.8
Tow bars are available in a variety of configurations, including telescoping self-aligning models that remain connected to the towed vehicle.

jackknifing the towed vehicle into the rear of the motorhome during tight turns.

Most small trucks and four-wheel-drive vehicles present no significant installation challenges for tow-bar manufacturers. These vehicles have body-on-frame designs, offering a system of steel girders in the front of the vehicle for attachment of the tow-bar baseplate (mounting platform). Ideally, the tow-bar manufacturer should supply a **baseplate** (mount) designed specifically for the vehicle so that few, if any, additional holes must be drilled in the vehicle's frame. The baseplate generally is bolted into place utilizing Grade 5 bolts, lockwashers, and Loctite thread sealant as added insurance against loosening (or locking nuts may be used).

The design of baseplates for cars with unitbody construction presents a real challenge because such cars do not have conventional frames. The sheetmetal body itself provides the vehicle's rigidity, and the engineers do not allow stress loads of engine and suspension mounts to concentrate too heavily at single points. Unfortunately, front ends of unitbody cars typically are not designed with tow-bar attachment in mind, and the tow-bar-baseplate designer faces a real challenge. Care must be taken to distribute stress loads properly. Failure to do so can result in the baseplate mounting bolts being pulled out of the body. Or, in extreme cases, major front-end sheetmetal components may be torn off the car.

In situations where a prefabricated baseplate is not offered by the tow-bar manufacturer, a local welding shop or hitch shop can be contracted by the tow-bar purchaser to build the baseplate. Master welders usually have an excellent understanding of stress loads and can come up with designs that offer acceptable durability. However, mediocre welders have been known to create unsafe designs. Unfortunately, the typical motorhomer may not be knowledgeable enough to choose a competent welder. Thus, it's best to choose a tow bar that is supplied with a prefabricated baseplate. If that's not practical or possible, at least choose a welding shop that does a large volume of tow-bar installations or hitches for vehicles that are used to tow large trailers.

Tow-Bar Inspection

It's important while traveling that the motorhome owner visually inspect the tow bar every time the vehicle is stopped (see boxed copy below).

Although it includes several points, this inspection takes less than a minute. The walkaround inspection should also include the motorhome's tires and a quick look underneath the chassis for signs of oil or coolant loss. A more detailed mechanical inspection should be performed periodically, as common sense dictates, or once every week while traveling. It should cover these points:

- Inspect all bolts underneath vehicle or otherwise out of sight that are used to attach tow-bar baseplate to car or truck. Inspect vehicle body or frame for deformation caused by stress on the bolts.*
- Inspect bolts securing hitch platform to motorhome.
- Check wiring for chafing or damage.
- Inspect all tow-bar pivot points for excessive wear.

* All bolts should have several threads protruding beyond the nuts. Fewer threads protruding provide a danger signal without having to retorque each nut with a wrench (although that should happen periodically). Deformation of metal components indicates improper design of baseplate.

Tow-Bar Inspection Checklist

The owner should perform a walkaround that covers these visual inspection points:

- Coupler secured on hitch ball
- Tires appear to have normal inflation pressure
- Pin (or bolt) securing coupler in locked position
- Hitch ball nut tight
- Ignition key positioned so steering column is unlocked
- Transmission shift lever and/or transfer case shift lever (four-wheel-drive only) still in desired position
- Hand brake in "off" position
- All bolts, nuts, and pins on tow bar and baseplate tight
- Wiring harness connected and lights operating properly

Dollies and Trailers

Dollies became popular with motorhome owners when only a few manufacturers of small front-wheel-drive cars approved of their cars being towed—even those with manual transmissions. Many motorhome owners prefer automatic transmissions in their towed cars, limiting them to Honda models unless they choose to use an automatic-transmission lubrication pump or a driveshaft-disconnect device. A dolly immobilizes the front (drive) wheels of the car (Figure 9.9), eliminating any concern about transmission damage while towing.

Dollies basically are small trailers equipped with ramps that haul one axle of a vehicle. The dolly will tow either end of a car. For example, a rear-wheel-drive car can be backed onto the dolly. However, at least one manufacturer recommends against towing a car backwards due to the possiblity of sway (yaw) that may occur if the car's front suspension has worn components or is misaligned.

One of the most significant advantages of a dolly or a trailer is availability of brakes, either hydraulically actuated via a surge-type coupler, or electric, which can make a sizable difference in braking capacity while traveling over mountainous terrain.

Trailers are used by a small number of motorhomers who want the best protection of the car against damage to the drive-

Figure 9.9
Dollies are designed to immobilize the drive wheels of the towed vehicle to prevent transmission damage.

train as well as to the paint while towing—motorhomers who don't mind the inconvenience of parking a trailer after arrival at a destination. Trailers of various weight capacities can be purchased for towing a wide range of car sizes and weights. The weight of a towed car on a trailer is more apt to exceed the motorhome manufacturer's GCWR, which is still an important factor even though braking is not a limitation.

Lights

Most states require the motorhome's light system to activate the towed vehicle's legal tail-, brake-, and turn-signal lights. Even in states that don't have the requirements, a full lighting system is necessary for safe towing. Dollies and trailers are fitted with appropriate lights by their manufacturers, and a four-wire plug can be installed at the rear of the motorhome to include the four lighting circuits necessary.

The motorhomer who tows a vehicle on its own wheels with a tow bar must either use the towed vehicle's taillights or add a light bar, which is an independent tail/signal-light system. When utilizing the towed vehicle's lights, the common wiring method is to splice three wires from the motorhome (tail, left turn and right turn) into the wiring harness leading to the towed vehicle's rear lights. The splice point may be in the engine compartment or slightly to the rear, under the floor.

Electrical feedback problems can occur with late-model vehicles utilizing transistorized ignition systems. Current from the motorhome may feed back through the towed vehicle's lighting system into ignition components or other control systems. This can be prevented by using a taillight wiring kit (Figure 9.10) that includes diodes (one-way electrical valves). Such kits are available from a variety of sources, including at least one manufacturer of widely used tow-bar products. Light bars require a simple four-wire hookup that is identical to the system used for a dolly or trailer.

Motorhomes utilizing turn signals that are separate from brake lights require the use of a solid-state converter to provide compatibility with the conventional lights of a dolly or trailer in

Figure 9.10
Special kits with diodes
can be used to prevent
electrical feedback when
hardwiring to utilize the
towed vehicle's lights.

which the same light is used for brakes and turn signals. Such converters are available from the same companies that make light bars and wiring kits.

Braking

With extra weight tagging along behind, it's always best to allow an additional margin of stopping distance than normally would be required. Any motorhome towing a vehicle should always have the capability of making an emergency stop on a downhill grade even though service brakes have been used intermittently to retard speed. It's usually necessary to use service brakes frequently to retard speed on downhill grades in mountainous terrain, sometimes to the extent that partial brake fade occurs. Fade is caused by overheating of brake pads, shoes, drums, and rotors to the point where friction between the two is partially or fully lost. Although the brake pedal may feel firm, little or no reduction of speed occurs.

The motorhomer who is towing a vehicle on its own wheels must use lower gears to retard speed and minimize the use of service brakes. If weight is too high to avoid excessive use of service brakes, additional braking using a brake-equipped dolly, a brake-actuating tow bar, or an engine-braking (retarder) system for the motorhome is needed.

Tracking

While towing with a tow bar or dolly, don't back up. The car or dolly will not steer in the motorhome's intended direction, and the car will be dragged sideways.

Some compact cars and trucks track better than others while being towed, due to differing steering geometry. If a vehicle does not track well, have an alignment shop set the front-wheel caster to the maximum factory-recommended setting. Maintain maximum air pressure in the tires to help reduce tread wear.

If the towed vehicle's front wheels have a tendency to **reverse steer** (crank all the way in the wrong direction) in driveways, it may be necessary to use a stretch cord to anchor the steering wheel to a point behind the driver's seat so the wheel cannot make a full revolution. This is not ideal because it accelerates tire wear, but it will prevent an annoying lockup situation in driveways and on other uneven terrain.

While maneuvering the motorhome, avoid sharp turns at slow speeds. Motorhomes have long rear overhangs, and sharp turns cause rapid lateral movement of the hitch ball. This tends to drag the towed vehicle sideways. While towing with a tow bar or dolly, don't back up. The car or dolly will not steer in the motorhome's intended direction, and the car will be dragged sideways. Be sure transmission lubricant is kept up to the recommended fill level to insure lubrication of the tailshaft during towing.

Automatic-transmission cars must be towed on dollies or trailers unless one of the above-mentioned add-on items is used. Yet another option is an automatic-transmission lubrication pump system (Figure 9.11). Such systems, operated by 12-volt DC power from the motorhome, circulate the towed vehicle's transmission fluid to prevent bearing damage. These systems are available for many models of conventional automatic-transmission cars. Automatic transmissions made by Honda differ from others in that the input shaft from the engine need not be turning to operate the transmission's built-in fluid pump.

Figure 9.11
Special lubrication pumps can be used to circulate oil in an automatic transmission to guard against internal damage while towing on all four wheels.

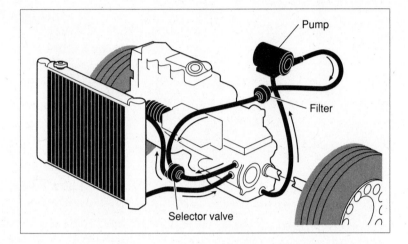

The reasons why dinghy towing has grown so popular are obvious: it adds greatly to the convenience and adventure of motorhoming. With proper equipment, maintenance, and precautions, the motorhome owner can be reasonably well assured that towing will be trouble free.

10

Safe Towing

B y its very nature, towing a travel trailer requires special attention. After all, a tow vehicle and trailer form an articulated vehicle—that is, two vehicles joined by a flexible link. Although the vehicle dynamics of trailering can get rather complex, it's possible to analyze tow vehicle/trailer potential for proper handling in terms that are easily understood by the layperson. That's what we'll do here—a step-by-step procedure for evaluating tow-vehicle/trailer-designed stability, followed by procedures for making trailers handle better.

Both trailers and tow vehicles have certain drawbacks: Trailers vary widely in weight distribution, while tow vehicles can vary substantially in basic roadworthiness. Being confronted by one of these situations is unfortunate; suffering with both can be dangerous. However, improvements can be made, even in a worst-case situation, that will dramatically improve safety and the enjoyability of trailering.

WEIGHT AND BALANCE

Trailers are available in two types: conventional travel trailers and fifth-wheel trailers (Figure 10.1). (Included in the travel-trailer category are folding camping trailers.) Primarily we'll discuss stability of conventional travel trailers here, since by design they are more vulnerable to destabilizing forces than are fifth-wheelers. This statement might be construed to suggest that fifth-wheel trailers are much preferred. (Owners of fifth-wheelers undoubtedly would agree.) However, travel trailers have many positive attributes, one of which is that various types of tow vehicles can be used, including pickup trucks whose beds are not occupied by a hitch and by the trailer's front overhang, allowing for storage. With proper balance and hitch equipment, conventional travel trailers will handle properly and are safe.

The problem that can occur with travel trailers that typically does not occur with fifth-wheel trailers is a phenomenon called **sway**, technically known as **yaw**. Sway is a fishtailing (sideways see-saw) motion of the trailer caused by external forces that set the trailer's mass into lateral motion with the trailer's wheels serving as the axis or pivot point (Figure 10.2). All conventionally hitched travel trailers will sway slightly in response to

Figure 10.1
Of the two types of popular trailers, travel trailers are more vulnerable to destabilizing forces.

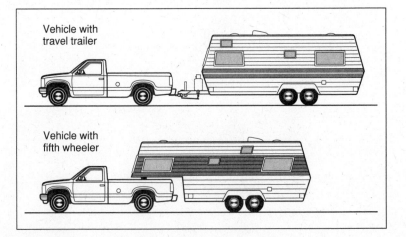

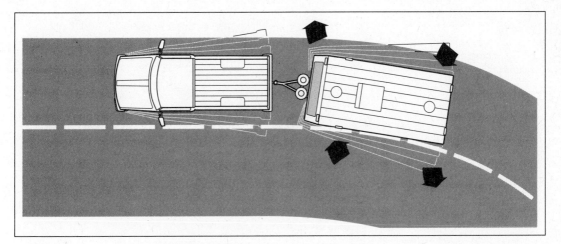

Figure 10.2
The lateral see-saw motion of the trailer exerts steering input on the
tow vehicle.

crosswinds or the bow wave of an 18-wheeler overtaking from
the rear. The good ones will need little correction by the driver
and will quickly restabilize. Only poorly designed trailers will
continue to sway after the force that caused the instability has
ceased. In fact, in poorly balanced trailers, the sway motion
may increase until control is lost.

There are several ways to judge a good travel trailer or correct a problem in a trailer that you may already own.

A TRAILER-STABILITY CHECKUP

A trailer's inherent stability is part of its design, based on the
amount of weight in front of the axles versus the amount of
weight behind. The difference between these two weight
masses is the amount of weight on the trailer's hitch, called
hitch weight or **tongue weight** (Figure 10.3). Trailers with
insufficient hitch weight have two deficiencies:

1. The weight mass behind the axle(s) is too high; when set
   in motion it acts as a pendulum.

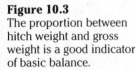

Figure 10.3
The proportion between hitch weight and gross weight is a good indicator of basic balance.

500 lbs hitch weight + 4,500 lbs trailer weight = 5,000 lbs gross weight

2. The distance between the hitch ball and the trailer axles is insufficient.

Elementary physics helps explain why distance between the hitch ball and axles is important. We all know that we can use a board (lever) positioned on a rock (fulcrum) to move another rock that is too heavy for us to lift without assistance. The lever gives us a mechanical advantage (leverage) on the rock. Likewise, trailers that have considerably more length in front of their axle(s) than in the rear give tow vehicles a mechanical advantage: the tow vehicle has a long lever with which to steer the trailer. This balance question is dealt with in terms of pounds of hitch weight.

Simply stated, *trailers with a high proportion of hitch weight to gross weight usually have more of their length ahead of the axles, and they handle better.* The generally accepted industry standard is that hitch weight should be approximately 10% of gross weight. In fact, that is a bare minimum, and some trailers with 10% hitch weight don't handle well. Hitch weights of 12% or higher (up to the weight limits of the hitch being used) assure proper handling. In marginal situations, the owner's ability to handle an unstable trailer will depend on the inherent stability of the tow vehicle, which is another variable.

A truck or van with long wheelbase, relatively short rear overhang, and stiff springs will, at least partially, make up for a trailer's lack of inherent stability. But if the trailer is towed by a softly sprung truck or van with a long overhang, or a passenger car, the trailer's shortcomings will be more obvious.

A brief driving test on a section of straight road with no other traffic in sight will give you an assessment of your trailer's inherent stability. The trial should be conducted with the tow vehicle and trailer loaded normally for travel. Make sure the refrigerator door is secured and that contents of cabinets will not be dislodged. If you have a friction-type sway-control device, set the adjusting lever so the device is not functional. A sway-control device is a valuable asset and should be used continually. But for the purposes of this test it should be disconnected so it does not camouflage inherent trailer instability.

For this trial, trailer brakes should be working effectively, and the manual control lever on the brake controller should be within easy reach of the driver (Figure 10.4). If your brake controller does not have a lever that allows you to actuate trailer brakes independently of tow-vehicle brakes, it's important that you change to a controller that does. *Independent use of trailer*

Figure 10.4
The brake controller should be within easy reach of the driver.

*brakes is the single most effective countermeasure to reduce or
eliminate trailer sway.*

Begin the test at about 20 miles per hour and crank the
steering wheel sharply to the left, simulating an attempt to avoid
an obstacle in the road. Note the reaction of the trailer. Repeat
the experiment while increasing speed, but take care not to
overdo it. Practice actuating the trailer brakes independently of
the tow-vehicle brakes so you can do it almost instinctively. As
speeds increase, the trailer will sway more dramatically. With
each trial, note the severity of trailer sway and how many oscillations occur before the trailer restabilizes. Again, take care
not to exceed the limits of your tow vehicle and trailer.

The most pronounced sway oscillations should be the ones
produced by your sharp steering input; subsequent oscillations
should diminish rapidly. If the second and third sway oscillations are equally as severe or worse than the first, the trailer is
unstable (or marginally stable at best) and needs correction.
Don't be lulled into complacency by the fact that the trailer
handles much better when your sway-control device is in use.
Sure it does! But an emergency maneuver may overcome the
effect of the sway-control unit and result in an accident.

HOW A TRAILER SHOULD HANDLE

Many trailerists become accustomed to being uncomfortable or
even frightened by trailer sway when they encounter strong
crosswinds, trucks overtaking from the rear, or mountainous
roads. They think it's normal—the way all trailers handle. Not
so! Properly designed, well-matched tow vehicles and trailers
have positive control, good road manners, and are fun to tow.
Certainly, strong crosswinds may tend to push the tow vehicle/
trailer combination laterally, and it may end up partially in the
next lane if the driver isn't paying close attention. But the rig
should be sufficiently controllable so that the driver can use
corrective steering without the uneasy feeling produced by
sway. Likewise, it should be possible to drive a mountain road
at brisk speeds while being able to keep the tow vehicle in the
proper position on curves.

Speeding 18-wheelers present hazards to travel trailers that don't handle well, particularly while descending mountain grades. A tow vehicle/trailer rig is most susceptible to destabilizing forces while descending a grade at highway speeds, and such conditions are the true test of inherent stability. It's natural for the bow wave (air pressure) of a speeding 18-wheeler to have an effect on a tow vehicle and trailer (Figure 10.5)—an effect that requires steering correction. But the effect should not be destabilization that makes the tow vehicle feel as if steering control is minimal and unpredictable. A properly balanced rig will not handle that way, although it will always be necessary to monitor one's rear-view mirror and anticipate the effects of an 18-wheeler overtaking from the rear. Drivers of all kinds of high-profile vehicles must do this; drivers of marginally stable vehicles who are caught napping usually are the ones who have control problems.

Figure 10.5
The bow wave (wind pressure) of an 18-wheeler overtaking from the rear can require defensive steering.

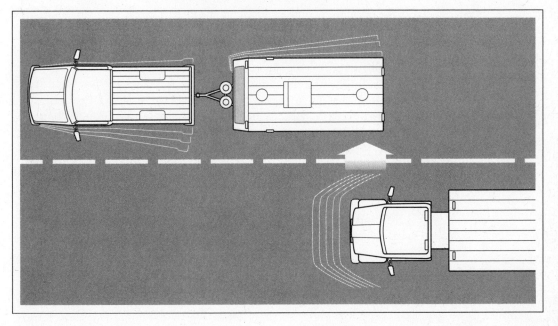

EVALUATING THE TRAILER AND HITCH

Even if your road trial produced good results, it's wise to check your trailer's weight and balance. The first step in evaluating a trailer for correction of stability is a trip to the scales (see Chapter 7, "RV Handling, Safety, and Weight Ratings," pages 163–165, for the proper weighing procedure). If your hitch-weight percentage is down around 10% (or less), it can explain a trailer's unstable behavior. If hitch weight is 10% to 12%, towing stability still could be a problem if the tow vehicle is marginally stable. If hitch weight is 12% to 15%, the trailer should handle well and not be the cause of an instability problem. Exceptions are trailers that have high weight masses, such as the water tank in the rear, serving as a pendulum and partially overcoming the relatively lengthy steering lever (distance between axles and hitch ball) that otherwise would assure good stability. Trailers with 15% to 20% hitch weight are even better, but it's important that hitch weight does not exceed the rating of the hitch, which ranges between 800 and 1,200 pounds, depending on brand and model. Hitch ratings are stamped on hitch receivers.

In Table 10.1, hitch weight is marginal but acceptable. This trailer should handle well behind a truck or van with long wheelbase, but may not be ideal behind a short-wheelbase tow vehicle such as a sport-utility General Motors Blazer or Ford Bronco.

Table 10.2 illustrates a trailer that clearly has insufficient hitch weight and is undoubtedly prone to sway. The only solution is to move weight forward. This may be accomplished by moving supplies or a rear-mounted spare tire. The worst place for a tire, or anything else that is relatively heavy, is on the back of the trailer. Carry it in the tow vehicle unless it can be

Table 10.1
Calculating Hitch-Weight Percentage, Example 1

Gross trailer weight	5,400 pounds
Hitch weight	620 pounds

Hitch-weight percentage: $620 \div 5,400 = 11\%$

Table 10.2
Calculating Hitch-Weight Percentage, Example 2

Gross trailer weight	6,200 pounds
Hitch weight	550 pounds

Hitch-weight percentage: 550 ÷ 6,200 = 9%

mounted on the trailer's A-frame (front). Another possibility is the battery; if carried in the rear, it could be relocated to the trailer A-frame. The fresh-water tank should not be located behind the trailer axles. This does occur, however, when designers don't pay proper attention to roadworthiness. If a rear water tank can be replaced by one of a different shape that will fit under a sofa in the forward section of the trailer, the positive effect on stability will be dramatic. Ideally, the water tank should be located over the axles, so its varying content does not affect hitch weight. Of course, it's wise to empty holding tanks before traveling to minimize weight in the rear.

Assuming hitch weight is raised to at least 12%, use of an effective sway control should give the trailer reasonably good road manners. Two types of sway controls are available: friction-type controls from Reese and Eaz-Lift (Figure 10.6) and the Reese Strait-Line (Figure 10.7). Both are effective, but since the Reese Strait-Line depends on adequate hitch weight for its effectiveness, it's most suitable to trailers with high hitch weights. Proper adjustment of the friction cams of the Strait-Line sway control also is very important for best stability. When it's not possible to achieve adequate hitch weight through relocation of supplies or appliances, two friction-type sway controls may be used as a stop-gap measure.

PROPER HITCH ADJUSTMENT

Yet another important factor in tow vehicle/trailer stability is proper adjustment of a conventional load-distributing hitch. Proper adjustment means that the trailer is level and that the

Figure 10.6
The Eaz-Lift friction sway control dampens the pivoting motion at the hitch coupler.

Figure 10.7
The Reese Strait-Line sway control utilizes friction between cams and brackets at the ends of spring bars.

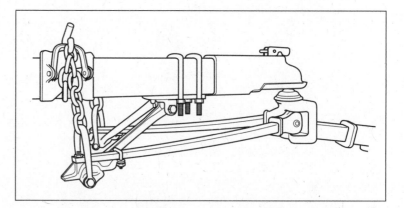

Figure 10.8
A load-distributing hitch distributes trailer hitch weight to all axles of the tow vehicle and trailer.

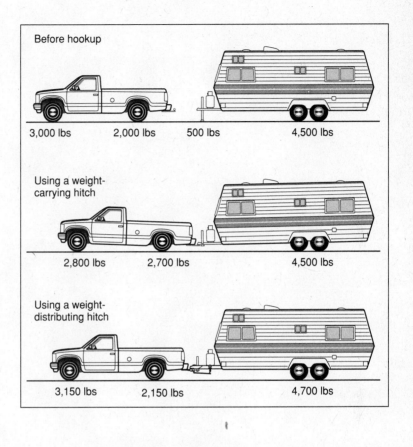

Before hookup

3,000 lbs   2,000 lbs   500 lbs   4,500 lbs

Using a weight-carrying hitch

2,800 lbs   2,700 lbs   4,500 lbs

Using a weight-distributing hitch

3,150 lbs   2,150 lbs   4,700 lbs

tow vehicle remains in the same attitude as before hitching. For example, if the tow vehicle was canted up at the rear before hitching, it should remain at that angle after hitching. The concept of a properly operating load-distributing hitch is that it should distribute hitch weight to all axles of tow vehicle and trailer (Figure 10.8). To make certain that happens, follow these steps:

1. Measure the vehicle at reference points on front and rear bumpers with the vehicle loaded for travel, but prior to hitching (Figure 10.9).
2. Hitch the trailer and adjust the spring-bar tension so the weight appears to have been added to the front as well as the rear of the tow vehicle.

Figure 10.9
Measure the tow vehicle at reference points, front and rear, to evaluate hitch adjustment.

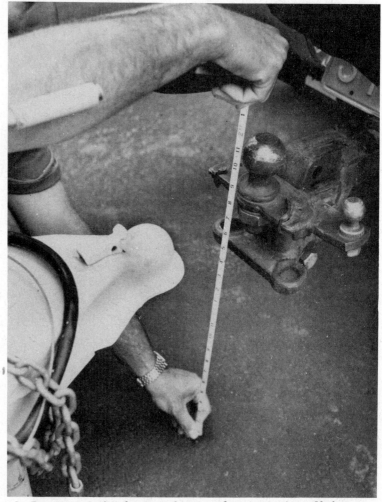

3. Remeasure the front and rear reference points. If, for example, the rear of the vehicle has dropped one inch and the front has only dropped one-quarter inch, add more tension to the spring bars, which will raise the rear and lower the front. Continue adjusting until the measurements are approximately the same. If a discrepancy is unavoidable, the rear of the vehicle should drop slightly more than the front.

Figure 10.10
Proper tow vehicle-trailer matchup is aided by an adjustable ball mount.

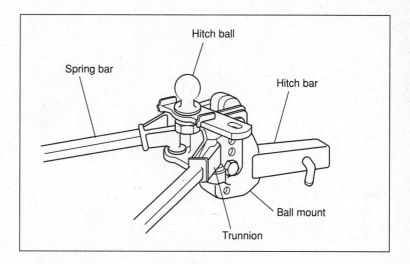

If the spring bars cannot be adjusted tight enough to achieve similar or identical vehicle height reduction, stiffer spring bars may be needed. The spring bars should be rated for at least the amount of the hitch weight of the trailer, plus about 200 pounds if the tow vehicle is softly sprung. If, after proper adjustment of tow-vehicle attitude is achieved, the trailer is not level, the ball mount should be raised or lowered. Adjustable ball mounts permit ball-height adjustment (Figure 10.10). If the ball mount is welded to the shank, replace it with an adjustable ball mount, available at hitch shops.

SWAY-CONTROL ADJUSTMENT

A sway control should be used, no matter how good trailer stability appears to be. The sway control dampens or slows the pivoting motion of the trailer coupler on the ball and is very valuable during emergency maneuvers to counteract driver steering overreaction, not to mention its role in helping the tow vehicle and trailer to act in concert with each other.

With a friction-bar sway control, tighten the control until you notice that the tow vehicle doesn't quite straighten out after completing a sharp turn at slow speeds. Loosen the control a bit, to the point you feel comfortable. With the Reese Strait Line sway control, the adjustment procedure involves driving straight forward very slowly while aiming the vehicle at a fixed object. Thus, with the tow vehicle and trailer in near-perfect longitudinal alignment, the sway-control brackets are centered over the friction cams. If the brackets aren't centered, loosen the hold-down bolts and move the cams forward or aft as necessary.

THE PULLRITE HITCH

The most effective sway control actually is a very unconventional hitch called the PullRite (Figure 10.11). The unique feature of this hitch is that it relocates the tow vehicle/trailer pivot point from its usual location behind the bumper to a point immediately behind the rear axle. The trailer no longer pivots on the hitch ball, so it's necessary to visualize the trailer A-frame having been extended about five feet underneath the tow vehicle to the pivot point. With the trailer, in effect, lengthened, a

Figure 10.11
The unique PullRite hitch pivots under the vehicle, behind the rear axle.

certain amount of maneuverability is sacrificed. The PullRite also functions as a load-distributing (equalizing) hitch.

The PullRite has a dramatic effect on towing stability. Even a basically unstable trailer is cured of its bad road manners. The principle is similar to that of fifth-wheel hitching, although the applications differ widely. The fifth-wheel hitch pin normally is positioned a couple of inches ahead of the rear-axle center line, topside in the bed of the truck, while the PullRite pivot point is underneath the vehicle, a few inches to the rear of the axle housing. Results are similar; on the road, directional control of the tow vehicle is not significantly affected by the steering forces of a marginally stable trailer.

The PullRite also differs from conventional load-distributing hitches in the amount of hardware installed under the tow vehicle. The PullRite utilizes a long draw bar and a radius bar, adding about 60 pounds beyond the weight of a conventional hitch receiver. The draw bar extends 11 inches behind the vehicle's bumper when the bar is straight to the rear. It can be swung out of the way when the hitch is not in use and locked in a stored position at the right rear corner of the unit.

While making turns, the PullRite causes the trailer to follow the tow vehicle farther toward the inside of the turn, similar to the way a fifth-wheel trailer behaves. This requires some re-learning by the driver to keep from towing the trailer over curbs and into obstacles.

EVALUATING THE TOW VEHICLE

Tow vehicles come in all shapes and sizes and with varying inherent stability for trailer towing. Factors that affect stability include wheelbase length, rear overhang, steering characteristics, and center of gravity. The most significant factor is the proportion between wheelbase and rear overhang (Figure 10.12). A longer wheelbase makes a vehicle respond more slowly to steering input. A short rear overhang gives the trailer less mechanical advantage over the tow vehicle. The combination of the two—long wheelbase and short rear overhang—provides the greatest stability. These two proportions are usually best in vans.

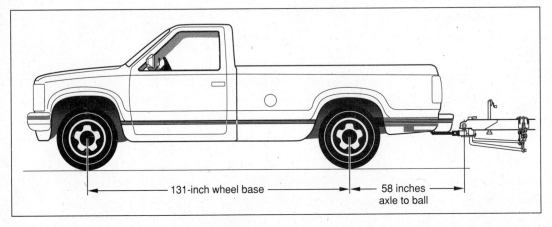

131-inch wheel base — 58 inches axle to ball

Figure 10.12
The proportion between wheelbase and rear overhang indicates potential for towing stability.

Typically, short-wheelbase sport-utility vehicles such as the GM Blazer/Jimmy, Ford Bronco, and Dodge Ramcharger are not as stable as vans, trucks, and Suburbans built by the same manufacturers. It's possible to tow successfully with the sport-utility vehicles, but they are less forgiving of poor trailer balance and/or improper hitching and sway control.

If sway tends to be a problem even though the trailer has a good proportion of hitch weight versus gross weight and hitching is proper, it may be necessary to raise the trailer's hitch-weight proportion still higher. The sway-control device being utilized should be very effective. If a Reese Strait-Line is used with a trailer that has less than 15% hitch weight, it may be necessary to add a friction-type sway control and use both sway-control devices.

For the tow vehicle itself, use the air pressure (stamped on tire sidewalls) in rear tires to stiffen their sidewalls; use the vehicle manufacturer's recommended pressure in front. Use effective shock absorbers, which tend to keep the vehicle in better control on unlevel road surfaces. If the vehicle responds too quickly to steering input, as many of the sport-utility vehicles are prone to do, have an alignment shop set the front end to the manufacturer's maximum positive caster setting. Additional caster tends to reduce steering response. A friction-type sway control adjusted to a stiff setting is especially important for comfortable towing with four-wheel-drive sport-utility vehicles.

CORRECTIVE DRIVING TECHNIQUES

The best defense against sway is a good offense—correction of weight distribution, proper hitching, and use of a good sway control. When stability remains in question under exceptionally bad driving conditions, the driver must compensate.

In any marginal driving situation, reduce speed, which will slow the reaction of your vehicle to external forces, while also giving you more time to react.

When sway occurs, the best technique for counteracting it is independent actuation of trailer brakes, even though it requires removing one hand from the steering wheel. In an emergency situation, this may require exceptional self-control. The driver who is vigilant about monitoring driving conditions and the scene in his rear-view mirror will be better prepared to use defensive techniques than the driver who is caught napping by a sudden change in driving conditions.

Although few hitch shops give it much thought, the location of the brake controller is a critical safety consideration. If it's positioned far under the dash and is hard to reach, relocate it to a better position, accessible to the hand you can most comfortably remove from the steering wheel—usually the left hand. With a properly balanced rig, you probably won't need to use the manual brake-control lever. But being capable of using it as a natural defensive maneuver is your insurance policy against loss of control in an emergency situation involving trailer sway.

If severe sway occurs, don't step on the tow vehicle brake pedal unless you're in danger of hitting something. Just lift your foot from the accelerator pedal and apply trailer brakes sharply via the hand control. During adverse driving conditions such as severe crosswinds, reduce speed and anticipate terrain that can produce sharp wind blasts. Be prepared to use trailer brakes if necessary.

FIFTH-WHEEL TOWING

Directional stability with fifth-wheel trailers is usually so good that it's hardly worth discussing. Only in cases where the fifth-wheel hitch pin is located behind the center line of the truck's rear axle does stability become a factor, and even then it's rarely a problem. Safety factors that definitely are worth discussing include secure attachment of the hitch, proper tire pressures, and proper tire/wheel compatibility.

Fifth-wheel hitches should be bolted through the truck bed to the truck frame for rigidity. If there is any doubt about your installation, contact the manufacturer of your hitch and ask for installation instructions.

Maintenance of proper tire pressures is important with any vehicle, but especially for the larger trailers. Low tire pressures, even for just a few hours, can cause insidious damage that can lead to a blowout later, when the low-pressure incident is long forgotten and there appears to be no explanation for the tire failure. Also, especially with the larger fifth-wheel trailers, wheel suitability may be questionable. This is particularly the case with styled wheels, many of which are rated for 2,000 to 2,200 pounds each and 40 psi maximum pressure, whereas the tire may be rated for considerably more weight as well as pressure. See Chapter 6, "Tires—And How to Care for Them," pages 143–146, for more information on tire/wheel suitability.

FREEWAY HOP

A bouncing, jerking motion commonly known as **freeway hop** occurs in some trailer rigs enough to become uncomfortable. The problem is very difficult to solve, even though it has existed for many years. It's caused by poor highway design—unfortunate spacing of the seams in the concrete (typically, 15-foot sections) so they set up a rhythmic bounce that reverberates throughout the tow vehicle and trailer (Figure 10.13). Whether or not it happens—and in what severity—depends on the spacing of tow vehicle and trailer axles and how they strike the pavement seams.

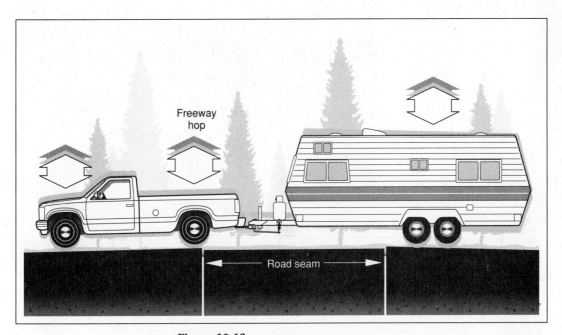

Figure 10.13
Spacing between seams in a concrete expressway can set up a rhythmic bouncing of tow vehicle and trailer.

Theoretically, changing the distance between tow vehicle and trailer axles should have an effect. However, the amount of that effect is impossible to predict. The simple way to change this distance is to extend the ball three or four inches farther behind the bumper. This can be done by changing to a longer hitch bar. The downside of this is that extension of the hitch can adversely affect towing stability.

Short of the hitch length change, good shocks and 1,000-pound hitch spring bars are recommended. Another change that improves some rigs and not others is the addition of shock absorbers to the trailer (assuming it does not already have them). Check with the manufacturer of your trailer chassis (contact your trailer manufacturer) to see if a shock absorber parts kit is available.

Changing to better shock absorbers for the tow vehicle also has the potential to improve the situation, although again, what helps one rig may not help another.

Figure 10.14
Spring shackles and bolts wear rapidly and should be inspected frequently.

EQUIPMENT MAINTENANCE

Maintenance procedures for tow vehicle chassis usually are very clearly defined in owners' manuals. In contrast, few trailer manufacturers offer advice on chassis maintenance.

In fact, very little is necessary, except for trailer brakes, which should be checked at least once a year. However, regular inspection is necessary because trailer springs and particularly shackles, the brackets that attach the springs to the trailer axles and frame, are subject to wear. Make it a point to regularly inspect the shackles (Figure 10.14), as well as the bolts used to secure them. Since shackles often become elongated, check them at the bolt holes and replace any that have elongated holes. Also check for spring wear and breakage. If a trip over exceptionally rough roads is planned, buy a couple of spring leaves for use in emergencies.

By evaluating trailer stability and taking the proper steps to assure better handling, towing travel trailers can be much more enjoyable.

Selecting a Motorhome Chassis

The cornerstone of any motorhome is the chassis, which is a sizable proportion of the vehicle's cost. For many years, motorhome designers have faced a variety of challenges when available chassis did not meet their needs. The limited number of chassis and weight ratings reduced the motorhome industry's ability to produce quality, variety, and load capacity in motorhomes. In turn, it limited the motorhome buyer's ability to get the most for his or her money.

Today, there are more chassis on the market than ever, in more configurations than ever, which is good news for motorhome builders and customers alike. See *Trailer Life's Towing Guide* for a complete listing of the latest motorhome chassis specifications.

Chassis manufacturers are paying particular attention to the needs of motorhome buyers, realizing that more and more of them are asking, not only about such items as headroom in the unit, but how much load capacity is available. With the advent of basement-style motorhome designs (voluminous storage capacity between the coach floor and the chassis rails), motorhome buyers became more aware of load ratings, ride, handling characteristics, and overall performance. Chassis manufacturers have come up with higher load ratings that fill the demands of both the motorhome builder and the consumer.

Designs and specifications differ among the various chassis, and the prospective motorhome buyer is wise to closely examine all the various models and features listed in *Trailer Life's Towing Guide*. Shop carefully, ask questions, and demand accurate answers. By all means, know what the motorhome of your dreams weighs before you make a purchase decision. No matter what the chassis's gross vehicle weight rating (GVWR) happens to be, it can still be violated by coach builders who don't pay enough attention to how their customers use their motorhomes.

GASOLINE VERSUS DIESEL

Sooner or later you'll have to face the chassis shopper's dilemma: Whether to chose gasoline or diesel power, and which engine among the two types best suits your needs (see pages 224–225). The choice is quite easy for gasoline power since there are only four contenders.

Chrysler offers its 360-cid (5.9-liter) electronic fuel-injection

---

Advantages of Diesel-Engine Power

Durability. The engine is designed to operate continuously under severe conditions at full power. If you're planning to keep your rig for many years and roll up lots of miles, diesel is the obvious choice.

Torque. Diesel-engine horsepower ratings appear low when compared to gas engines of the same displacement, but horsepower is not as important as torque, which is the name of the game in heavy vehicles. Torque is twisting force applied to the driveshaft and hence to the wheels, propelling the coach. Higher torque means more energy applied to the wheels. Diesels produce high torque at low engine RPM, providing a strong, steady, driving force.

Economy. A gallon of diesel fuel contains more energy than a gallon of gasoline, and the diesel engine makes better use of it, via higher compression. Diesels will get better fuel mileage than gasoline engines under the same weight and road conditions. Situations vary widely, but an example would be the Cummins 6CBTA in a 31-foot motorhome weighing 17,000 pounds, which typically gets 11 to 12 MPG, while the same motorhome with either of the aforementioned gasoline V-8s will usually do 6 to 7 MPG. Of course, the buyer must pay more for the diesel engine at the outset, which must be amortized by the fuel savings.

(EFI) V-8 and three-speed TorqueFlite automatic transmission. Several manufacturers are using this combination in their relatively new low-profile Class A motorhome chassis. The 360 engine is very reliable and has an excellent track record.

Ford and General Motors supply Class C chassis (cutaway van chassis) powered by several well-proven fuel-injected gasoline engines: the Ford 351 (5.8 liters) and 460 V-8s, and the GM 350 (5.7 liters) and 454 V-8s. Class C chassis also are available with the 6.2-liter diesel (GM) and the 7.3-liter diesel (Ford).

Disadvantages of Diesel-Engine Power

Cost. The cost to manufacture a heavy-duty diesel engine is several times that of a gasoline engine because compression in diesel engines is very high (20 to 1) compared to compression in gasoline engines, usually around 8 to 1. The additional cost for a diesel usually is about $2,500 in chassis that also can be fitted with gasoline engines. Top-of-the-line powerplants identical to those found in heavy-duty commercial trucks add considerably to the cost of the chassis, but such chassis usually are designed for motorhomes that are too heavy for gasoline engines. Thus, the gasoline option is not available.

Maintenance. Diesel fuel produces more combustion by-products than gasoline, and the crankcase usually contains more than twice the oil capacity of a gasoline engine, raising maintenance costs. The price of engine components is higher for diesels than for gas engines, as is repair work; neglecting maintenance can be very expensive.

Noise. Diesel engines produce a higher level of noise than gas engines, although while traveling, the noise is isolated from the driver and passenger in rear-engine motorhomes. This noise may be difficult to tolerate for some, but it's music to the ears of others. Diesels are coupled to special automatic transmissions that are designed to transmit their tremendous torque. The transmissions usually have four speeds, but five- and six-speed models also are available. Two manufacturers dominate the diesel transmission market: Allison, a division of General Motors, and ZF of Germany.

Diesel engines do not offer as much compression braking force (drag) as gas engines do, and many times the transmission builders offer optional speed-retarder systems built into the transmission. These worthwhile systems virtually eliminate the need to ride the brakes on long, downhill grades. Another diesel-brake device known as the "Jake Brake" is an engine-valve-control system that, when activated, changes the valve timing, turning the engine into a compressor. This causes the engine to provide much greater resistance to rotation than that which occurs when the driver lifts his foot from the accelerator pedal.

In the Class A motorhomes, the gasoline-engine choices are the Ford 460-cid V-8 (7.5 liters), with either a three-speed automatic or the new electronically controlled four-speed overdrive automatic transmission, and the General Motors 454-cid V-8 (7.4-liter) with three-speed automatic or four-speed automatic with overdrive. As of 1990, both Ford and GM offer electronic fuel injection as the standard fuel-delivery system for the gas engines. Ford utilizes a port fuel-injection system while GM uses a throttle-body system. Both accomplish the same task, but in a slightly different manner. The port system uses electrically controlled injectors just ahead of the engine's intake valves in the manifold passageway. A computer monitors the throttle position (opening), intake air temperature and volume, oxygen content of the exhaust, engine-cylinder timing, and coolant temperature. Depending on the combination or conditions of all these items, the computer will make a decision and signal the injector to spray fuel at the correct timed interval into each intake port.

The GM throttle-body system monitors the same engine variables, but controls fuel flow through a special fuel-metering device on top of the intake manifold. The injectors release fuel at a steady rate of flow to the engine on command from the computer system, depending on the engine-operating variables.

Both of the big-block engines have enough stamina to drive Class A motorhomes with gross combined weight (GCW) up to about 18,000 pounds. The **gross combined weight** is the gross weight (loaded) of the motorhome plus the weight of anything the motorhome tows. When you pass the 18,000-pound GCW threshold, it's time to start shopping diesel power because the torque output of both gasoline engines is insufficient for good performance, especially in mountain travel.

During the past few years, the diesel-motorhome market has exploded with choices. The proliferation has occurred mainly in the luxury motorhomes, where a wide variety of large-displacement engines is available from famous makers such as Detroit Diesel, Cummins, and Caterpillar. Torque output is very high, and motorhomes powered by these engines are known to perform very well despite their high weight plus the additional weight of a towed vehicle. In mid-priced motorhomes, the Cummins 6BT has found acceptance as an alternate.

SUSPENSION SELECTIONS

Several types of suspension systems are available on motorhome chassis. Selection is limited on the Class C and Class A rails, but for high-line coaches, many innovative systems offer features that improve ride quality as well as handling.

The types of systems that you'll run across while chassis shopping are:

1. Coil-front/rear-leaf springs
2. Coil-front springs with air-bag-assisted rear-leaf springs
3. Coil-front/rear-leaf springs with air-bag assist
4. Leaf springs, front and rear
5. Air bags, front and rear
6. Torsion bar front, leaf spring rear
7. Coil front, rubber rear
8. Rubber torsion, front and rear

Type 1 is found on Ford Class C and Ford's E33 Class A and the Vironex low-profile. Coil springs generally offer a smoother ride than do leaf springs, since they have less internal friction when the axle moves through its range of travel. In some respects, coil springs have a greater tendency to bottom on rough road surfaces. Leaf springs have a great deal of internal friction (the leaves must slide against each other when pressure is applied or released from the spring), and the ride quality usually is not as good, unless their higher load-carrying capacity prevents the bottoming problem.

Type 2 is used exclusively by General Motors on its Class A chassis. GM attempts to get around the bottoming tendency of the coil spring with the use of a heavy rubber air bag in the center of the spring. This does add capacity to the spring to help prevent bottoming, but it also stiffens the spring, reducing ride quality.

Type 3 involves installation by the coach builder of an add-on air-bag kit on the rear suspension of the coach. This is often intended to prevent rear sag, and it adds the ability to inflate the left bag at a different pressure than the right bag in order to level the coach laterally. These bags *do not* increase the chassis

GVWR. Suspension stiffness is increased when the bags are inflated normally (60 to 90 psi).

Type 4, leaf springs on all wheels, is a typical truck-type suspension that has been around for decades. It offers high durability, with some sacrifice in ride quality. Recently, new anti-friction materials have been used between the spring leaves. This offers a slight improvement over older methods, but the only way you'll know whether the ride is acceptable on any type of chassis is to take a thorough test drive and compare carefully.

Type 5 is usually found only on the high-line Class A coaches. Large air bags used as the primary suspension method offer a soft, smooth ride with resistance to bottoming. As the suspension is compressed, the air pressure rises rapidly to resist suspension travel and prevent bottoming. Niceties such as a built-in leveling system are included. Some systems offer pressure control that allows the owner to adjust pressure in each bag as desired while traveling or parked.

Type 6 is found only on the front of the Toyota micro-mini cab and chassis. Torsion bars are, in a sense, a straight coil spring. A spring-steel bar connects a front suspension member to the vehicle frame. When the suspension must move, the bar must be twisted. Thus, resistance is offered. Torsion-bar suspensions are efficient and usually adjustable for ride height. Ride quality seems to be a bit lower than that provided by a coil spring, but it's a good compromise between leaf and coil suspensions.

Type 7 is usually found in one brand, MOR/ryde. The rubber-block system is added by the coach builder and is designed to replace the existing leaf springs on the rear of the coach, or, it's utilized to support tag axles. The advantage of this system is nearly friction-free action of the rubber spring, which tends to smooth even the smallest road imperfections, resulting in an extraordinarily smooth ride. Another advantage of the rubber block is its sound insulating/absorption ability, resulting in a quieter ride.

Type 8 is an independent rubber-torsion suspension system developed by BFGoodrich. The system, which has been used in bus conversions for many years, is starting to show up under higher-priced Class A's. BFGoodrich's Velvet-Ride Torsilastic suspension system is designed around a Torsilastic spring, consisting of an inner metal shaft, surrounded by a molded rubber cylinder with an outer metal tube. The outer tube is fastened to the vehicle axle, and the inner shaft is attached to the chassis via suspension arms and special shackles. Impact is absorbed by the rubber.

THE CHASSIS

Computer-Designed Chassis (CDC)

Offering a low-profile chassis for compact Class A motorhomes, (Figure 11.1A) CDC can supply either leaf-spring or air rear suspension along with coil-spring independent front suspension. The optional air suspension is mounted outboard of frame rails. GVW ratings are 11,500 pounds and available wheelbases are 145, 158, and 176 inches.

The chassis, featuring a twenty-three-inch frame rail height, are available either with the Chrysler 360-cid fuel-injected V-8 or with the Cummins 5.9-liter turbocharged diesel.

Ford

Like GM, Ford produces both Class C and Class A chassis (Figure 11.1B).

In Class C chassis, the 460 and 351 gasoline engines, both fitted with EFI, and the 7.3-liter diesel are available. In the Class A chassis, only the 460 is available.

The 460 Ford has proven itself over many years as a reliable, high-torque engine, well suited for heavy RVs. The Class C chassis is available with GVW ratings up to 11,500 pounds, which makes it suitable for coaches in the 24- to 26-foot range. Several manufacturers have officially raised Ford's GVW rating as high as 14,500 pounds when utilizing a tag axle, which is designed to carry some of the load that normally would be handled by the rear-drive axle. In these situations, coach lengths range up to 30 feet. Ford's proven Twin-I-Beam suspension with coil springs up front and leaf springs in the rear allows the chassis to provide a comfortable, stable ride.

Ford offers two Class A chassis, the E-33 chassis, designed to support coaches up to 27 feet (GVW ratings limited to 11,500 pounds), and the Super-Duty Class A chassis, with GVW ratings up to 17,000 pounds. The Super-Duty Ford chassis is available in 178- and 208-inch wheelbases, and has a standard 75-gallon fuel tank, 100-amp alternator, and Ford's new electronically controlled, heavy-duty, four-speed automatic transmission. The suspension is leaf all the way around, and the front axle is a heavy-duty single I-beam.

General Motors

There are more GM chassis carrying either the GMC or Chevrolet logo under motorhomes than any other brand. General Motors produces both the Class C, which they call the RV cutaway van chassis, and Class A frame rails, which they refer to as the motorhome chassis (Figure 11.1C).

The Class C cutaway is available with the 350-cid (5.7-liter) and 454-cid V-8s, both throttle-body EFI engines. The transmission of choice is the GM Turbo Hydramatic three-speed automatic transmission. The GVW ratings range from a low of 8,600 pounds to a high of 10,500 pounds. Usually you'll find that motorhome builders will construct a coach up to about 24 feet in length on the GM Class C chassis. This is all the length that can be handled on this chassis and still leave a reasonable load capacity for the consumer. The GM Class C chassis with a GVWR of less than 10,000 pounds has a wheelbase of 125 inches, while the chassis with the 10,500-pound GVWR has a wheelbase of 146 inches.

Three rear-axle ratios are available: 3.73:1, 4.10:1, and 4.56:1. The usual choice is 4.10, which is a good compromise between power and fuel economy. The 4.56 gears provide good power, but at the expense of extra fuel. The GM Class C chassis features coil-spring independent front suspension and leaf springs in the rear.

GM's venerable Class A chassis is the workhorse of the RV industry. Wheelbases range from 137 to 208 inches. GVW ratings start at 10,500 pounds and range up to 16,000 pounds.

The transmission for the lower-rated units is the three-speed Turbo Hydramatic while the top-of-the-line 16,000-pound chassis gets a heavy-duty four-speed automatic from GM's Allison Transmission Division.

Gillig

Gillig Corporation has been building vehicles for more than 100 years, specializing during recent years in high-quality luxury diesel-pusher chassis (Figure 11.1D).

The Gillig high-line chassis are available with the computer-controlled GM 6V-92 350-horsepower diesel backed by an Allison HT700 computer-controlled transmission. The chassis is well suited to high-line coaches and long-distance cruising. Jake Brake systems are standard with the 6V-92.

LGS

Used only for the Ameri-Cruiser line of compact Class A motorhomes, the LGS chassis is a low-profile design in 135, 145, 159, and 173-inch wheelbases (Figure 11.1E). Standard power is the Chrysler 360, and the Cummins 5.9-liter turbocharged diesel is optional.

GVW ratings are 10,100 pounds when single rear wheels are ordered and 11,500 pounds when dual rear wheels are specified. Suspension are front coil springs (Dodge truck front end) and leaf rear springs.

Oshkosh

Oshkosh offers perhaps the widest range of GVW ratings and engine/transmission combinations (Figure 11.1F). The lineup, which includes the chassis Oshkosh bought from John Deere in 1989, has front- and rear-engine configurations with gasoline or

11.1A CDC Low-Profile

11.1B Ford Super-Duty

11.1C General Motors CP31832

Figure 11.1.
Late-model motorhome chassis range from compact gasoline-powered units for lightweight motorhomes to the heavyweights with large "pusher" diesel engines.

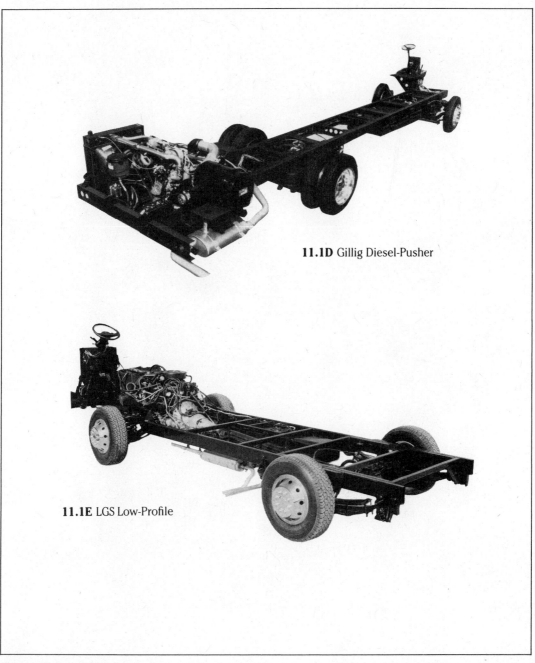

11.1D Gillig Diesel-Pusher

11.1E LGS Low-Profile

Figure 11.1, *continued*

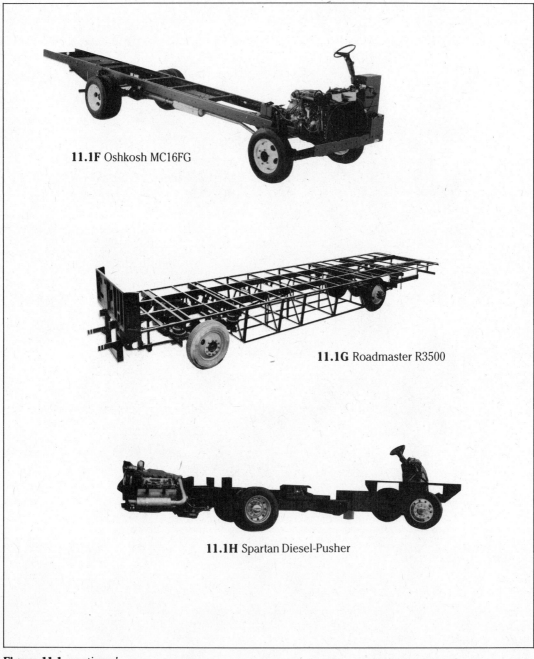

11.1F Oshkosh MC16FG

11.1G Roadmaster R3500

11.1H Spartan Diesel-Pusher

Figure 11.1, *continued*

11.1I Toyota Cab and Chassis

11.1J Vironex Low-Profile

Figure 11.1, *continued*

diesel power. Oshkosh models are offered from 10,300 to 26,000 pounds GVWR and in wheelbase lengths ranging from 145 to 276 inches. The gasoline engines used by Oshkosh are the Chrysler 360-cid EFI V-8 and TorqueFlite three-speed automatic and the Ford 460-cid EFI V-8 with the Ford E4OD four-speed automatic. For larger chassis, the Cummins 8.3-liter turbo-diesel is mated with an Allison four-speed automatic.

Chassis are divided into three categories: the L-Line with GVWRs up to 11,500 pounds, the gasoline-powered 360 V-8 for compact motorhomes; the M-Line, with GVWRs up to 18,000 pounds, with the gasoline-powered 460 V-8 or the Cummins 5.9-liter turbo-diesel for medium to large Class A motorhomes; and the V-Line, with GVWRs up to 26,000 pounds, with the Cummins 8.3-liter turbo-diesel in pusher configuration for large Class A motorhomes.

Roadmaster

Roadmaster (Figure 11.1G) uses three of the popular Cummins diesels in their pusher chassis: The 6CTA (8.3 liters), 250 horsepower; the L-10 (10 liters), 300 horsepower; and the 444XT with 444 horsepower.

Gross vehicle weight ratings range from 28,000 to 34,700 pounds, and equipment choices include air-ride or leaf-spring suspension.

Spartan

Spartan's high-line 32,000-pound-GVWR chassis features the Cummins L-10 engine and an Allison MT 647 transmission (Figure 11.1H). The Cummins powerplant is high tech and state of the art, rated at 300 horsepower at 2,100 RPM and 780 foot-pounds of torque at 1,300 RPM.

The company offers GVW ratings ranging from 18,000 to 33,000 with air-ride suspensions, Allison transmissions, and engine choices that also include the Caterpillar 3208 and Detroit-Diesel 8.2 liter.

Toyota

The Toyota cab and chassis, designed for micro-mini motorhomes, has a 6,000-pound GVWR and features a heavy-duty truck rear axle with full floating axle shafts, designed to prevent durability problems that occurred when earlier chassis equipped with semi-floating axles were overloaded (Figure 11.1I). Wheel bearings have higher load capacity, and braking power is upgraded via larger front-disc rotors and rear-brake drums.

Early micro-mini chassis were built with single rear wheels, which motorhome manufacturers converter to duals. Some of the aftermarket dual wheels were of dubious quality, resulting in breakage problems that have been prevented by the factory duals of the new Toyota chassis. Toyota uses a 3-liter V-6, which performs satisfactorily with the design weight capacity and still offers fuel economy of between 15 and 18 MPG.

Vironex

The Vironex chassis has found a home under the compact Class A motorhomes that have grown rapidly in popularity (Figure 11.1J). Built mainly with Chrysler components, the chassis is serviced by Chrysler dealers. The chassis features a 10,400 GVWR and is well suited to the aerodynamic designs of the low-profile coaches. Powered by Chrysler's 360-cid EFI engine and TorqueFlite three-speed automatic, the Vironex rails offer good handling and fuel economy.

When chassis comparison shopping, remember that all motorhome manufacturers are required to display a certification sticker that lists information regarding the GVWR and axle capacities. Different coach builders opt to place the sticker in different locations; ask your coach dealer to show it to you and explain the meaning. You should also attempt to determine the weight of the coach with all fluids on board; this will tell you the cargo-carrying capacity of the rig (see pages 161–167 on weight ratings).

If at all possible, take a test drive to a public scale and weigh the coach. Then calculate the additional weight of water and fuels, based on tank sizes, and add them to the weight figure. Gasoline weighs about 6.2 pounds per gallon, diesel fuel, 7 pounds per gallon, and water weighs 8 pounds. The sum of these figures is the "wet" weight of the coach. Subtract the wet weight from the GVWR to determine the payload capacity, which is the allowable weight of supplies and passengers. There should be about 300 pounds of capacity for every seating (seatbelted) position in the coach.

The wide variety of motorhome chassis gives the prospective buyer more choices than ever before, which can translate into a motorhome that is a better value and more enjoyable to drive.

Understanding Propane

The most commonly available form of liquefied petroleum gas (LP-gas) in the United States, propane, has been used in RVs for several decades as a source of energy for cooking, heating, and refrigeration. It's difficult to imagine how we would keep ourselves warm, clean, and well fed without this versatile, relatively inexpensive fuel.

Of course, propane can be dangerous if handled carelessly or used improperly. *Very* dangerous. So can gasoline. RV owners' attitudes about propane range from lackadaisical to paranoid. Both attitudes usually are based on lack of knowledge of the fuel's characteristics.

Gasoline and propane are cousins. The same people who may view propane as a mysterious unexploded bomb awaiting accidental ignition may pay little attention to safety when handling gasoline. Of course, there are people who pay scant attention to safety with either fuel. To help you understand propane better, possibly saving you from a very serious accident, this chapter will cover:

- The way propane works, its benefits, its characteristics, and its hazards
- Inspection and maintenance of storage or propane containers; proper marking and filling, plus information about service valves

- The pressure regulator: its function, protection, and inspection
- Testing you can do on your gas system; when to seek a competent professional

THE FUEL

Liquefied petroleum gas consists of a number of hydrocarbon gases that will turn to liquid under pressure. The gas used in RVs is called **commercial propane**. It consists of 95% propane and/or propylene and 5% other gases, mainly of the butane family. All of these gases are petroleum products separated out of the natural-gas or crude-oil streams. Butane is a close cousin to gasoline; propane is closer to the natural-gas side of the family. The chemical formulas may help us understand the relationship of this hydrocarbon family. Natural gas is a mixture of gases resulting in a C_2H_4 range of hydrocarbons. Propane is C_3H_8. Butane is C_4H_{10}, and gasoline blends are about C_6H_{14}.

Propane is a colorless, odorless liquid that looks somewhat like water. One *big* difference is its boiling point. Water boils at 212°F, and propane boils at −50°F. The vapor that comes from propane will burn. So, above −50°F we have a flammable gas under pressure.

The pressure varies with temperature and volume, as you learned in your high-school physics class. Remember Charles's and Boyle's laws on gases?* A closed container of propane at −50°F will have zero pressure. At 0°F, pressure will be 24 pounds, and at 100°F it will be over 200 pounds. The higher the temperature, the more pressure we have. Tanks are even painted in light, reflective colors to keep pressures lower in summer.

* **Charles's Law,** sometimes known as Gay-Lussac's Law, states that the volume of an enclosed gas is directly proportional to its temperature, or $V = kT$; this expression is strictly true only if the temperature is defined in such a way that zero degrees corresponds to zero volume.

Boyle's Law states that the pressure and volume of a gas are inversely proportional to one another, or $PV = k$, where P is pressure, V is volume, and k is a constant of proportionality.

An odorant is added as a warning agent so you can detect leaks. Make sure you recognize the smell (it's similar to rotten eggs), and be aware that your nose doesn't always work well. If your sense of smell is poor, you should consider installing a gas detector.

Since propane boils at −50°F, the liquid absorbs heat when the pressure is released. You have seen the stream of liquid at your outage valve (also called 20% valve) when the tank is being filled. It looks like steam, but instead of being hot, it is very cold. *Remember, it's flammable, it's under pressure, and it can freeze your skin.*

Expanding Liquid = Gas

The propane liquid expands 270 times to form the gas. One gallon of liquid propane makes 36.6 cubic feet of gas with 2,500 Btu's. Natural gas has 1,000 Btu's per cubic foot, so propane has twice the heat.

The one characteristic everyone seems to know about propane is that it's heavier than air—about 1½ times as heavy, while natural gas is about as half as heavy as air. This feature is usually exaggerated with both gases. We are sometimes taught that propane fumes collect on the floor. If the fumes are what make it dangerous, then beware of gasoline fumes, which are 2.6 times as heavy as air and almost twice as heavy as gaseous propane. The truth is that all these gases continue to expand as the temperature increases, as described in Charles's and Boyle's laws, and they don't usually collect near the floor because of constantly moving air currents caused by convection. Regardless of where the gas concentrates, don't turn on light switches, don't light matches, don't provide any source of ignition—high or low—when you detect escaping gas.

If you think you have a leak, get out, turn off the gas, and leave doors open to ventilate the coach. Don't use fans and don't turn off the refrigerator because it might trigger an automatic spark igniter.

Liquid propane weighs 4.24 pounds per gallon, about half the weight of water. Propane liquid expands dramatically when it warms, growing 1½ times bigger for each 10°F it is warmed

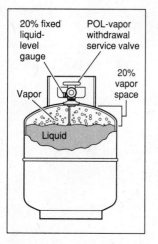

20% fixed liquid-level gauge

POL-vapor withdrawal service valve

20% vapor space

Vapor

Liquid

Figure 12.1
To compensate for expansion, propane cylinders are filled to only 80% capacity.

(Figure 12.1). This is why we only fill propane tanks 80% full; that level is indicated by the fixed liquid-level gauge, also called the outage valve or 20% valve. *Do not allow your tanks to be overfilled beyond the fixed liquid-level gauge* (see also pages 248–251).

Another propane characteristic that needs some understanding is the rate of vaporization in a container. Many propane tanks are built to the ASME code for unfired pressure vessels; in other words they are boilers. As with RV water heaters, these "gas boilers" are limited in size and output. The heat that causes the gas boiler (propane tank) to operate is also the heat that causes the container to be above −50°F. In zero-degree weather, the tank sometimes cannot collect enough heat to provide all the pressure (fuel vaporization) needed to operate the appliances. When the propane tank runs low, this problem worsens due to the reduction of surface area of propane exposed to absorb heat. One step that will help in cold climates is to fill your tanks when the gas level drops below 30%.

You may have noticed frost on your tanks during use in cool, moist weather. When the liquid propane cannot absorb the heat needed to create the amount of gas your appliances are demanding, it becomes refrigerated. This is the same action as moisture collecting on a glass of iced tea. There is no cause for alarm, and in fact this refrigeration can be useful in showing you the level of liquid propane in the tank if you don't have a gauge.

More than ten years ago, the RV code required the use of two-stage regulators to provide appliances with their required gas pressure even when this vaporization rate drops. Without a two-stage regulator you will experience appliance problems generally referred to as **freeze-up**. (See also pages 256–257.)

When It Won't Burn

One other important characteristic is propane's rather narrow limits of flammability, saving many a careless act from becoming an accident. Sadly it has made many believe their careless acts were acceptable behavior, leading to the classic post-accident statement: "But I've done it this way for thirty years!"

The limits of flammability are from 2.2% to 9.6% gas in air. Mixtures that are too rich or too lean won't burn. On some burners, the air adjustments can be opened so far that they dilute the mixture, causing the burner to go out. Too little air to the burner causes sooting. When there is more than 10% gas in a combustion chamber, the fire goes out or the flame travels, trying to find air to burn.

You should always shut off pilots and electronic re-igniters before entering gasoline or propane refueling facilities. Don't drive into the yard as if you're searching for an area that has a combustible mixture. You just might find it.

THE PROPANE TANK

Figure 12.2
Often called tanks or bottles, propane cylinders (DOT) are used on trailers.

All propane vessels are manufactured in accordance with strict quality codes. The first of these two codes is the DOT (Department of Transportation) specification. DOT (formerly ICC) vessels are called **cylinders** (Figure 12.2). They can only have openings in their hemispherical portions or heads. ASME (American Society of Mechanical Engineers) vessels are correctly called **tanks** (Figure 12.3) and can have openings in their shells as well as their heads.

Container thickness is related to the diameter and the code. DOT cylinders used on travel trailers, campers, and other RVs are usually about 12 inches in diameter. The minimum allowable thickness for a steel DOT cylinder is .078 inch, or about the same thickness as the guard or foot ring on the cylinder. Aluminum cylinders are .140 inch thick.

Rust pits, gouges, scrapes, or sharp dents can seriously compromise the safety and integrity of this vessel. Do yourself a favor and keep it rust free and painted a heat-reflective color. Especially check the tank bottom where condensation collects and where it is harder to paint under the foot ring.

The DOT requires visually checking each tank for these obvious defects and for leaks before filling. Furthermore, filling personnel are not allowed to fill a DOT cylinder that is more than 12 years old unless it is requalified, recorded, and stamped. Unfortunately, many refillers fail to observe the requalifying requirement, and the conscientious refiller may have to take a

Figure 12.3
Propane (ASME) tanks
are frame-mounted on
motorhomes.

lot of abuse from the customer when he refuses to fill an illegal container.

The Compressed Gas Association (CGA) and DOT are rewriting the rules on this recertification process, and the results probably will be stricter and costlier for cylinder owners. Accidents involving older, damaged cylinders have caused the Consumer Product Safety Commission to recommend they be tested at 12 years.

Whatever the outcome of these regulatory bodies' deliberations, you should check your cylinders for leaks and damage. If you are concerned they are unsafe, take them to a qualified propane dealer for checking and if necessary, disposal.

Both DOT cylinders and ASME tanks must have valve guards intact. Do not cut away portions of a guard or alter it in a way that weakens its strength. Screw caps are used on some cylinders, and these caps must be in place when transporting.

Cylinders of 45 pounds propane capacity or less must have the valve plugged or capped when not hooked up for use, empty or full. A plastic POL plug (Figure 12.4) is an inexpensive way for RVers to protect their families from accidents in which the valve is opened by a child. This plug also keeps air and moisture from entering the cylinder when empty, thus eliminating the opportunity for internal rust, false container pressure, or odorant oxidation.

Figure 12.4
A plastic POL plug must be used to keep air and moisture from entering the cylinder when not connected to the system.

ASME horizontal tanks are most commonly found on motorhomes. These tanks need to be inspected and maintained free of rust and leaks; however, the ASME rules do not require the 12-year recertification. The metal in ASME tanks is almost half again as thick as the metal in DOT cylinders of the same diameter. Even so, ASME rules for dents and corrosion are very strict. Give your motorhome tank an annual inspection; clean and repaint in a light color. Be sure to check the mounting brackets and bolts. Loose brackets not only cause a tank to fall off, they can also lead to stress cracks in the vessel.

Welding a propane container can only be handled by a certified shop. The container must be heat-treated after being welded to relieve the welding stresses. Both types of vessels must be retested according to their manufacturing codes.

The racks that hold cylinders on a trailer A-frame are designed to hold eight times the filled containers' weight. (Old racks were designed for four times full weight.) Make sure your hold-down bars are properly positioned and the wing nut is securely tightened before travel. Make this check a routine part of your trailer hookup procedure. Hold-down bars that fit into the square holes in the tank guard are somewhat forgiving, but the more common saw-blade-shaped hold-downs must be secure.

Mount your cylinders with the openings of the relief valves pointing away from the trailer. The guard opening will be toward the trailer, allowing better protection for the valve from flying debris; the regulator will also be better protected between the cylinders and the trailer wall.

A fairly common service-valve complaint is a leak around the valve stem. When the O-ring seal becomes cold, dirty, old, or worn, it may leak at the stem threads. Happily this leak can be controlled by opening or closing the valve all the way. Gently backseat the valve stem when opening to prevent stem leakage; you can then operate safely until proper repair or replacement can be made. Sometimes opening and closing the valve a few times will remove dirt from the internal O-ring.

The service valve should close off gas flow when hand tight; avoid the use of tools. If tools are required, the valve should be replaced.

POL Service Valves

The threaded high-pressure connector of this service valve is a special bullet-nosed part called a POL (Figure 12.5). The name originated with the Prest-O-Lite Company, but it's helpful to remember it as "put-on-left" to designate its left-handed-thread feature.

If the male end of the pigtail gets nicked by dropping or from a blow, and it will not seal, replace it. If that's not possible, there is an appropriate O-ring that can be inserted in the valve to fix the leak. Check your POL connection after each hookup. Sniff, listen, and coat the connection with soapy water to detect any leakage.

Fixed liquid-level gauges are called a variety of names, most of them usable in polite company. Spit, bleed, outage, 10%, 20%, 80%, and release are just a few. This valve was operated by a small finger-operated knurled knob for many years. More recently it is a screwdriver-operated valve (Figure 12.6) that helps avoid liquid burns and smelly fingers, an improvement that has also eliminated some of their more salty names.

Figure 12.5
This bullet-nosed left-hand threaded connector is called a POL valve.

Figure 12.6
A liquid-level gauge is
operated with a screwdriver
on newer cylinders.

This valve opens a small passageway to an internal tube extending into the tank to its 80% level or the maximum safe filling level. When filling a cylinder by volume (as opposed to filling by weight), the filling must stop when a steady stream of white liquid appears. Many accidents involving propane are caused by overfilling. As the warning decal shows, any overfill should be discharged through the valve in a well-ventilated area until the white liquid stops and the stream is only vapor. Open the outage valve from one-half to one turn. If opened too far it will come out, and you will add to its list of names as you search for it. On most cylinders, this valve is in the left side of the service valve body; however, on some vertical and most horizontally used cylinders, the valve is a separate part screwed into a ¼-inch NPT (National Pipe Thread) opening.

The proper length of this valve's dip tube (in inches) is stamped in the guard of the cylinder. DT 3.5, indicating a 3.5-inch dip tube, would be the likely stamping for a 20-pound cylinder, commonly called 5 gallon. Another stamping in the guard shows water capacity in pounds—WC 47.7 pounds. By moving the decimal one place to the left, we get the *propane capacity in gallons*. There are 4.77 gallons in a 20-pound cylinder, about 7.2 gallons in a 30-pound cylinder, and 9.2 gallons in a 40-pound cylinder.

Figure 12.7
The pressure-relief valve
must vent excess pressure
if the tank is overfilled or
subjected to excessive heat.

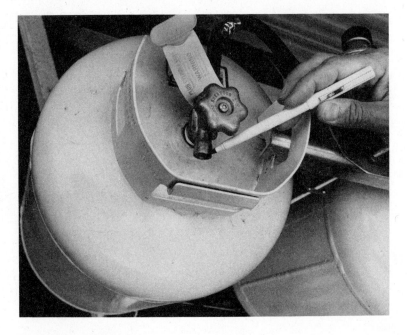

Another component of the cylinder valve, the **pressure-relief valve** (Figure 12.7), is the small opening facing opposite the threaded opening for the POL nut. This automatic spring-loaded valve is installed to keep the pressure from bursting the cylinder in case it is overfilled or subject to excessive heat. Never plug, tamper, or attempt to adjust this valve. If it is leaking, cool the tank with a water stream.

Caution: Take care and stand back as you do this. If practical, seek the assistance of trained gas- or fire-fighting personnel. If not, check the fixed-level gauge for overfilling, move the cylinder to an open area, and bleed it as discussed on page 251.

Pressure Relief and Overfilling

The activation of a relief valve signifies a potentially serious problem. This valve can open suddenly and discharge large amounts of liquid. Keep in mind that liquid expands 270 times and can freeze your skin. Keep the cylinder upright. *Remember:*

Don't allow overfilling of any of your tanks or cylinders! This is the most common cause of accidents. Due to the previously discussed natural expansion of the fuel in response to temperature changes, the relief valve of an overfilled cylinder or tank that is subjected to a large temperature change is liable to open and unexpectedly release a large amount of gas. This situation can be created by very simple, understandable circumstances, but it's the reason why some users believe the fuel is unpredictable.

For example, a service attendant carelessly overfills an RV owner's tank early one morning in a location where overnight temperatures have dropped to near zero. The next day, the RVer may have covered hundreds of miles and reached an area where daytime highs are near 100°F. If little or no propane is used, the volume of fuel in the overfilled tank will increase 15%—enough to force the relief valve open and release enough gas to fill a small house. When that happens, all that's needed to complete the scenario for a disastrous fire is an accidental source of ignition. *Take personal responsibility for making sure the service attendant does not overfill your tank!*

Proper filling should not be determined by a gauge. Some cylinders and most motorhome tanks have gauges that are operated by floats inside the tanks. The accuracy of these gauges is similar to a car's gasoline gauge: They are not precision instruments and are not to be used for filling. However, the dramatic expansion rate of the liquid can make a gauge change as much as 10% from cool night to warm day. Use the gauge to check when you are running low and need to refill. Only three methods are used to determine when a tank is full: When white liquid appears at the 20% valve; when a stop-fill valve automatically shuts off the gas flow (on motorhomes equipped with such valves); or when the filling station is equipped with an accurate scale to weigh a cylinder. When the appearance of white liquid at a 20% valve indicates a full tank, the filling service should be shut off *immediately*. Any delay will require that the excess fuel be bled off.

ASME tanks on motorhomes utilize a service valve somewhat similar to a DOT cylinder; however, they are not interchangeable. The relief on a DOT cylinder is set at 375 psi and RV-size

(45 pounds or smaller) cylinders have small-capacity relief-valve openings. ASME tanks have larger opening relief valves set for 312 psi, and the valve is larger and heavier.

Fixed liquid-level (20%) gauges on ASME tanks are separate from the service valve. They are still the knurled-knob type, since some are not easily operated with a screwdriver because of their location.

Permanently mounted ASME tanks have fill fittings separate from their outlet valves, and since 1983, the fill fittings are required to include automatic stop-fill devices—a code change necessitated by overfilling, fires, and explosions. Like many safety devices, these are frequently misunderstood and abused. Also, as with many other new items on the market, early stop-fill devices were troublesome. Even so, do not remove or obstruct these devices. To do so is to cause a perilous situation. Read and follow the operating instructions, especially with the Auto-Stop valve. You already learned to open an outage valve only a little, and here comes a device that won't allow any gas to enter the tank unless the outage valve is open all the way (about three turns). Don't worry, this one won't come all the way out.

All fill valves are sensitive to dirt, but automatic stop-fills must have their dust caps on when not being filled (Figure 12.8). Also, the hose nozzle can catch rain or dirt and inject it in the next fill if the nozzle is not properly plugged or protected.

Figure 12.8
The automatic stop-fill valve must be protected by a dust cover.

The Auto-Stop can be easily serviced and parts can be replaced without emptying the tank. Only trained service people should work on these devices, but if the serviceman knows the valve and has the parts, it can be completely rebuilt in 30 minutes.

The other float-type stop-fills cannot be repaired—only replaced. The gas must be used or flared to zero pressure before removal. Don't blow gas into the atmosphere unless you want to get rid of your RV quickly. Static electricity may automatically ignite a large release of gas. The rule is to bleed through an opening not larger than a Number 54 drill (the size of your outage valve). A torch can be used by a professional technician to flare this gas when necessary.

PRESSURE REGULATORS

The proper control of your propane-system pressure is the work of the **regulator** that is connected to the service valve of the cylinder or tank. The correct operation of your appliances, as well as your safety, depend on this device. For this reason it's often called the heart of the propane system. Its job is to reduce tank pressure to the appliance-operating pressure of 11 inches water-column (WC) pressure or about ⅓ of a pound.

When RVing became a popular winter activity about 15 years ago, the regulator had great difficulty maintaining a constant outlet pressure with low inlet pressures caused by cold weather; these regulators were designed for inlet pressures of 60 psi or more.

In 1977 the design code was changed to require the use of two-stage regulators (Figure 12.9). These are really two regulators in one: The first stage reduces the varying tank pressures to about 10 to 15 pounds, and the second stage reduces pressure to the desired 11 inches WC pressure.

The first stage can take the form of an automatic cylinder changeover device on trailers or a rectangular section attached to the second stage on units that don't have automatic changers.

If your RV doesn't have a two-stage regulator, you should replace the old one at the earliest opportunity. Regulator man-

Figure 12.9
A two-stage regulator maintains constant gas pressure for the proper operation of appliances.

ufacturers believe a 15-year life is about maximum for this product, so a 1976 or earlier single-stage model has reached the end of its useful life. RV regulator life is most likely less than 15 years due to intermittent use, exposure to road spray (salt), and contaminants that come loose from the vibration and shaking. Regulator failure not only can cause inconvenience but is dangerous. Don't wait until you have trouble. Each time you turn on the container, open the valve slowly for the first turn. Quick opening causes excessive pressure, and may cause regulator-diaphragm leaks.

The industry quit using copper pigtails in 1977 because the sulphurs in the odorants could cause a black graphite-like flaking that fouled the regulator seats. If you still have copper pigtails, replace them with rubber ones. Be sure to get UL/CGA-approved pigtails with excess-flow devices in the POL spud (Figure 12.10). The UL label is a silver band about ½ inch long around the pigtail.

The required excess-flow device is a spring-loaded metal component in the POL nose that will close automatically when a sudden surge of gas occurs. This device is designed to close automatically if the cylinder(s) gets knocked off in a collision, and it will work to protect your regulator if you open your service valve too quickly. The excess-flow device will not close and protect you from leaks in the pipeline. It can't tell a leak from a furnace burner coming on. Should you hit your excess flow device with sudden pressure by turning your valve on too

Figure 12.10
An excess-flow device
automatically reduces the
gas flow if a sudden surge
occurs.

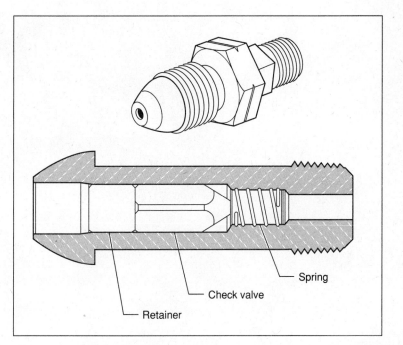

Spring

Check valve

Retainer

quickly, you may find only a small amount of gas coming to your appliances. The excess-flow device doesn't shut off all gas flow. Turn the service flow off, listen for a click, then slowly reopen to reset the check valve. Sometimes you can also hear the click of the excess flow when it closes.

When you turn on the service valve, always listen to the regulator for the sound of gas flowing. While this is only a rough leak indicator, you can usually hear flow if a burner is open or a line is disconnected. If you hear a leak, turn the gas off. Check your range valves and inspect your lines for damage. Don't plug in electrical power, and don't light matches.

Checking for Leaks

You can check the regulator connections, diaphragm seals, and vents for leaks by using soap and water or special leak-detecting solution. A bottle of Mr. Bubble does not contain

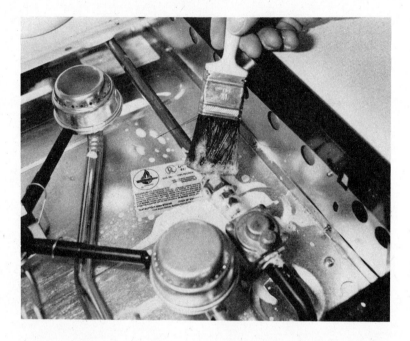

harsh chemicals, such as ammonia, that may corrode lines and
brass fittings, and it mixes into a reliable bubble-mix consistency (Figure 12.11). Leaks at the diaphragm seal or vents indicate the regulator should be replaced.

Regulators that are not enclosed in compartments, such as
those in campers and some fifth-wheel and travel trailers using
cylinder covers, are required to have regulator covers. Several
types of inexpensive plastic covers are available (Figure 12.12).
An RV serviceman or parts dealer can help you select the
proper one for your application.

Regulator vents must point downward within 45 degrees of
vertical to drain any moisture from the diaphragm. The drip-lip
design on the vent prevents ice from forming over the vent
screen. You must select the correct design for your application.
A motorhome regulator will have vents on the side, and an
automatic regulator will have a vent on the bottom, next to the
gas outlet. Water from wheel spray can otherwise collect in the
diaphragm area, causing rust on the metal parts and rotting the
diaphragm rubber, thus reducing useful life.

Figure 12.12
The regulator must be covered for protection against dirt and debris in its vent.

Figure 12.12
The regulator must be covered for protection against dirt and debris in its vent.

Regulator manufacturers do not make any replacement parts available and specifically advise against attempting any repairs. If you have reason to suspect your regulator, have it checked or replaced by a qualified service technician.

Regulators should be checked with an instrument called a **manometer** (Figure 12.13). The pressure output should be 10½ to 11½ inches of water-column pressure when about half your appliances are operating (measured by Btu rating). When everything is turned off, the "lock-up" pressure can be measured. This must not exceed 14 inches WC or ½ pound.

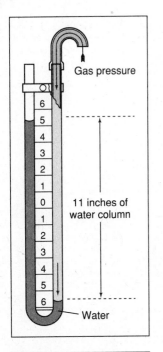

Figure 12.13
A manometer measures gas pressure in inches of water column—the differential between one column of water and the other.

These tests could be performed properly at a gas-range orifice on most RVs until about 1987. Then gas regulators were added to all ranges, making orifice readings inaccurate, so a test must be performed elsewhere. A manometer leak test is required when a gas line is temporarily disconnected; be sure this test is performed by a competent serviceman when work has been done on your system.

Low operating pressure can be the result of improperly sized, damaged, or crimped pipelines. Check them if your operating pressure drops when you turn on more equipment. Do not attempt any of these regulator tests or adjustments. We have not tried to cover the many additional steps required to perform these tests safely and properly; this should be left to qualified service people.

There is a generic term called **"freeze-up"** that applies to regulators. True freeze-up alludes to moisture in the tank that freezes in the regulator inlet orifice where expansion of the gas causes refrigeration. This phenomenon occurs most commonly when the air temperature ranges from 30°F to 40°F. If you can restore gas pressure by pouring a pint of warm water on the regulator, you have moisture in your gas. Have some gas-line dryer (methyl alcohol) injected by a propane refiller. Only 1 pint per 100 gallons is needed, so the serviceman must measure with a shot glass, not a milk bucket. Be sure it comes from a sealed container, since alcohol stored in a barrel will already be saturated with water.

Other gas interruptions also are referred to as freeze-up. They may be the result of a regulator vent being plugged so the diaphragm cannot breathe. Look for signs of bug nests in vents. Also, mud or salt corrosion in the vent screen will restrict breathing.

Finally, liquid propane being fed to the regulator may create interruption of flow. Liquid can enter the regulator if the tank or cylinder is used in an improper position. Observe the arrows and warning decals (Figure 12.14). Horizontal DOT cylinders are constructed with internal tubes so they can be used either vertically or horizontally. However, when used horizontally, they *must* be in their correct orientation (directions state which posi-

Figure 12.14
Propane cylinders and tanks must be kept in the proper position while being used, transported, or stored.

tion is up). Liquid propane reaching the regulator may indicate overfill. Check the liquid level by using the outage valve, and bleed as described on page 251 if necessary.

Small amounts of liquid can splash into the **drop tube,** the tube within the tank that goes up into the vapor space of ASME tanks or horizontal cylinders. This normally does not affect a two-stage regulator but can cause a possible gas interruption if you use a single-stage regulator.

Vibrations can cause a drop tube to crack or even break off. If this condition is suspected, have your tank checked by a qualified technician. Continuing regulator problems would indicate that this is a possibility. Your regulator may also show frost or feel cold even when the air temperature is above 40°F.

TESTING AND INSPECTING PROPANE SYSTEMS

There are several testing and inspection procedures for propane tanks that are necessary for safe and efficient operation.

Checking Gas Quantity

A test to determine the quantity of gas in a DOT container requires a scale (bathroom scales are usually accurate enough for this check). Merely weigh the cylinder and subtract the tare weight as stamped on the guard, for example, T.W. 18; the difference is the weight of the fuel. (Propane weighs 4.24 pounds per gallon as previously mentioned.)

Moisture on your container may be visible on cool, but not freezing, mornings, after overnight use of your furnace. The visible demarcation line between the moisture and the dry upper surface of the tank will indicate the liquid level. A frost line may be visible in cold weather.

In warm weather, you can pour a glass of water over your tank after use and there will usually be a visible area of difference in the way the water shows bubbles, indicating the liquid level.

The Automatic Regulator

The **automatic regulator** (Figure 12.15) is designed for use with two cylinders connected by high-pressure lines (pigtails). With both valves turned on, the regulator will use the cylinder (called the **service cylinder**) indicated by the arrow on the regulator. As long as there is fuel in the service cylinder, the full–empty indicator on top of the regulator will show white (silver). When the service cylinder goes empty, the indicator will show red, and the regulator will change the gas supply to the reserve cylinder without interruption.

When you observe the red indicator, you may close the service-cylinder valve. Rotate the selector knob so the arrow points to the reserve. This transforms the reserve cylinder to the service cylinder. Now disconnect the POL pigtail on the empty tank. Refill, reconnect, open the valve, test the connection, and you have a full tank in reserve again.

If you experience a gas leak when disconnecting the pigtail, you have forgotten to turn the arrow or close your empty tank valve. The full–empty indicator on the changeover regulator is simply a pressure gauge calibrated at about 10 pounds. It can be used as a leak-detecting device. Check that all burners and

Figure 12.15
An automatic changeover regulator changes gas feed from one tank to the other when one is nearly empty.

A Propane-System Checklist

- Storage in cold climates subjects the copper tube fittings to stresses that can crack them, so an annual spring inspection is a necessary precaution. Check your rubber flex hoses as well as your pigtails for signs of rot or weathering. Replace as necessary with UL/CGA-approved parts.
- Check the tubing where it connects to the pipe manifold at several points. These connections are usually below the belly of a trailer or in the storage compartments in motorhomes. Check for kinks or dents or evidence of damage.
- Always store an RV with the gas turned off. It helps prevent accidents, such as a child entering unnoticed and turning on a gas range. In addition, it would prevent accumulations due to slow leaks or line breaks. Air enters gas lines when they are not in use, so purging your system of air is necessary when you turn the gas on. The easiest method is to turn on a range burner and hold a match or lighter near it so the gas will ignite when it arrives. Then allow the burner to operate for a few minutes before attempting to light another appliance.
- Light the appliance at the end of the gas line, probably the water heater, before lighting the refrigerator. This large-Btu appliance will purge the line. It is not safe to disconnect gas lines in order to speed purging.
- If your range has a top burner pilot, always use it for its convenience and added safety, helping prevent inadvertent range valve turnon without lighting the burner.
- New gas containers need to be properly purged of all air before they are used. Also, purging must be done for containers that have been improperly stored with their valves open and unplugged. When air enters open propane containers, it can lead to internal rusting and a chemical process of oxidation of the odorant, called odor fade. Tell your refiller if your container is new or needs this additional attention because the service valve was left open. When DOT cylinders are first filled with propane, the filler should install a DOT Flammable warning decal to advise emergency personnel of the contents of the cylinder (Figure 12.16).
- Be aware that your sense of smell can be affected by age, colds, allergies, use of tobacco and drugs, and that the gas odor can be masked by other strong smells. If your gas-detector alarm sounds, investigate thoroughly and do not disable the alarm. The alarm sound of a gas detector and a smoke detector are very similar, so investigate carefully should either alarm sound. Don't decide your detector is giving a false alarm until you check everything thoroughly.
- Gas detectors sense any hydrocarbon fuel vapor, so alarms can be caused by other than their designed purpose—alcohol, glues, paints, cleaners, sewer gases, new carpet, pressure sprays, Freon leaks, exhaust, and carbon monoxide, to name a few. Low battery or voltage drop can also cause alarms. If an alarm sounds, air out the coach and take a few minutes to see what might be wrong. Never store propane cylinders inside your RV or home.

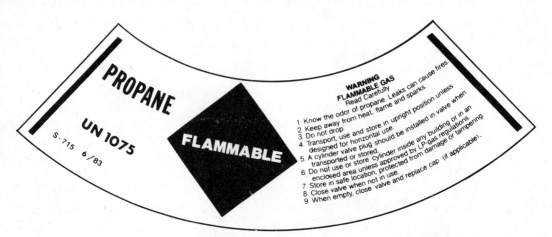

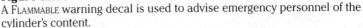

Figure 12.16
A FLAMMABLE warning decal is used to advise emergency personnel of the cylinder's content.

pilot lights are turned off. Then turn on your cylinder valve *slowly*. Listen to the regulator for the sound of gas flow. If you hear no flow, turn off both tanks. Wait 30 minutes and check the full–empty indicator. If it has turned red, you have a leak.

Try this test with a range pilot turned on: either the top-burner pilot or oven pilot will do. The gas that escapes through one of these pilots will take about 10 minutes to turn the indicator red. The larger the leak, the earlier the red will show. Doing the test with a gas leak of known size (pilot) will help you better understand the process.

Gas controls have minute leaks, so don't test with a match; leave power disconnected while testing.

Motorhomes do not have automatic regulators. However, other devices can be used as leak detectors on motorhome systems. The Rosen bubble-type detector or a pressure gauge installed ahead of the propane regulator will allow proper leak checks; the devices are available at many RV-supply stores.

Caution: Installation of the pressure gauge may move the regulator out of its protective compartment.

The propane system provides a dependable, safe fuel that adds comfort and convenience to our RV experience, no matter where we choose to camp. A little knowledge and care will add to its reliability and our peace of mind.

RV Electrical Systems

M any RV owners feel the same about their electrical systems as they do about filing their taxes—pay someone else to deal with it and hope everything works out all right. That's one way to look at it, but what happens when you're in the middle of nowhere on a weekend and nothing works?

The best insurance against such a dilemma is a fundamental knowledge of what happens in your electrical system. You don't have to be an engineer to grasp the basics of electrical systems and to figure out what may be wrong. It could be something simple that appears complex, but even if it's a major problem, knowing what's wrong and how the system works will be quite valuable when you begin dealing with a repair facility.

HOW ELECTRICITY IS SUPPLIED

Most electricity is produced by generators (or alternators—another type of generator). When we want to save some of this power for later consumption, we use storage batteries. Virtually all RV storage batteries are the lead-acid type, with lead plates and sulphuric acid as an electrolyte. These batteries convert electrical energy to chemical energy. Then, on demand, they reconvert the energy back to electrical energy.

Alternating and Direct Current

Batteries can only store and supply direct current. Mechanical generating devices can produce either direct or alternating current.

Electrical power (or current) can be produced and transmitted in two different forms: **alternating current** (AC) and **direct current** (DC). Direct current is constant; the electrons flow steadily in one direction. With alternating current, the electrons rapidly and constantly reverse direction. The frequency with which they reverse direction is measured in cycles per second, or hertz (Hz). The standard frequency for alternating current in the United States, 60-hertz standard house current, commonly known as "110," actually is 110-to 120-volt 60-hertz AC.

Batteries can only store and supply direct current. Mechanical generating devices can produce either direct or alternating current. DC generators were commonly used on cars and trucks through the 1960s to charge the batteries and provide for the electrical needs of the vehicles. With the advent of solid-state electronics, compact, efficient AC generators (commonly called alternators) were introduced because they were more efficient than DC models. Alternators produce alternating current and usually employ diodes to convert it (rectify it) to direct current for automotive 12-volt DC systems.

Units of Measurement

When you work with electricity, an understanding of the following terms will be helpful:

Voltage can be defined as electrical pressure—the amount of electrical force pushing the electrons through the circuit. In principle, it's the same as pounds per square inch in a water system.

Amperes (amps) are units of electrical flow, or volume. This is analogous to gallons per minute for water.

Ohms is a measure of resistance to flow, or restriction. Think of it relative to the size of the pipe or how far the faucet has been opened.

The **watt,** the fundamental unit of electrical power, is a rate unit, not a quantity. Volts multiplied by amps equal watts. Larger units are the horsepower and the kilowatt.

All of these terms are interrelated. Amperage is directly proportional to how much voltage is applied and is inversely proportional to resistance (ohms). The relationship can be stated in several ways:

- When voltage goes up or down, current goes up or down with it, assuming resistance doesn't change.
- When resistance goes up or down, current flow goes up or down, assuming voltage stays the same.
- When voltage goes up or down, wattage goes up or down, assuming resistance stays the same.

When dealing with these concepts, Ohm's Law can be helpful. The formula, invented by German physicist George Ohm in 1826, can be used in several ways, with these values:

R = resistance, measured in ohms.
E = voltage.
I = current, measured in amps.

$$\frac{E}{IR}$$

The formula can be altered for various purposes by using any of the three values as the unknown element: $E = I \times R$; $I = E \div R$; $R = E \div I$.

Example: You want to know the voltage required to drive a 6-amp current through a resistance of 2 ohms. Use E as the unknown; 6 (amps) × 2 (ohms) = 12; the voltage needed is 12.

Example: How much resistance occurs when 12 volts push 2 amps of current through a wire? Use R as the unknown; 12 (volts) ÷ 2 (amps) = 6; the answer is 6 ohms.

AC AND DC SYSTEMS

RVs utilize three separate electrical systems: two 12-volt DC (12VDC) systems and one 120-volt AC (120VAC) system.

The 12-Volt Direct-Current Chassis System

The 12-volt DC system is used to provide power for chassis components such as the ignition system, electronic fuel injection (if so equipped), running lights, air conditioning, etc. (Figure 13.1). It includes an alternator, a battery for engine starting, and all the necessary wiring, fuses, circuit breakers, and other components common to an automotive system.

Trailers utilize a tow-vehicle electrical system to operate their electric brakes and turn signals and stop- and running lights.

The 12-Volt Direct-Current "House" System

The other 12-volt DC system has its own batteries and is often referred to as the "house" system (Figure 13.2). This system operates such accessories as the furnace, water pump, interior lights, and fans. It's usually isolated from the chassis electrical system so the house appliances cannot accidentally drain the engine-starting battery. The house batteries are charged by the same engine-mounted alternator that charges the vehicle battery, via an isolator that prevents any interconnection between batteries in the two systems. The house batteries also can be charged via an RV electrical converter, which changes 120-volt

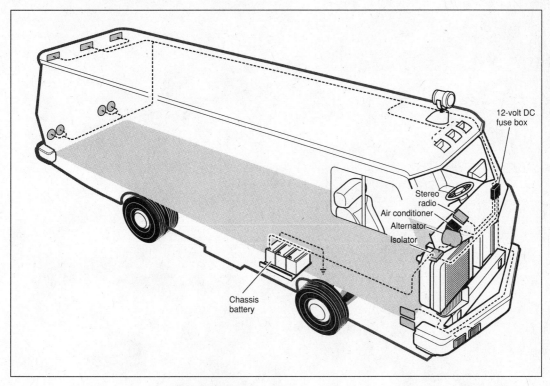

Figure 13.1
The chassis 12-volt system in a motorhome or tow vehicle provides power for automotive systems separate from the 12-volt RV-accessories system.

AC to 12-volt DC, if the RV is connected to a 120-volt power source.

The wiring layout for this system is similar in principle to that of the chassis system, but less complex since it doesn't involve an engine. Typically, a deep-cycle RV battery provides the power, which is channeled to one or more fuse panels via positive and negative wires of appropriate size.

From the fuse panel(s), power is routed to various 12-volt appliances (the furnace, interior lights, water pump, fans, and outlets for 12-volt portable appliances, such as a television or radio). The stereo AM/FM tape unit built into the dash of a typical motorhome usually is connected to the chassis 12-volt system rather than to the house system.

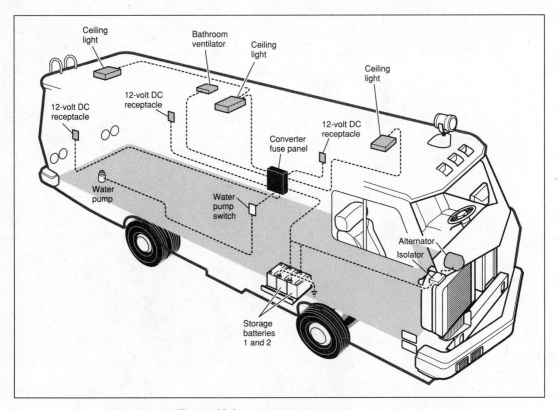

Figure 13.2
The 12-volt RV-accessories system is fed by the vehicle alternator via a battery isolator, which keeps it separate from the 12-volt chassis system.

The 120-Volt AC System

The 120-volt AC system (Figure 13.3) allows the use of household-type AC appliances and motors and is very similar in concept to the electrical system in a home, except that the source of power for the system is not a utility pole in the backyard, but an umbilical cord designed to be plugged into a campground receptacle or an AC-generator electrical system. The AC system usually has circuits for such permanent appliances as air conditioners and microwave ovens and wall outlets for many

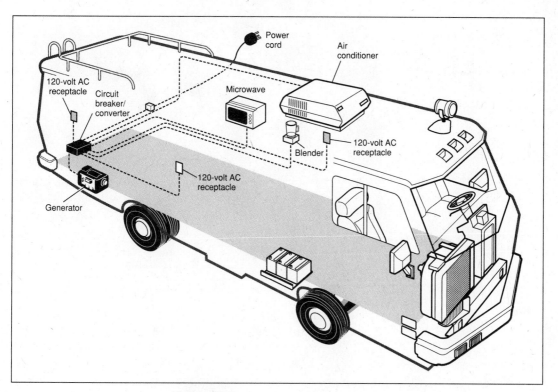

Figure 13.3
An RV's 120-volt AC system is similar for motorhomes and trailers, except that trailers usually do not have AC generators.

other appliances. Most RVs include an electrical converter that is powered by the 120-volt AC system, and it converts 120-volt AC into 12-volt DC. Thus, when a source of 120-volt AC is present, the AC system provides power for appliances such as those found in a home, while also supplying power for the DC system. The converter also may serve as a battery charger for the house batteries, although few converters are very effective in this role.

Power for the 120-volt AC system may come from an outside utility hookup in a campground or an on-board engine-powered AC generator. The more sophisticated RVs may also include inverters, which change 12-volt DC (taken from batteries) into 120-volt AC.

Figure 13.4
In many RVs, the main
power-distribution panel is
combined with a converter/
battery charger.

The heart of the 120-volt AC system in an RV is the main distribution panel (Figure 13.4), into which the input lines from the RV hookup cord and the AC generator (if so equipped) feed. There are three incoming lines from either source, two for power transmission and a third (ground) for safety. All appliances and wall outlets in the RV should have the three lines. The power is fed to several circuit breakers that serve as the source for all the individual circuits that feed appliances and the wall outlets.

The primary difference between this system and one in a home is that the homeowner hardly ever has to contend with overloads. Although it can occur more readily in an RV, it's unusual. If, for example, the receptacle in a campground and the hookup cord on your RV are rated at 30 amps, it's possible to turn on enough appliances to exceed that rating. If an RV has two roof air conditioners, most manufacturers wire the coaches so only one can be operated from the campground hookup; the other must be operated from an on-board AC generator. The arrangement is designed to keep people from operating both air conditioners and then turning on yet another appliance, such as a toaster or the convection-oven feature of a microwave/convection oven. Two AC units will operate from a 30-amp circuit, but with little unused capacity.

Table 13.1
Common RV Appliances and Their Power Requirements

Appliance	Watts	Appliance	Watts
Air conditioner	1,000 to 1,300	Ice maker	600
Blender	1,000	Microwave oven	800 to 1,500
Coffee maker	1,400	Popcorn popper (air)	1,400
Computer	100	120-volt refrigerator	600
Drill motor	350	Satellite dish	200 to 300
Electric blanket	120	Soldering iron	50
Freezer	500	Trash compactor	800 to 1,000
Hair dryer	1,500	Videocassette recorder	200

A list of common appliances used in RVs and their common power requirements can be found in Table 13.1. Appliances differ, and power requirements will vary. For more specific ratings, refer to the identification plate on the appliance.

ELECTRICAL SAFETY

Unlike a snarling Doberman, electrical hazards are silent and invisible. The two prevalent dangers are fire and shock. Electrical fires are caused by short circuits and overloads. Shock is caused when electricity finds an easy path through a person to ground.

Short Circuits and Shock Hazards

A **short circuit** occurs when a power or "hot" wire comes in contact with a ground (return) connection. This can occur when wires come loose or insulation is rubbed through. When the short circuit occurs, the safety device (circuit breaker or fuse) should prevent any problems.

Shock and electrocution are virtually nonexistent with 12-volt systems, but 120-volt systems can knock you for a loop. To protect yourself from shock, disconnect the power source before working on any electrical device. Before you plug your rig

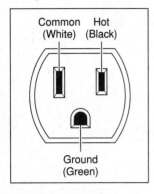

Figure 13.5
The correct polarity of a
120-volt AC system can
be checked at a typical
wall outlet.

Figure 13.6
Wiring-check devices
plugged into wall outlets
indicate proper polarity
and functional ground
connection.

in, be sure all major loads are shut off. Check the electrical outlet, plug, and wire for damage and fraying. The insulation on all wires should be intact and unbroken. Cover the exposed spots with electrical tape, and replace any wiring if the conductors are damaged.

Beyond personal danger, the result of a short circuit can be very high current flow, melted insulation, and fire at the place of contact if the circuit is not properly protected by a circuit breaker or if the circuit breaker is rated for more current than the circuit can handle.

Problems can be caused by improper wiring in the receptacle at a campground, and it's wise to check the receptacle with a wiring-checking device *before* plugging into it. Although you should not attempt to correct a fault in a campground receptacle, you should know that 120-volt AC wiring is conventionally color coded with black as "hot" or positive, and white as return or neutral. These are the two flat prongs on a common three-prong plug; the green pin, the ground connection, is round (Figure 13.5).

Wiring-check devices (Figure 13.6) are available at most RV-supply stores. If the circuit does not check out properly, don't plug into it. Find another that checks out properly, or ask the campground management to repair the problem receptacle.

To protect against short circuits, inspect the electrical system for loose connections and damaged or chafed insulation. Be sure all circuit breakers and/or fuses are the correct capacity.

Overloads

Overloads occur when circuits are forced to handle more current than they are designed to carry. The more amperage, the hotter things get. If the fuse or circuit breaker doesn't shut the circuit down, the insulation on the wiring will melt, and the wires may touch, causing a fire. Although we commonly think that only 120-volt AC systems have the capacity to cause fires, the 12-volt DC system also can create enough heat to do so. A shorted 12-volt wire functions as a heating element unless it is properly protected by a fuse or circuit breaker.

Table 13.2
Amperage Load in Circuit

Gauge	1	1.5	2	3	4	5	6	7	8	10	12	15	20	24	30	36	50	100	150	200
							Allowable Conductor Length—Feet in Circuit Before 1-Volt Loss													
20	106	70	53	35	26	21	17	15	13	10	8	7	5	4	3	3	2	1	0	0
18	150	100	75	50	37	30	25	21	18	15	12	10	7	6	5	4	3	1	1	0
16	224	144	112	74	56	44	37	32	28	22	18	14	11	9	7	6	4	2	1	1
14	362	241	181	120	90	72	60	51	45	36	30	24	18	15	12	10	7	3	2	1
12	572	381	286	190	143	114	95	81	71	57	47	38	28	23	19	15	11	5	3	2
10	908	605	454	302	227	181	151	129	113	90	75	60	45	37	30	25	18	9	6	4
8	1452	967	726	483	363	290	241	207	181	145	120	96	72	60	48	40	29	14	9	7
6	2342	1560	1171	780	585	468	390	334	292	234	194	155	117	97	78	65	46	23	15	11
4	3702	2467	1851	1232	925	740	616	529	462	370	307	246	185	154	123	102	74	37	24	18
2	6060	4038	3030	2018	1515	1212	1009	866	757	606	503	403	303	252	201	168	121	60	40	30
1	7692	5126	3846	2561	1923	1538	1280	1100	961	769	638	511	384	320	256	213	153	76	51	38
0	9708	6470	4854	3232	2427	1941	1616	1388	1213	970	805	645	485	404	323	269	194	97	64	48

The above table is computed for a 68°F (20°C) ambient temperature.

Overloading often happens when an RV owner adds lights and appliances and raises ratings of fuses or circuit breakers to handle the additional load. Fuses and circuit breakers are supposed to be the weakest link in a circuit; they should stop the flow of current to prevent the wiring from getting too hot. Before adding any electrical devices to a circuit, be sure the added load will not exceed the rating of the wiring and circuit breaker or fuse. And never replace a circuit-protection device with one of a higher amperage rating! See Table 13.2 for wiring loads.

120-Volt AC Cords

Sometimes an extension cord is needed as an add-on to the RV power cord so it will reach a power outlet. The extension cord must be heavy enough to carry the expected loads. To feed an RV with 30-amp service, the cord should be 10-gauge or heavier wire. The cord should also be as short as possible; the use of long or undersize cords results in additional voltage drop, which reduces the voltage available to appliances, possibly causing damage through overheating.

When using adapters, be aware of their ratings, and match your loads to the ratings. Make sure the adapter is in good condition.

Adapters

Low voltage may also be caused by the risky practice of using an adapter for connecting a 30-amp power cord to an outlet rated lower—usually 15 amps. Most of us do it, because 30-amp outlets are not always available. The use of an adapter is not liable to cause problems unless we use the rig as if we were still plugged into 30-amp power. An air conditioner alone will consume most or all of the power supplied through a 15-amp circuit, and the 15-amp plug will become warm, indicating excessive resistance to current flow. It's not wise to run an air conditioner from a 15-amp receptacle.

When using adapters, be aware of their ratings, and match your loads to the ratings. Make sure the adapter is in good condition. Loose connections create high resistance and heat. Be wary of the odor of hot electrical equipment, and investigate any popping sounds emitted by such equipment.

Load-Shedding Devices

Load-shedding devices are available to automatically turn off the air conditioner if current flow exceeds a preset amount. If your RV is not equipped with such a device, that control is left to you. To determine the load, add the total amp draw of every appliance you plan to operate simultaneously. Keep that total at or below the rated limit of the power supply and wiring. If you only have the rating of the appliance in watts, divide that rating by the voltage (120) to determine the amperage rating.

Ground Fault Interrupters

Most newer RVs are equipped with 120-volt Ground Fault Interrupter (GFI) outlets where receptacles are located in the bathroom, with outdoor plugs wired from them (Figure 13.7). They can be identified by the little buttons marked "T" for test and "R" for reset on the faceplates. The GFI monitors the variance in current between the "hot" and "common" wires in the outlet. If

Figure 13.7
The ground fault detector, usually found in the bathroom, helps protect against electrical shock.

something is drawing current to ground (such as a human body), the levels of current in the two wires will differ. Sensing this, the GFI will shut down the outlet. To be sure the GFI is working properly, press the "T," or test, button. When you do this, the "R," or reset, button, should pop out and the outlet will go dead. Pressing the "R" button again should lock it in and restore power. If the GFI doesn't work properly, have it replaced. Older RVs may have GFI circuit breakers in their main distribution boxes. Such circuit breakers will have white reset buttons.

Preparing for an Emergency

If an electrical fire occurs, first disconnect the power source by unplugging the power cord, shutting off the generator, or switching off the batteries. Then aim a dry chemical, carbon dioxide, or Halon fire extinguisher at the base of the flames. Read the instructions on your fire extinguishers now; don't wait until there's a fire! Never use water on an electrical fire while the electricity is on. After the electricity is unplugged, the fire is no longer electrical in nature and water may be used.

To assist someone who has received a severe shock, shut off the power source *first* if they are still connected to the electrical source, then check for breathing and pulse. Call for help and begin artificial respiration and cardiopulmonary resuscitation if you know how. (The Red Cross offers classes on these subjects.)

ELECTRICAL PROBLEM DIAGNOSIS

The goal of electrical diagnosis is to find the faulty component that keeps the current from flowing through the circuit as originally designed.

As manufacturers load up modern RVs with electrical devices, the potential for problems increases. Given the complexity of these systems and the high cost of many replacement parts, a "hit-and-miss" approach to troubleshooting must be avoided. An organized and logical approach to diagnosis is essential to repair these electrical circuits quickly and cost effectively.

Since electricity is invisible, special testers are needed to check circuits and components.

Test Equipment

Before you begin chasing electrical gremlins, you have to know how to use the test equipment. Most testers come with instructions. If they differ from the general procedures described here, follow the specific instructions provided by the manufacturer of the tester.

Caution: Never connect solid-state circuits to battery voltage, and never test them with any device other than a good meter, such as a digital multimeter.

Test Lights

Test lights are used to check for voltage in AC and DC circuits while power is connected (Figure 13.8). Test lights for 12-volt DC and 12-volt AC should be included in every toolbox unless a multimeter is included. In that case, the 120-volt AC test light can be omitted. Although accurate voltage measurements aren't possible with a test light, large differences may be detected by the relative brightness of the lighted bulb. Before using a test light for diagnosis, check it by connecting it to a known source of power, insuring that the bulb is functional (see page 275).

Figure 13.8
Test lights for AC and DC circuits are essential tools unless a multimeter is available.

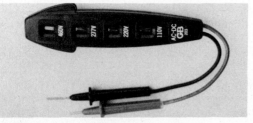 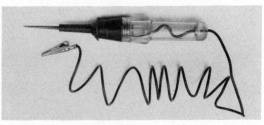

Using a 12-Volt Test Light

Twelve-volt test lights have a multitude of uses, including this common example:

1. Connect the ground wire of a test light to a clean, bare metal ground.
2. With the circuit switched on, insert the probe into the 12-volt terminal or socket to be checked. If necessary, the probe may be pushed through the insulation to make contact with a wire (some testers have a special insulation-piercing probe).
3. The bulb should light if there is sufficient voltage present.
4. After testing is complete, tape over any wires exposed by the probe. Test lights are not sensitive to polarity and can be connected either way.

Uses for a 120-volt test light are more limited. Such a light can be used, for example, to test for power to all circuit breakers in a power-distribution panel.

Continuity Testers

Continuity testers, also known as self-powered test lights, are used to check for open or short circuits on 12-volt systems (Figure 13.9). *Continuity testers must not be used on powered circuits;* battery voltage will burn out the low-voltage bulb in the tester. Never use a self-powered continuity tester on circuits that contain solid-state components, since damage to these components may occur.

Continuity (an unbroken circuit) may be checked with a number of devices. If the circuit has power in it, a voltmeter or test light may be used as described previously. If the circuit is not powered, an ohmmeter or self-powered continuity tester should be used.

To use a continuity tester, first isolate the circuit by disconnecting the battery or removing the fuse or circuit breaker. Select two points along the circuit through which power should

Figure 13.9
The continuity tester can be used to check for open or shorted circuits.

pass. Connect one lead of the tester to each point. If there is continuity, the test lamp will light, meaning there is a path for current flow.

Multimeters

Figure 13.10
The multimeter performs a variety of test functions on AC as well as DC systems. Digital models are preferred.

Analog multimeters (needle on dial) are suitable for most 12- and 120-volt RV test functions requiring the measurement of volts, ohms, and amperes. If you own an analog unit, use it for the tests described in this chapter. However, if you must buy a new multimeter, consider getting a digital model (Figure 13.10), which will perform all the tests of which an analog unit is capable, is more accurate, and is compatible with solid-state devices.

All multimeters are sold with instructions explaining how to perform a variety of tests. An example of multimeter use is measurement of voltage. The leads are pressed against the contact surfaces to be measured. If the power source is AC, be sure your hands are not in contact with the meter probes. Most multimeters will measure a broad range of DC- and AC-voltage levels, including battery and alternator voltage in the DC system of an RV. For example, a reading lower than 13.5 volts at either the chassis or house batteries while the engine is running at about 1,500 RPM or higher can indicate loss of alternator output. While AC voltage may be adequate (110 to 120 volts) without a load on the system, it may drop to 105 or lower when you turn on an air conditioner, indicating low voltage from a campground hookup.

ELECTRICAL TESTING

Testing for Open DC Ground Connections

To test for an open DC ground connection:
   Connect a jumper wire (Figure 13.11) between the component case or ground terminal and a clean bare metal spot on the vehicle chassis. If a circuit works properly with the jumper

Figure 13.11
Jumper wire can be used to verify ground connections.

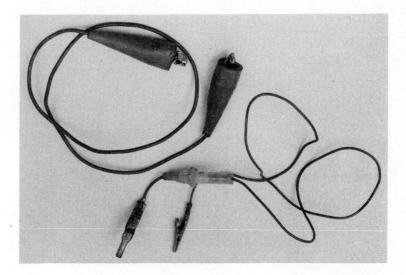

wire in place but doesn't work when the jumper wire is removed, the ground circuit has an open section (high resistance) that needs correction.

Testing a Battery-Voltage-Operated Component

To test a component designed to operate on battery voltage:

Ground the device with a jumper as described above and connect a fused jumper wire from the positive battery terminal to the positive terminal on the component being tested. If it now works normally, remove the ground jumper wire and, if the device stops working, repair the ground connection. If the device still doesn't work, look for a break in the positive side of the circuit.

Checking Resistance

Resistance is checked with the ohm-measuring function of a multimeter. Turn the scale-selector switch to the proper ohms range for the device you will be measuring. Insure that the wires are connected to the proper plugs on the meter and turn the meter on. Check that the meter reads "infinity" before testing is begun, and then touch the test probes together to insure that the meter goes to zero, which means no resistance.

Checking Voltage Drop

Perform this test for voltage that is lost when current travels through a wire, connection, or switch:

1. Connect the positive lead of a multimeter to the end of the wire (or to one side of the connection or switch) that is closer to the battery.
2. Connect the negative lead of the multimeter to the other end of the wire (or the other side of the connection or switch).
3. Select the multimeter range just above battery voltage.
4. Switch on the circuit.
5. The multimeter will show the difference in voltage between the two points. A difference (or drop) of more than about one volt indicates a problem, depending on the load. When heavy current passes through a wire, more voltage drop occurs.
6. Clean and repair the connections as needed or replace any faulty components.

When no current is flowing, there can be no voltage drop.

Warning: On 120- or 240-volt AC systems, do not touch test leads while they are connected to power.

Checking Direct-Current Flow

Ammeters are always connected in series with the circuit being tested (except units with inductive pickups).

1. To place an ammeter in a circuit, unplug one of the connectors in the circuit and attach the test leads to the two connectors.

2. Switch on an appliance connected to the circuit and read the amperage (or current draw) shown on the meter. If it shows a negative reading, reverse the test lead connections. No reading indicates an open (incomplete) circuit.
3. Compare the reading to the specified current rating (when available) to determine if the component is defective. Many electrical components have voltage and amperage ratings stamped on their cases.

ELECTRIC TROUBLESHOOTING STRATEGIES

Before you begin troubleshooting a circuit, formulate a plan of action. Let's take a look at some of the methods pros use when tracking down problems.

Intermittent Electrical Problems

The toughest type of electrical problem to diagnose is an intermittent one. Intermittent opens or shorts are usually caused by something rubbing or a component that changes resistance when it heats up. Corroded and loose connections are also frequently the cause of such problems.

Observe when the problem occurs, and try to discover how to duplicate the problem. For example, does it only happen when going around a corner or over a rough railroad crossing? Sometimes, wiggling the wiring harness or tapping your hand on the fixture will locate the problem. Once you can duplicate the problem, follow the test procedures that follow. (Any items that have recently been disturbed or worked on are prime suspects.)

Identify the Problem

Operate the problem circuit in all modes. What doesn't work properly? Is it a complete or partial failure? Which systems does it affect? When does it occur?

Determine which components in the circuit, if any, still work. For example, if you find that only one device in the circuit is out, you have eliminated the fuse, switch, and main wiring harness as potential sources of the problem.

Obtain the wiring diagrams for the specific vehicle you are working on, when possible. Familiarize yourself with the current flow in the circuit by tracing the path in the wiring diagram. Determine where the circuit receives current, what the circuit protection is, which switches and/or relays control current flow, and how the components operate.

Check the fuses and/or circuit breakers. If the circuit-protection devices are blown, look for a short circuit; if they are intact, look for an open circuit.

Test the Cause

Most electrical failures are caused by these four items:

1. *The wire or component is not receiving current.* Test for voltage at the component.
2. *The component is not grounded properly.* Test for voltage drop between the component and its ground connection with power on, or check for resistance between the component and ground with the power off.
3. *The component itself is faulty.* With the power on, check for voltage drop. With the power off, check for resistance.
4. *The wiring is faulty.* With the power on, check for voltage drop. With the power off, check for continuity or resistance.

As a general rule, if the fault affects a single component of a circuit, begin testing at that component. If the fault affects several components of a circuit, begin testing at the point where the circuit draws its power. Check for obvious problems first, such as corroded connections, broken wires, or burned-out bulbs.

Elusive Problems

If access to a circuit is a problem, it may be easier to disconnect an old, damaged circuit at both ends and create a new circuit— in effect, wiring around the problem. Check the wiring diagram (if available) to determine how circuits are connected. In absence of a diagram, check all the connections at both ends to insure no other circuits will be affected and that no feedback problems will occur.

Always use wire of at least the same size as the original. If you're not sure, use the next-size-heavier wire. Consult Table 13.2, page 271, to determine the proper gauge based on round-trip length of the circuit and the fuse rating. For example, if the circuit and fuse must handle 15 amps and the circuit length is 24 feet, use 14-gauge wire.

12-Volt Lighting Circuits

Interior lighting on RVs is fairly trouble free, but exterior lighting requires more attention because of weather and physical damage. The most common types of problems are burned-out fuses or bulbs, damaged fixtures, corroded terminals, and pulled-out or broken wires. Check the obvious items first. If the fuse is good, check for voltage at the socket with a test light. If voltage is present, try a new bulb. If no voltage is present at the fixture, check for power at the switch. Does the switch look or feel damaged? If so, replace the switch. Also look for a bad ground-return path, which is very common in taillights and turn signals. When a tow vehicle and trailer are involved, make sure the ground connection between tow vehicle and trailer is valid. Checking for proper ground is easily done with a jumper wire connected to a known good ground and to the external surface of a light socket.

If power is not present in a light socket or other terminal, work your way backward in the circuit toward the fuse panel, paying special attention to connections.

Charging Systems

The alternator supplies electricity for charging batteries and operating accessories when the engine is running. Alternators are usually mounted on the front of the engine and driven by a belt off the crankshaft pulley.

A voltage regulator is used to limit the current output of the alternator. Older or modified vehicles usually have externally mounted voltage regulators, while in newer models they are inside the alternator housing. The voltage regulator automatically limits alternator output voltage to a preset level, varying from 14 to 14.8 volts depending on brand, type, and operating conditions.

If the vehicle is equipped with a charging light on the dash, it should come on when the ignition key is turned on, then go out after the engine starts. If the light fails to go out after the engine starts, the alternator, voltage regulator, or connecting wiring is faulty. If the light comes on when the ignition is turned off, one or more diodes is defective.

Begin your charging-system inspection by checking the cleanliness and security of the battery terminals and the connections on the back of the alternator. Then check the drive belt for tension, glazing, and cracks. Adjust or replace as necessary.

If the vehicle's lights are excessively bright and bulbs burn out frequently, the voltage regulator may be faulty. Connect a voltmeter to the battery terminals with the engine off and note the reading. Start the engine and again take a reading. On a normally functioning 12-volt system, starting battery voltage at rest should be about 12.6, unless the battery is depleted. When the engine is started, voltage should rise steadily to the aforementioned 14- to 14.8-volt level. The higher levels usually are reached only in cold weather by a voltage-compensating alternator such as those used on General Motors vehicles. Those same temperature-compensating alternators may cut voltage below 14 volts during hot-weather driving. However, a voltage reading of at least 14 when the engine has not heated the alternator to high levels indicates that the alternator is working properly. Low alternator-voltage output causes inadequate battery charging.

Begin your charging-system inspection by checking the cleanliness and security of the battery terminals and the connections on the back of the alternator.

Excessively high voltage with the engine running indicates a need for regulator replacement. If the voltage is too low, the alternator, regulator, or wiring could be defective.

Battery Isolators

Because RVs have battery-powered appliances that must be operated while the vehicle is parked, a battery isolator is necessary to make sure only the house batteries are used for RV appliances (Figure 13.12). An isolator allows one battery to be kept fully charged for engine starting. Through the magic of electronics, the one-way electrical valves (diodes) of a solid-state battery isolator allow power to flow from the engine-mounted alternator to charge all the batteries while preventing electricity from flowing out of one battery into another. This function also may be provided by an electrical relay. When triggered by the ignition switch, the relay contacts close and bring all batteries into parallel for charging by the alternator. When the ignition switch is turned off, contacts open and the house batteries are separated from the engine-starting battery.

Figure 13.12
The battery isolator uses diodes to allow charging while preventing inter-connection between batteries.

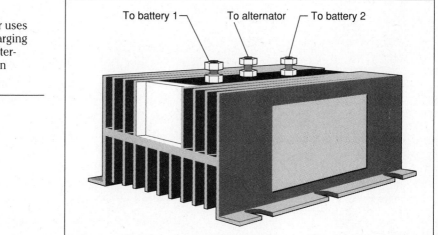

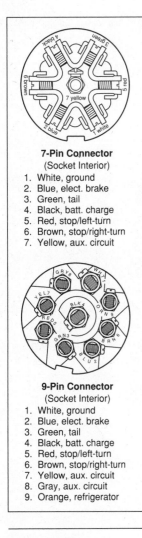

7-Pin Connector
(Socket Interior)
1. White, ground
2. Blue, elect. brake
3. Green, tail
4. Black, batt. charge
5. Red, stop/left-turn
6. Brown, stop/right-turn
7. Yellow, aux. circuit

9-Pin Connector
(Socket Interior)
1. White, ground
2. Blue, elect. brake
3. Green, tail
4. Black, batt. charge
5. Red, stop/left-turn
6. Brown, stop/right-turn
7. Yellow, aux. circuit
8. Gray, aux. circuit
9. Orange, refrigerator

Figure 13.13
Wiring diagrams are shown for the 7-pin plug, used for most travel trailers, and for the 9-pin plug, needed for travel trailers with 12-volt automatic refrigerators.

Trailer Wiring Connectors

The trailer wiring connector must be capable of carrying power from the tow vehicle to the trailer lights, brakes, and batteries. Inspect it thoroughly every time you connect it. Insure that the plug is clean, tight, and the prongs are undamaged.

Most travel trailers use seven- or nine-pin Bargman or Pollak flat-pin plugs and receptacles. The nine-pin plugs are used only when a trailer is equipped with a refrigerator that is operated on 12-volt power while traveling. To simplify matters, color codes have been standardized by the RV industry (Figure 13.13).

Some late-model vehicles have separate brake lights and turn signals. An electrical converter sold at RV-supply stores must be wired into the harness to make this system compatible with most trailers.

To troubleshoot trailer-connector electrical problems, have an assistant operate each circuit, one at a time, from the tow vehicle. With the trailer plug disconnected, use a test light to probe the tow-rig side of the connector for power in the appropriate terminal. If the terminal doesn't have power, the problem is in the tow vehicle wiring. If the terminal has power, check the trailer connector and wiring harness for continuity. The most common problem is a faulty ground connection.

Trailer Brakes

There are two types of trailer-brake operating systems: electric and surge. **Surge brakes,** found only on small folding camping trailers and on rental cargo trailers, use the force of the trailer pushing the tow vehicle to provide mechanical actuation of a trailer-mounted master brake cylinder. **Electric brakes** utilize a revolving armature located in the brake drum. An electromagnet pivots on an arm with a cam that is attached between the brake shoes. When the magnet is energized, current flows through it, causing a magnetic attraction between it and the armature. The magnet attempts to follow the rotation of the armature. This causes the cam to rotate, actuating the primary brake shoe into the drum and energizing the secondary shoe, resisting the rotation of the drum.

Most problems with electric brakes are electrical, occurring in the connecting wiring or the brake controller (Figure 13.4). To test electric brakes, connect an ammeter in series between the controller and the electric brakes. Actuate the controller with the manual lever and note the reading. Current should vary depending on how hard the brakes are applied. The minimum current should be about 1 to 1.75 amps. The maximum depends on the size and number of brakes (Table 13.3).

If a high or low current is registered, check for faulty wiring, bad grounds, and corroded trailer plugs. If an electrical problem is isolated to the trailer, check all exposed wiring for electrical short circuits caused by chafing of wires against metal. Use a multitester to check for resistance of wiring inside axle tubes where they sometimes chafe and make contact with the metal tube. Inspect the electromagnets for wear or shorting.

Figure 13.14
Most trailer-brake problems are electrical in nature, involving wiring and connections.

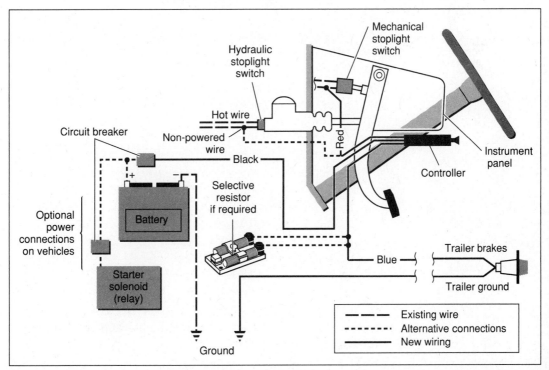

Table 13.3
Trailer Brakes—Maximum Current

Brake Size (in inches)	Two Brakes	Four Brakes	Six Brakes
7	3.8–4.4	7.6–8.8	11.4–13.2
10, 12	6.0–6.5	12–13	18–19.5

Brake Controllers

An electric-hydraulic brake controller utilizes an integral hydraulic cylinder to control the amount of braking force directed to the trailer brakes. As the brake pedal of the tow vehicle is depressed, hydraulic-fluid pressure from the vehicle's master cylinder moves the piston inside the brake controller's hydraulic cylinder. Movement of this piston pushes the controller's manual control arm toward the unit's wire-wound resistor assembly, activating the control automatically.

Electronic brake controllers utilize a pendulum weight to detect the rate of deceleration caused by tow-vehicle braking, and they meter an appropriate amount of current to the trailer brakes for braking effort that is comparable to the level of braking in the tow vehicle. With the electronic controllers, following the manufacturer's instructions for adjustment of the unit is particularly important for proper brake performance because a variety of factors, including off-level mounting of the controller, affects their performance.

Twelve-gauge automotive-grade wire (or larger) should be used to make the connection between the brake controller and the electrical connector. Circuit protection is essential. An automatic-reset circuit breaker should be installed in the black wire between the battery and the brake controller to protect the brake controller and the vehicle wiring from short circuits. Use a 15-amp circuit for two brake trailers, a 20-amp circuit breaker for four-brake trailers, and a 30-amp circuit for six-brake trailers.

The use of a variable resistor may be necessary in order to prevent excessive brake actuation when a hydraulic-electric controller is used.

The use of a variable resistor may be necessary in order to prevent excessive brake actuation when a hydraulic-electric controller is used.

Trailer Breakaway Switch

A breakaway switch automatically applies the trailer brakes if the trailer becomes uncoupled from the tow vehicle while the vehicles are in motion. The switch is mounted on the trailer tongue, and a lanyard runs from the switch to the frame of the tow vehicle. If the trailer breaks away, the lanyard pulls a pin out of the switch, engaging the brakes. In this situation, power for the trailer brakes comes from the house battery through the breakaway switch.

Be sure the lanyard is connected to the frame of the tow rig, not to some part of the hitch. Clean the inside of the switch with electrical contact cleaner on a regular basis, and lubricate the pin with light oil. Test the breakaway switch occasionally by pulling the pin and trying to drive the tow vehicle forward with the trailer hitched. If everything is working properly, you won't be able to move.

Converters and Inverters

All RVs are equipped with electrical converters designed to transform 120-volt AC to 12-volt DC power that can be used to operate DC appliances in the RV and charge batteries. Inverters change 12-volt DC battery power to 120 volt AC power to operate household-type appliances without an auxiliary generator or "shore" power (Figure 13.15). Concepts of both appliances are described in Chapter 14, "How to Live Without Hookups."

Simple troubleshooting of both appliances can be performed with a multimeter. When a converter malfunctions, the result usually is improper voltage output, which is relatively simple to check. Single-output converters are designed to produce voltage of 13.8 to 14 (Figure 13.16). The rated output voltage should be listed on the identification label. The older units usually are designed for 13.8 volts output, and newer ones may be set for 14 volts. These voltage levels will be reached when the converter has been operating long enough to bring the battery to a high state of charge.

The converter's output should be within 0.2 volt of its rating if the input AC voltage is 110 to 120 volts. If a converter rated at

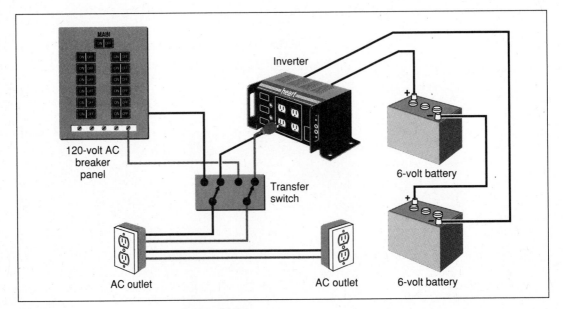

Figure 13.15
Inverters transform 12-volt DC power into 120-volt AC power for RV
appliances such as microwave ovens and videocassette players.

13.8 volts produces about 14 volts, that shouldn't cause immediate problems. But any converter that produces more than 14
volts has the capability of causing excessive loss of battery
electrolyte in open-cell batteries if the converter is in continuous operation. Common complaints of excessive loss of electrolyte and shortened battery life are usually due to high voltage. Dirty power from the appliance circuit of a dual-output
converter (Figure 13.17) may shorten the life of electronic
appliances.

If voltage is lower than 13.8, the converter will not effectively
replenish the battery's state of charge. Adjustment of output
voltage must be handled by the converter manufacturer.

Incorrect input voltage to a converter can cause its output to
vary if the converter is a dual-output type. If you see the converter's output drop to 12.5 or 13 volts, check input voltage and
you'll probably find it low as well. If the converter is a single-

Figure 13.16
Single-output converters usually are limited to DC output voltage of about 14.

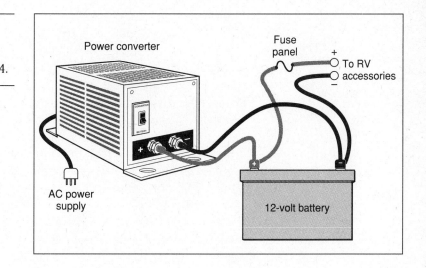

output type (battery floater), its DC output should be unaffected by moderate changes in its AC input.

Troubleshooting inverters involves a few fundamentals, since most owners are not capable of evaluating glitches inside the unit. We can check input- as well as output-voltage levels and the inverter's built-in circuit protection.

Figure 13.17
Dual-output converters have separate circuits for batter charging and for RV appliances.

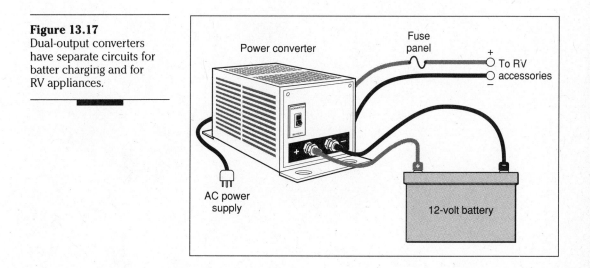

Inverters must be connected to the battery(ies) with electrical cable of appropriate size. For example, for inverters rated for not more than about 300 watts output, 6-gauge cable is suitable if cable length is limited to 9 feet. For an inverter rated at 1,200 watts output, the cable requirement would be 1 gauge with length held to about 9 feet. A fuse of proper size to handle the inverter's maximum DC amp draw should be installed at the battery to protect the circuit in case of a short to ground.

In addition to being near the batteries, an inverter installation requires an area that is cool and dry since an inverter produces a limited amount of heat while operating under heavy loads.

While electrical circuits in RVs are many and varied, an understanding of the basic principles of operation can help the owner solve problems. The tools described in this chapter are neither expensive nor difficult to use. Combined with a basic understanding of the RV and automotive systems, they should help you become more self-sufficient.

How to Live Without Hookups

B y their very design, RVs are "independence machines," equipped with relatively sophisticated systems that support habitation in all kinds of places, under all kinds of conditions. RVs take us to the desert in the summertime in temperatures well above 100°F, or to the ski resorts in winter where temperatures may fall well below zero. While RVing in such extreme temperatures usually requires special knowledge and preparation, it can be done in comfort. Beyond comfort, pushing the self-sufficiency limits of our RVs can create our most enjoyable experiences!

Even if we have no intention of pushing our limits climatically, our RV still is our ticket to independence. It would appear that many owners don't fully appreciate how much freedom their RVs can offer. Although campground hookups are convenient, they are not a necessity. Many RV owners who stay almost exclusively in commercial RV parks may believe they can't make it without umbilical cords connected to outside services. Some just prefer full-hookup campgrounds, which is fine. For those of you who would like to do some solo flying, this chapter will explain how. Certainly it's necessary to fill gasoline, water, and LP-gas tanks occasionally, but an RV can provide comfortable accommodations for several days without the need for the owner to add *anything*!

RV owners who take their self-contained RVing seriously are those who congregate on free or nearly free public land sites in the more temperate parts of the United States, notably in southern California, Arizona, and Florida. These people are ingenious adventurers who enjoy their freedom and independence to the utmost. Many have sold their homes and live on a fraction of their former living costs. This is not for everyone. But it proves that RVs can be used for full-time habitation for long periods with no hookups. All RVs aren't ideally suited to this kind of long-term use, but nearly all have self-containment capabilities that may extend well beyond their owners' expectations.

Following are discussions of the basic self-containment needs—electrical power, water, LP-gas—and how to stretch our self-sufficiency.

BOOSTING BATTERY POWER

The RV life-support system that causes the most consternation for RV owners who spend much of their time without hookups is the 12-volt system, including the batteries reserved for operation of RV accessories, the **auxiliary** (house) **batteries** (Figure 14.1). How much power is stored in a battery? How long is it liable to last? How can we quickly replenish batteries when they are depleted? Losing battery power may be a minor frustration on an occasional basis under moderate climatic conditions, but repeat occurrences can put a lid on our enthusiasm for "unplugged" RVing.

First, let's examine how to understand and make the best of our factory-installed 12-volt systems.

Eliminating Handicaps

Some RVs are fitted with a single house battery (in addition to the engine-starting battery), while others may have two. Unfortunately, improper battery care takes its toll, especially on the house batteries, and they often don't supply the power they were capable of when new.

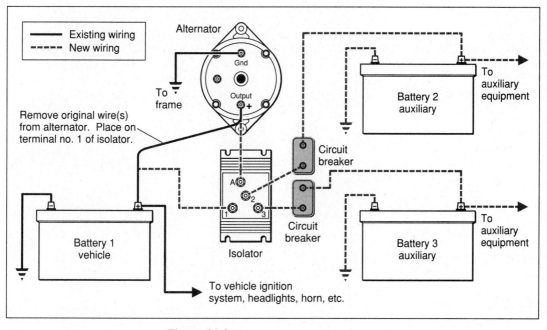

Figure 14.1
The auxiliary (house) batteries are the key to successful self-contained camping.

Improper Handling

The first handicap that many RV owners incur is loss of battery capacity due to improper charging, and improper charging may result when the battery connectors and the terminals become corroded.

The advice that has been issued for so many years about cleaning battery connectors and terminals is more than just idle commentary; corroded connectors can de-rate a battery to a fraction of its original capacity. This is the most common cause of inadequate battery reserve power.

"I've been driving for at least four hours, but the battery didn't even get us through one night!" is a complaint heard frequently regarding insufficient RV appliance power. The problem can be described in a water-system analogy: Although the pump (engine-driven alternator) had been functioning properly during the trip, the pipeline (wiring hookup) was restricted and the

Figure 14.2
The much-heard advice
about keeping batteries free
of corrosion cannot be
overemphasized.

tank (battery or batteries) was less than half full when the
owner assumed it was filled.

At the basic level, battery-maintenance chores should include simple cleaning of terminals and connectors with a solution of baking soda and water to remove corrosion (Figure
14.2). Use this solution to clean corrosion off the battery tray
and hold-down apparatus. Most corrosion occurs at the connection to the battery, but if problems persist, it's wise to check
other connections as well. You might add these two procedures
to the typical cleaning procedure:

1. Use a wire brush or sandpaper to roughen contact
   surfaces.
2. After reassembling, coat the *exterior* surfaces with grease
   or petroleum jelly to eliminate corrosion. Don't get any of
   the grease on contact surfaces because it can impede the
   flow of current.

Improper Storage

When placing batteries into storage, even for a couple of months, it's important that they are fully charged. Self-discharge rates decrease with temperature.

Even when batteries are clean and connections are well maintained, a small amount of self-discharge gradually occurs during storage, particularly in warm or hot weather. When placing batteries into storage, even for a couple of months, it's important that they are fully charged. Self-discharge rates decrease with temperature. When the temperature is under 50°F, a fully charged conventional open-cell battery usually is okay for several months; in higher temperatures a charger that delivers 14 to 14.2 volts should be used on the battery for three or four hours about once a month (operate the charger for at least twenty-four hours if voltage is less than 14).

Most maintenance-free batteries do not self-discharge as rapidly as conventional batteries, and the need for periodic charging may be reduced or eliminated.

Reserve Power

Continuing to visualize a battery as a water tank and the engine alternator as the water pump, we know the tank has a specific size. In battery terms this is known as the **reserve capacity**.

For example, a Group 27-size battery, the largest 12-volt battery typically used in RVs, may be rated at 160 minutes reserve capacity. This reserve-capacity rating describes how long the battery will sustain a 25-amp load at 80°F ambient temperature before voltage drops to 10.5. Introduced several years ago, this rating was intended to provide specific information on reserve capacity. Unfortunately, the 25-amp load does not necessarily represent the average RV load, which probably is closer to 10 amps. The difference is important because batteries last longer at lower discharge rates.

Helping to confuse the matter is the traditional ampere-hour rating, which has survived as the common battery descriptive term even though most manufacturers no longer list it. The amp-hour rating is another measurement of a battery's reserve capacity. It means that a battery rated at 100 amp-hours should be able to sustain a load of $\frac{1}{20}$ of its rating for 20 hours. For example, a 100-amp-hour battery should sustain a 5-amp load for 20 hours. There is no accurate, universal correlation between the old amp-hour rating and the new reserve-capacity rating listed in minutes.

Fortunately, most deep-cycle batteries are supplied by their manufacturers with data tables showing, by model, how long they will sustain a specific load. For example, a popular Group 27 battery will sustain a 10-amp load for 9.3 hours. That's 93 amp-hours for the practical purpose of calculating your 12-volt needs in a given period of time during which you expect to rely solely on battery power, and it's the information necessary to calculate your battery needs. (See also pages 302–303.)

Although a new battery may begin with the ability, for example, to sustain a 10-amp load for 9.3 hours, that's not usually the performance the consumer will receive. Due to ineffective charging, the battery's reserve capacity is reduced. If connections are corroded, reducing the effectiveness of the vehicle's alternator, the effect is like having a 93-gallon water tank that can be filled only to the 60-gallon level because the pipe that connects the pump to the tank is restricted.

Battery Depletion

How does the RV owner determine if a battery has been derated, other than assuming that's the case when the battery repeatedly goes flat prematurely? A depletion test can provide a rough answer. Most battery manufacturers list performance tables for their deep-cycle batteries. House batteries should always be the deep-cycle type for anyone who expects to do much self-contained camping. The term *deep-cycle* means that the batteries are designed for deep or prolonged discharge, followed by recharge, without excessive loss of battery life and potential for storing energy that can occur when starting batteries are subjected to this type of use.

As examples of how deep-cycle batteries can be expected to perform, the GNB Action Pack-80 is a Group 24 battery rated at 125 minutes reserve capacity, and the GNB Action Pack-105 is a Group 27 battery rated at 160 minutes (see Table 14.1). The

Table 14.1
Capacities of GNB Action Pack-80 and Action Pack-105 Batteries

If your accessories draw:	Based on peak performance, continuous power will be provided for:	
Amps	*AP-80 (Hours)*	*AP-105 (Hours)*
5	16.0	21.0
10	6.9	9.3
15	4.2	5.8
20	2.7	3.5
25	2.0	2.7

reserve-capacity test, conducted at 25 amps, is not realistic for typical RV use, but it's the published rating of the battery's ability to sustain RV electrical loads.

If your battery performs to about 80% of the GNB values, it's probably okay. New batteries usually will not perform fully to manufacturer's specifications, but their performance improves with use. If you find that your battery will sustain considerably

A Battery-Depletion Test

The average rate of power consumption for RVs may be 5 to 10 amps, with the exception of large, luxury motorhomes. With these figures in mind, here's a test that will give you an idea of how your batteries compare:

1. The battery should have been charged with the engine alternator, a portable battery charger, or the RV built-in charger/converter for an appropriate amount of time to insure maximum charge level. You'll need a multimeter (electrical test meter) to conduct this test, because the voltmeter on the instrument panel is not accurate enough. The multimeter is essential for much more than this test if you intend to understand and trouble-shoot batteries and electrical systems. See also pages 298–299, "Accurate Monitoring."

2. With the battery fully charged, turn on a sufficient number of interior lights to create a 5-amp load, measuring the load accurately with the multimeter. Note the time. Monitor time and voltage periodically until the voltage level drops to 10.5 volts, which is the end of the battery's useful capacity.

less load than the performance figures indicated here—or, better yet, the figures the battery's manufacturer issued for it—check for corrosion and/or inadequate charging (see also pages 299–300). You may recall that your battery sat in a discharged state for several months, incurring sulfation, which would explain the poor performance. If so, replacement is in order.

If your average load is higher than the 5- to 10-amp range, perform your test at higher rates, to simulate your specific situation.

Accurate Monitoring

The **multimeter**, a portable test meter essential for understanding, maintaining, and troubleshooting batteries and charging systems, can perform a number of functions, including voltage measurement of both direct-current and alternating-current systems, as well as measurement of electrical resistance (Figure 14.3). For example, it allows you to monitor the state of charge of your batteries. The meter should include an ammeter function that will handle up to 10 amps so loads can be accurately measured for battery-depletion tests. Adequate multimeters are available from Radio Shack and other electronics supply stores

Figure 14.3
The digital multimeter is invaluable in evaluating battery- and charging-system performances.

Table 14.2
Open-Circuit Voltage

Charge Level	Voltage	Specific Gravity
100%	12.7	1.265
75	12.4	1.225
50	12.2	1.190
25	12.0	1.155

for $40 to $60. The accuracy of less-expensive meters may be questionable. Good-quality meters with digital readouts are most effective for accurate measurement of voltage.

One of the primary benefits of an accurate multimeter is the ability to monitor a battery's **state of charge**. If you want to know the state of charge, it's merely a matter of reading the battery's voltage according to Table 14.2. These numbers must be interpreted based on experience. If the meter indicates your battery is 50% charged, you must estimate how long it will sustain your typical needs based on your experience.

Note: Readings must be taken with no load on the battery and are not accurate if taken within twenty-four hours after the battery has been charged unless surface charge has been depleted by turning on a load of about 10 amps for five minutes. **Specific gravity measurement** is a method of checking status of the electrolyte in open-cell batteries. A temperature-corrected battery hydrometer (available on order at auto-parts stores) is needed for this testing method.

Proper Charging

Our ability to properly charge batteries changes with the weather, which is why some vehicle alternators (mainly General Motors) are temperature compensating; they raise output voltage as ambient temperature drops because a battery's willingness to accept a charge is reduced in low ambient temperatures. Other alternators maintain a constant output of 14 to 14.2

volts, which is sufficient in warm or hot weather to charge a battery to or near its full capacity if driving time is adequate. Higher voltage levels are more effective in cold weather.

Most electrical converters built into RVs limit voltage to 13.8. In some late models, the voltage limit is 14. These voltage limits are intended to prevent excessive gassing and loss of water from the electrolyte of a conventional open-cell battery when the converter is in use continuously for weeks or months. Thus, the typical built-in RV converter is not as effective for raising a battery to its full capacity in a short time as the alternator. The alternator's voltage output can be slightly higher because it is not used on a long-term basis. Your multimeter will enable you to analyze the differences in voltage from various charging sources.

Aside from the question of adequate voltage output from the charging source—be it alternator or converter—the critical question is whether or not the voltage is seen at the battery—especially a battery located a considerable distance from the alternator. If alternator output is 14.2 volts, the voltage reading at the battery (which may be as much as 25 feet away) should not be lower than 14. The difference is known as voltage drop. Inadequate wire size and faulty or corroded connections are common causes of voltage drop in tow vehicle/trailer rigs, often exaggerated by faulty or corroded connections. Motorhomes usually are fitted with heavy cable (4 gauge or larger) for more effectiveness. However, corroded connections and inadequate attention paid to proper charging are typical causes of battery inadequacy in motorhomes. Just because you don't see corrosion on the exterior of the terminal doesn't mean it's not there, sandwiched between the terminal and the battery post. Remove terminals on batteries and check for corrosion periodically.

Testing for Voltage Drop

An accurate multimeter, used to measure voltage drop, will give a good indication of charging effectiveness. Different methods are used for vehicles with and without battery isolators. There are two types of battery isolators, and it's important to determine which kind your vehicle has. One is a **mechanical battery isolator**, which is a mechanical relay that makes clicking noises when the ignition key is turned on and off (Figure 14.4); the other is a **solid-state isolator**, which makes no sounds (Figure 14.5).

A Voltage-Drop Test

To test for voltage drop, follow these steps:

- For vehicles with either no isolator or a mechanical isolator, turn on several interior lights to deplete the auxiliary battery(ies) to a voltage level of about 10.5. Set engine RPM to about 1,500 (approximately double idle speed) and check the voltage at two points: the alternator output terminal and the positive post of the auxiliary battery. The difference in the readings is the amount of voltage drop, or loss of efficiency, in the wiring and in the isolator, if one is used. Bear in mind that voltage readings will be a bit lower with a depleted battery than the values quoted earlier for fully recharged batteries.

  If the voltage drop exceeds the values listed in Table 13.2, page 271, wire size is inadequate, connections are faulty, or a mechanical battery isolator (relay) is creating resistance.

  Check for voltage drop across the isolator by checking the voltage at both the input and the outlet terminals while the isolator is carrying a heavy load. The two readings at the two terminals should be almost identical.

- For vehicles with solid-state (diode-type) battery isolators, again use a depleted auxiliary battery.

  Test A: Set engine speed to about 1,500 RPM and check voltage at the output terminal on the alternator and at the alternator post on the isolator. Voltage drop in this short line should not be more than 0.2 volt.

  Test B: With engine RPM at about 1,500, check voltage at the auxiliary battery output terminal of the isolator and at the auxiliary battery lugs. Voltage drop will vary according to current flow and length of wire (see Table 13.2, page 271), but should be held to a minimum.

  Do not expect voltage levels taken in Tests A and B to be identical. Isolator diodes create a voltage drop of about one volt. However, the isolator causes alternator output to rise about one volt, compensating for the drop across diodes. For example, voltage at the alternator may read 15, compared to 14 at the output of the auxiliary battery terminal on the isolator. Recharge batteries when tests are completed.

Figure 14.4
The mechanical battery isolator basically is an electrical relay.

Figure 14.5
The solid-state battery isolator can be identified by its cooling fins.

Figure 14.6
The Group 24 battery (left) offers less reserve capacity than does the larger Group 27 battery.

Adding Battery Capacity

Now that we've discussed how to get the most out of what you have, let's consider increasing battery and alternator capacities to assure that adequate power will be available for accessories over long periods of self-contained camping.

Many RV manufacturers are using Group 24 batteries (11 inches long × 6¾ inches wide × 9⅝ inches long), rated at 125 to 130 minutes, rather than Group 27 batteries (12¾ inches long × 6¾ inches wide × 9⅝ inches long), rated at 160 to 170 minutes, to reduce costs (Figure 14.6). The smaller batteries may be sufficient in RVs that don't have a large number of appliances or are not used extensively for self-contained camping, particularly in winter, when the furnace usually creates the largest power demand. The smaller battery probably won't sustain an RV for more than a couple of days even with minimal 12-volt needs in warm weather.

Calculating Correct Capacity

Just how much capacity do we need? Arithmetic will provide the answer. We must estimate our total 12-volt needs during typical periods when neither the engine nor an AC generator will be used.

Table 14.3
Appliance Power Ratings

Appliance	Amps	Running Time (Hours)	Amp Hours
Lights (3)	4.5	4.0	18.0
Stereo	3.0	3.0	9.0
Television	4.0	3.0	12.0
Water pump	5.0	0.3	1.5
Furnace	7.0	4.0	28.0
Total amp hours			**68.5**

To evaluate our needs, we'll need to deal in amp-hours. For example, a single, fully charged, Group 24 battery is capable of delivering about 70 amp-hours if the average depletion rate is 10 amps and the battery is in top condition, that is, the battery will deliver 10 amps for 7 hours. That amount of battery capacity would be adequate for only one evening in cold weather (see Table 14.3). Further complicating matters in cold weather, low temperatures extend battery recharge time and reduce available capacity below the figures listed in this chapter.

Upgrading Batteries

Assuming an average depletion rate of 10 amps, the least expensive improvement in this case is to replace the Group 24 battery with a Group 27, expanding available amp-hour capacity from about 70 to about 90, and by learning to live with that level of reserve power. If still more capacity is needed, a pair of Group 27 deep-cycle batteries can be connected in parallel to serve as the house batteries, providing about 180 amp-hours (at the 10-amp depletion rate), while a 12-volt starting battery is reserved to crank the engine. All three can be charged simultaneously through use of a battery isolator, preferably a solid-state diode-type unit. Mechanical relay-type isolators function well when new, but their contact points gradually become corroded, causing electrical resistance.

Figure 14.7
Six-volt electric-vehicle
(golf-cart) batteries are
preferred for maximum
reserve capacity.

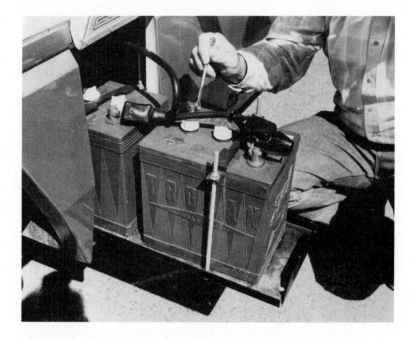

The use of two 12-volt batteries in parallel is the common
setup for RV use, even though it is not ideal over the long term.
A better auxiliary power setup consists of two 6-volt electric-
vehicle (golf cart) batteries wired in series for 12-volt output
(see Figure 14.7). These batteries are not interconnected when
they are at rest. Connected in series, the 6-volt batteries will
supply about 235 amp-hours of 12-volt power at a depletion rate
of 12 amps.

These batteries are $10\frac{3}{8}$ inches long $\times$ $7\frac{1}{8}$ inches wide $\times$
$11\frac{3}{16}$ inches high, which means they usually will fit in a compartment designed for typical 12-volt Group 27 batteries, although it will be necessary to build special accommodations if
four batteries are to be used. Most motorized RVs will accom-
modate two house batteries plus an engine battery.

Electric vehicle batteries aren't marketed with all the glamour
graphics and sales literature usually devoted to 12-volt batteries,
but they are designed for the ultimate in deep-cycle abuse that
occurs in golf carts. They have exceptionally thick lead plates in
addition to special thick glass separator mats. The batteries

shown in Figure 14.7 weigh 66 pounds apiece, compared to 55 pounds for a typical 12-volt deep-cycle battery.

Parallel hookup of 12-volt batteries tends to reduce their capacity on a long-term basis. The deterioration is worse when the two 12-volt batteries are not identical in size, type, brand, and age. Thus, the 6-volt series setup offers better long-term durability. With either setup, the ability to properly recharge the batteries is critical; wire size should be at least 8 gauge (preferably larger) between the alternator and the batteries. Welding-supply stores are a source for large-gauge wire and connectors.

Upgrading the Alternator

Here again, batteries and water tanks share theoretical characteristics. What if we were to add another tank (battery) only to find that our pump (alternator) is not capable of filling both tanks in a limited amount of time? Indeed, substantial additional battery capacity may be of little use without additional alternator capacity. Every situation is different, and a 55- to 60-amp alternator may be adequate for the owner who does not use a wide variety of 12-volt equipment while traveling and usually plugs in at commercial campgrounds. This greatly reduces the need for charging via the alternator.

The other extreme is limited driving time and/or heavy 12-volt equipment usage while traveling (air conditioner plus headlights and running lights), followed by heavy use of house accessories while camped. This situation requires the ability to recharge batteries at a higher rate while driving. High-output alternators do this job well (Figure 14.8). They're available at RV-supply stores and from RV mail-order catalogues, as are the other components described in this chapter.

In cases where increased output is needed, replacement of a standard alternator in the 50- to 60-amp range with a 105-amp model will cut battery recharge time. Voltage readings will tell the on-the-road recharge story. When voltage at the house batteries falls below 13.5 due to an excessive amperage draw from the chassis systems and RV appliances, recharge is restricted; when it falls below 13, recharging has ceased.

Figure 14.8
A high-capacity alternator can recharge batteries more rapidly when driving time is limited.

Regardless of the size and complexity of your system, the charging, maintenance, monitoring, and modification recommendations described here are the keys to making the most of your 12-volt system for maximum independence and comfort.

POWER FROM THE SUN

Only a few years ago, solar power for RVs seemed exotic. But the sun has been a practical source of electricity for RV owners for many years. It's relatively easy to assemble a system that supplies all the electrical needs of the RV except for air conditioners, whose amp draw usually is too high to be sustained by electrical inverters that transform 12-volt DC into 120-volt-AC power. Thus, AC generators still are needed, but only for air conditioning.

Several manufacturers of solar panels offer a variety of panels that range in output from a trickle of power to amounts that are limited only by the number of solar panels that will fit on the roof of the RV.

A typical system capable of producing a substantial amount of power from the sun consists of four 47-watt modules, a charge controller, and batteries capable of storing the power (Figure 14.9). The four panels (13 × 48 inches) and controller hooked to four 6-volt golf-cart batteries rated at over 200 amp-hours per pair when used in series for 12-volt output (a total of over 400 amp-hours) typically is adequate for even the most aggressive self-contained RV owner. About 100 amp-hours of battery capacity are recommended for each 47-watt panel installed to take proper advantage of each solar panel's output capability. The only practical way to have a battery for each of four panels is to connect the two banks of series-wired 6-volt batteries in parallel. Battery manufacturers usually recommend against parallel hookups because they shorten battery life. But in this case it's the only practical way to have battery capacity beyond the 200-amp-hour level.

Some solar panels are self-regulating, which means they do not require a charge controller. In contrast, the 47-watt panels must be used through a charge controller to prevent battery

Figure 14.9
Solar panels use silicon cells to convert sunlight into electrical energy for charging batteries.

overcharging. Several brands and types of charge controllers and batteries are sold by service firms for use in solar-panel installations. The addition of a charge controller capable of handling up to four of the 47-watt modules allows the owner to install less than four panels if he believes his needs can be met by fewer panels, and it allows expansion of the system later if necessary.

The panels are mounted on the roof, as near the refrigerator vent as practical, to minimize the length of wire needed to reach the charge controller installed inside the coach. The panels are supplied with mounting brackets, and electrical connections are made with 12-gauge wire. Four 47-watt solar modules, each rated at 2.94 amps (4 × 2.94 = 11.76), produce in excess of 10

Table 14.4
Power Requirements of Typical 12-Volt Appliances

	Amps
Incandescent light, each bulb	1.5
Fluorescent light	1.5
Color TV	4.0
CB radio (receive)	0.5
CB radio (transmit)	0.9
Videocassette player	2.5
Furnace	4.0–7.0
Water pump	8.0
Microwave oven (via inverter)	100.0

amps on bright, sunny days when a heavy load is applied to the batteries. Four panels typically will provide more power than the average RVer needs, even while periodically using an inverter to operate a television 2 to 3 hours a day, a microwave oven for 15 to 20 minutes each evening, as well as lights and common 12-volt appliances. Each motorhome owner's power requirements will differ, as will the power output of the panels in cloudy or partly cloudy weather. Thus, what is sufficient for one motorhomer may not be sufficient for another (see Table 14.4).

Because the variables are so numerous, manufacturers of panels offer detailed solar-system guides and worksheets to help prospective customers calculate energy needs and estimate how sun intensity variances affect power output of the panels in various sections of the nation. Solar panels are sold by many RV-supply stores, which can also furnish the worksheets.

Inverters that transform 12-volt-DC into 120-volt-AC power draw heavily from batteries. Motorhomes equipped with inverters will need the larger solar-power systems, such as the four-panel system described here, possibly even reaching the point where the batteries in the four-panel four-battery system must be periodically supplemented by use of the AC generator or engine alternator. The panels usually will recharge the batteries by midday or early afternoon, and the controller will limit the charge rate.

Large batteries with good storage capacity are critical to proper utilization of solar power, which is why electric vehicle batteries are popular.

GENERATORS AND POWER CONVERTERS

Most RV owners who intend to do much self-contained camping usually have an AC generator of sufficient size to operate one or two roof air conditioners. Generators that are built into motorhomes typically are four kilowatts or larger (Figure 14.10), while portables used by trailerists and carried in the tow vehicle tend to be smaller (Figure 14.11).

Use of an AC generator for self-contained camping does not require extensive explanation, except to specify that most generators do not have much, if any, 12-volt-DC output for recharging batteries, although they can capably provide 120-volt power to a power converter (transformer) for battery charging. Almost all manufacturers install converters at the factory, but few have adequate battery-charging capacity. The **converter** is an automatic electrical transformer that changes 120-volt-AC to 12-volt-

Figure 14.10
A four-kilowatt AC generator is a popular size for motorhomes equipped with roof air conditioners.

Figure 14.11
Available in many sizes, a portable AC generator can be installed in the truck bed to provide power to the trailer.

DC power (Figure 14.12). Most have the capability to perform some recharging of batteries, although few are well suited to that role.

The battery-charge ratings of converters range from about 5 amps to about 15—piddling capability even for RVs with only one house battery. Thus, the RV owner who runs his AC generator for extended periods for battery charging, possibly annoying his campground neighbors, usually is wasting time and fuel.

To evaluate your situation, inspect the converter's identification plate (Figure 14.13). It usually will specify battery-charging output. If the converter is the type with separate output terminals for RV accessories and battery charging, it may be rated at 30 amps, but only 7 amps of that is available for battery charging. The battery-charge rate usually will be listed on the identification plate.

Figure 14.12
In this application, a converter is combined with the main electrical distribution unit.

In contrast, the converter with a single output is much more effective because the total output of the unit, minus the load from RV appliances being used at the time, is available for battery charging (Figure 14.14). Thus, there will be no battery-charge rating because the converter's entire output is available for battery charging if the amp draw of appliances does not enter the picture.

In either case, effectiveness may be measured with an ammeter. Turn on several interior lights for a couple of hours—

Figure 14.13
The converter's identification plate lists its battery-charge rating.

Figure 14.14
With a single-output converter, voltage is more stable and battery-charge rates are considerably higher.

sufficient time to substantially deplete the house battery(ies). Place an automotive-type ammeter in the positive line leading from the converter to the house battery(ies). The ammeter on a multimeter typically won't be rated high enough to perform this task. Make sure all 12-volt appliances are turned off. Plug in the RV's power cord, which should automatically activate the converter. Check the ammeter; the charge rate should equal the rating listed on the converter/charger. If it is lower, inadequate wiring and/or placement by the manufacturer of the converter/charger too far from the battery(ies) usually is at fault.

If the converter's charge rate is equal to or near the rating stamped on the converter, it shows an effective wiring hookup, but you still must decide if the output is high enough for your needs. For rapid recharging in no-hookup situations, a converter with at least 30 amps of battery-charging capability is needed. RV-supply stores offer effective single-output converters. Installing such a converter as near as possible to the house batteries makes running an AC generator for battery charging worthwhile.

The same situation exists with portable AC generators. Their output for battery charging usually is about 10 amps, actually better than the output of many built-in RV converters.

Running the engine-driven alternator is usually the most effective way to recharge batteries, although it's impractical for the RV owner who spends considerable time without hookups. And, of course, it's inefficient to run an eight-cylinder engine for battery charging when it's possible to use a two-cylinder engine if you already have an AC generator. Effective single-output converters range in price from $225 to $300.

INVERTERS

For maximum convenience and minimum AC-generator usage (noise), many RV owners install **inverters** (Figure 14.15), those sophisticated transformers that change 12-volt-DC to 120-volt-AC power, the opposite of the converter/charger discussed previously. Inverters cost from $100 to $2,000 depending on their

Figure 14.15
An inverter changes 12-volt
DC power to 120-volt AC.

rated output, which ranges upward to 2,000 watts of AC power for most appliances, from microwave ovens to music systems, 120-volt televisions, videocassette recorders, and a wide variety of other items.

The most popular role for the inverter is to supply power for a microwave oven, eliminating the need to crank up the AC generator every time the owner decides to warm a cup of coffee. Thus, the inverter, although not a necessity, greatly reduces generator running time. If there are neighbors nearby, they will surely appreciate the benefits of an inverter for its generator-noise reduction. The only appliance that an inverter cannot handle is an air conditioner; an AC generator still is needed in climates where air conditioning is desirable.

All inverter manufacturers supply detailed installation instructions that call for use of heavy cables (4 gauge or larger) to connect the inverter with the batteries (Figure 14.16). Notice the plural, *batteries*. Since an inverter draws at least 10 amps of 12-volt-DC power for every amp of 120-volt-AC power it produces, power draw from batteries can be high. For example, a microwave/convection oven can draw 8 amps of 120-volt-AC power, which requires at least 80 amps of DC power—more if the inverter is inefficient. If the inverter is 90% efficient, the 8-amp microwave would require 88 amps of battery power. Without substantial battery capacity, the high amp draw of an inverter can pull batteries down quickly. Although microwave oven usage usually is of short duration, the power required to operate the oven, combined with 12-volt requirements of other appliances, make effective battery-recharge capability essential.

An inverter should be installed as near the house batteries as possible for minimum voltage drop in the 12-volt-DC wiring. For 120-volt-AC output, appliances may be plugged directly into the unit via extension cords, or the unit can be connected to the RV 120-volt power-distribution system by a qualified electrician. When choosing an inverter, check its efficiency—the ratio between input and output. A low-efficiency inverter is one that loses 20% or more of its input to heat. Good inverters lose less than 10% to heat. Some inverters are only 60 to 70% efficient, which can cause rapid battery depletion.

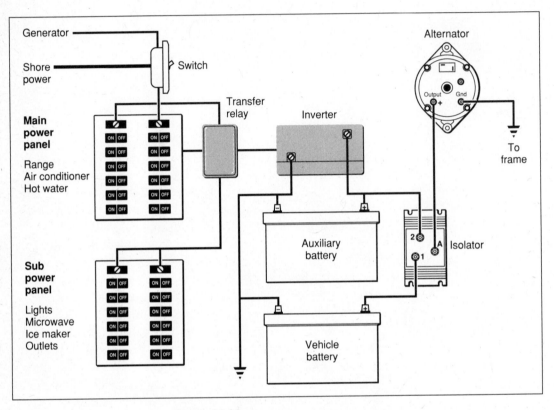

Figure 14.16
An inverter relies on heavy cables for power from the battery. One is shown here, but multiple batteries normally are used.

Camping without hookups in comfort and convenience requires that all three battery-recharging methods—engine alternator, RV converter/charger, and solar-power system—be available and effective, especially when an inverter is used.

WATER—THE LIFE SOURCE

An RV owner's supply of water is another of the essential ingredients of comfortable, enjoyable, no-hookup camping. Of course, the more water we carry, the less we have to worry about running out. How much water is adequate? That's a question that must be answered by the individual, because we all have different levels of efficiency when it comes to water conservation. Some RV owners may regard 30 gallons as adequate, while others may believe that 60 gallons are minimal. An "unplugged" camping trip or two will provide the answer.

Many RVs have water tanks of marginal size, and in some of those cases the tanks do not fill the compartments in which they are housed. In such cases it's wise to install the largest water tank that will fit in the compartment. Replacement tanks can be purchased from RV-supply stores.

If the existing tank cannot be replaced with a larger one, it may be possible to locate another tank in a storage area that is not essential—under a dinette seat, for example. It's best that the tank fill be located on the same side as the fill for the original tank. Of course, the new tank must have an air vent so it can be filled properly. Inspecting the installation of the original tank will be helpful in installing the new one.

When adding water capacity, weight is an important factor. Some RVs are overloaded already, and adding water (8 pounds per gallon) adds to the overload. Weigh the RV before deciding to add water capacity (see pages 163–167). Be sure to weigh the RV laterally (side to side) to make sure that an additional water tank added to the heavy side does not create a side-to-side imbalance of sufficient poundage to cause vehicle handling/ stability problems or tire overloading.

If water capacity is added, it doesn't mean the owner must travel with the tanks full. Twenty gallons might be an adequate amount until approaching the destination, when the tank(s) can be filled.

Conserving water may be an effective way to make do with what otherwise would be inadequate water capacity. Obviously, there are various levels of water conservation. One full-time RVing couple wrote that they re-use bath water, among their myriad conservation efforts. Most of us probably would rather stay in campgrounds with hookups than do the recycling bit. Fortunately it's possible to comfortably camp unplugged without going to such extremes.

LP-GAS

Even though **liquefied petrolem gas** (LP-gas), better known as **propane**, has been around for a very long time, it's still an amazing fuel when we take a moment to realize what it does for us. Our refrigeration, heating, and much of our cooking are made possible by this fuel, which is compacted into a relatively small tank.

Except in winter, when furnaces place unusually high demands on propane supplies, propane storage capacity is not a problem. A normal rate of usage normally allows us to fill the tank(s) before we're in danger of running out.

In winter, however, the story may be a bit different if the RV tank is relatively small. The definition of "relatively small" will vary from one rig to the next, but 15 gallons is small for winter usage, unless the RV and its furnace are very compact. In a 25- to 30-foot motorhome or trailer, 20 gallons should be the minimum for RV usage. For truly large RVs, 30 to 40 gallons of propane would be sufficient for long-term self-contained usage.

If you find that the propane level drops rapidly and you're constantly monitoring the content, consider using a spare tank. Ideally it should be at least a 7½-gallon DOT tank of the type fitted on travel trailers.

Note: *The tank must be transported the way it is designed to be used*. In other words, if the tank is designed to stand upright when connected to the gas system, it should be transported or stored that way. Instructions stamped on the tank's collar will identify the proper position. Don't store a propane tank in a closed storage compartment.

Although it requires more effort and planning, the ability to camp without hookups is the RV owner's ticket to more adventurous RV experience.

15

RV Service—Taking Command

No single aspect of RV ownership may be as important as adequate service. Good dealer service not only means a well-maintained rig with a high resale value at trade-in time, it may also be the deciding factor between enjoyable, trouble-free traveling or a trip that ends prematurely in frustration, disappointment, and anger.

Most RV owners also own at least one automobile, and while significant advances have been made in recent years in RV service, the contrast between the resources available for automobile maintenance and repairs and those available for RVs can be striking. Most obvious, of course, is that auto mechanics are available at virtually every wide spot in the road throughout the country. Contrast that with the effort still required to find a competent RV mechanic, and it is readily apparent that the auto and RV industries are still worlds apart, even though RV systems generally are considerably less complex.

In recent years, increased consumer awareness has called attention to the need for assuring reliable and honest service for motor-vehicle owners. A number of laws regulating automotive service and repair have been enacted on both the state and federal levels. Many states have now responded to the needs of consumers by establishing motor-vehicle complaint offices within their consumer affairs departments. Also forty-eight states have now passed automotive repair acts—commonly referred to as **lemon laws**—which have set specific guidelines for warranty service and other repairs, and have established penalties for those dealers, service technicians, and mechanics who, for one reason or another, fail to fulfill their obligations to the vehicle owner.

While much of the state legislation has been especially helpful for automobile owners, most state laws specifically exclude motorhomes and other recreational vehicles. Efforts have been made to amend many of these laws in recent years to include motorhome chassis, but, given the many different types of systems—some automotive and others relating to habitation—in the average motorhome, the laws are frequently impossible to enforce. When the exact source of the problem is difficult to diagnose, the owner often still ends up caught in the tug-of-war between the chassis manufacturer and the motorhome builder.

In an effort to address the unique problems of RVers and extend to them the same resources enjoyed by automobile owners under state laws, the major chassis manufacturers and the Recreation Vehicle Industry Association (RVIA) have entered into agreements that streamline the complaint process for motorhome owners. According to RVIA officials, these pacts provide that when a warranty dispute triggers the state law and a buy-back of the unit is ordered by a state arbitrator, the motorhome manufacturer will automatically be responsible for taking care of the consumer. Once the consumer has been reimbursed for the motorhome, the chassis maker and the motorhome manufacturer can then decide how they will share the cost of replacing the RV.

Although such a program is not available for trailer owners, it is worth noting that increased competition in the RV industry has made all manufacturers much more sensitive to all RV buyers. Most manufacturers now have customer relations departments, as well as established procedures for handling warranty and other service complaints. What's more, in sharp contrast to industry practices of just a few years ago, manufacturers today emphasize service when selecting a dealer to represent their line. In a recent random survey of a number of manufacturers, all of them indicated they are especially careful to pick dealers that have sound service experience, trained personnel, and adequate service facilities.

In addition, many manufacturers offer service clinics for dealers, in which service personnel are brought to the factory for extensive training. Of special note, RVIA has established a program of one-week, "troubleshooter" clinics aimed at enhancing the skills of experienced service technicians. The association has also assisted in the establishment of a National Recreational Vehicle Institute that offers a formal program of training for new and veteran service personnel. In conjunction

---

A Checklist for Better Dealer Service

Check the Dealer. Before buying your RV, check out the dealer's service area to make sure the facilities are adequate. Look for state and local licensing documents and any certifications for both the individual technicians as well as the dealership. Check to see if the dealer is a member of RVDA. While RVDA membership is not mandatory, it is generally a sign that the dealer is conscientious enough about his business to subscribe to a voluntary set of standards. If possible, check with others who have bought RVs from that dealer to see whether their service experiences have been satisfactory.

Check Your Warranty. Read your warranty documents on all components of the RV thoroughly so that you know exactly what is covered by the manufacturer and what the dealer's responsibilities are, as well as what the warranty excludes.

Get Written Estimates. If nonwarranty work is to be performed, get a written estimate and make sure the service writer understands that you want to be consulted if any further work is deemed necessary. In many states, the law now requires prior notification before any work is performed beyond that originally authorized. For your added protection, however, insist that the service writer make a written note that states that you must authorize any additional repairs not noted on the original work order.

Verify Replacement Parts. Ask that the service department save all old parts that are replaced so you can verify that replacement was necessary. Also, if the repairs are performed under warranty, the factory probably will ask to see the old part before authorizing a warranty payment to the service shop or a reimbursement to the owner.

If Problems Arise. If problems arise, approach the service manager in a courteous manner and present your case. If that fails, ask to speak to the manager or owner of the dealership. If that still does not lead to a satisfactory resolution of your complaint, contact the factory immediately and ask that the manufacturer's service or customer relations personnel take action. Finally, if all else fails, contact the automotive repair bureau of your state consumer affairs department to determine what regulatory remedies may be available to you. At that point you may also wish to seek assistance through one or more of the agencies or consumer advocates listed on page 334.

with those efforts, the Recreation Vehicle Dealers Association (RVDA), has begun a program to provide formal certification to service personnel who have completed a prescribed course of training. (See page 332 for a sample complaint letter.)

TIPS FOR BETTER SERVICE

In addition to the regulatory remedies provided on both the federal and state levels, as well as the industry advances in improving service, the guidelines detailed in the boxed copy on

---

Guidelines to Selecting an Independent Repair Shop

Check Your Warranty. If the RV is still within the manufacturer's warranty period, consult your owner's manual or warranty identification card for instructions on how to obtain warranty service when it is impossible for the vehicle or any of its components to be repaired by a factory-authorized service facility. A telephone number for the factory customer relations department is usually listed with the warranty documents.

Ask for Recommendations. Before contracting for work through an independent service facility, ask managers of the nearest campground for service recommendations.

Check for Certification. Check to see if the mechanic displays any documents of certification. For instance, the National Institute for Automotive Excellence offers tests on a voluntary basis. Anyone who successfully completes that test is certified as competent in engine, brake, transmission, and other specialty repairs. Display of such a certificate

should also be an indication that the mechanic cares enough to be certified.

Check Accreditation. Check to see if the shop displays a registration by a state bureau of automotive repair or a seal from an association, such as a vehicle owner's club or the Better Business Bureau.

Check Business Record. Inquire locally to see how long the shop has been in business. Reliable shops with good reputations generally have been around for a while and have an established record of expertise. Bear in mind that gas stations may not have the facilities to perform the specialized repairs needed on an RV.

Check Alternative Shops. Remember that specialty shops, such as transmission centers and muffler and radiator shops, may charge lower prices than service stations. These shops may also be in a position to do the work faster.

page 319 will help assure that the service you receive at your selling dealer is competent and thorough.

INDEPENDENT REPAIR SHOPS

Given a choice between getting repairs at their selling dealer or having the work performed by an independent repair facility, most RV owners would opt for the former. However, all too frequently, breakdowns occur at a time and location that precludes getting the work done by a home-based dealer. For those who are faced with such a circumstance, the guidelines listed on pages 320–321 may help in getting reliable service on the road.

Get a Written Guarantee. Ask if the shop guarantees its work, and get that guarantee in writing so you can have some leverage in getting a refund if the work has to be redone when you return home.

Talk to the Mechanic. Try to talk directly to the mechanic to make sure you both understand what is to be done.

Get a Written Estimate. Get a written estimate before approving the repairs and, if time and circumstances permit, use it to compare prices at other facilities in the area.

Check Repair Rates. Be aware that most automotive-repair shops estimate charges based on a flat-rate manual. That manual tells the shop how many hours a particular job should take. However, many repairs are completed in less time than the flat-rate manual indicates. If the shop you are dealing with charges on an hourly basis, see if you can be charged only for the actual time worked, rather than the time indicated in the flat-rate manual.

Keep Copies of All Receipts. Be sure you keep copies of all work orders and repair receipts, and make sure the mechanic or service manager has detailed each charge. Separate costs should be listed for parts and labor. The mileage of your vehicle should be noted, as well as the terms of any warranty on the repairs. Also, ask for the old parts and keep them at least until the warranty runs out.

Consider Repair Programs. Finally, consider enrolling in a program such as the Good Sam Emergency Road Service (ERS), which provides members with a toll-free number that can be used twenty-four hours a day from any place in the country for towing any type of RV to a Good Sam-approved repair facility. For additional information about Good Sam's ERS program, write: Good Sam, Box 700, Agoura, California 91376; or call the club toll free at (800) 234-3450.

YOUR RESPONSIBILITIES AS A CONSUMER

While RV owners would like to have all manufacturers and dealers adhere to the old adage "the customer is always right," the fact is that RVers sometimes are wrong in their service desires and demands.

Asked to list their pet peeves regarding RVers, dealers consistently noted that they are especially irritated by the RV owners who lie about a particular problem. Owners may have failed to read their manuals on the coach or on a particular component and thereby caused the problem, yet they want it repaired under the warranty.

Some dealers are irritated by RV owners who insist on staying with their rigs while they are being repaired, and then talk incessantly to the mechanic while he is trying to work. Not only does that slow the repair process, it also presents a potential liability problem for the shop if the RV owner should be injured while he or she is in the service area.

Other dealers have a more liberal view and recognize that to many RVers, their rigs are also their homes. They ask owners to wait elsewhere if hazardous work is being done, but arrange to allow owners to occupy their rigs at least while they are not actually being repaired.

Topping the list of pet peeves about RVers is the nearly unanimous complaint concerning those who make appointments for service and then fail to show up or call the dealership to cancel.

Topping the list of pet peeves about RVers is the nearly unanimous complaint concerning those who make appointments for service and then fail to show up or call the dealership to cancel. It's an especially troublesome problem during the summer because many dealers are trying to service their own customers, as well as travelers who need attention immediately so they can get back on the road.

Recognizing that the RV owner does play a key role in determining whether he or she has an unsatisfactory service experience or ends up driving out of the service facility a happy and satisfied customer, the Consumer Care Commission of the Recreation Vehicle Dealers Association, an organization founded in 1986 to promote better service for RV owners, recommends that consumers follow these guidelines:

- Be able to better identify the value of reliable products and good service.

- Be willing to pay the necessary costs for reliable products and good service.
- Accept the responsibility for knowledge of all aspects of the vehicle's operation before leaving the dealership.
- Become better informed about the product by studying the owners' manuals provided by manufacturers and suppliers.
- Be more aware of the realistic limitations of the vehicle.
- Be prepared to accept responsibility for the basic vehicle maintenance.

REPAIR SCAMS

Each year thousands of motorists—and a good many RVers among them—fall victim to repair scams perpetrated by disreputable service-station attendants and independent repair facilities. Some of the more common ploys include squirting oil on the inside of a wheel hub and telling the vehicle owner that

How to Guard Against Repair Scams

- Beware of overeager service-station attendants, especially in self-service stations; avoid high-pressure sales tactics (for example, when the attendant warns you it is "too dangerous" to continue your trip if you don't buy a particular component or agree to a repair).
- Never leave your rig unattended in a service station; this is an open invitation for the dishonest attendant to sabotage the unit.
- Don't allow anyone to check under the hood unless you are by his side. This especially holds true for self-service operations where an attendant comes out to "help you out" while you are busy filling the gas tank.

- If you find yourself faced with the purchase of parts and/or repairs, take a couple of minutes to phone other service facilities or parts suppliers in the area to get a cost comparison.
- If possible, pay for repairs with an oil-company credit card. If a dispute arises later over the cost, you may be able to recover some of your money since the oil company can usually reverse an overcharge. If you pay with cash or another type of credit card, the oil company supplying the station can not legally force the dealer to refund your money, and your only recourse may be the courts.

there is a problem with a "leaky brake cylinder," puncturing a tire with a sharp instrument such as an ice pick and then charging for a repair or complete replacement of the tire, or puncturing the radiator. The advice listed on page 323 will help you guard against these frauds.

CONSUMER WARRANTY RIGHTS

One of the most perplexing problems for the RV owner is fully understanding the warranty coverage on trailers or motorhomes. The task can be confusing and overwhelming because every RV comes with multiple warranties. While motorhomes have two main warranties—one for the chassis and one for the coach portion—all RVs have separate warranties for all major components. The terms and duration of all those warranties can vary greatly.

Bear in mind that one of the most important things a prospective RV buyer can do is review and compare the various warranties before the purchase. Since 1975, consumers in the United States have been given the right of prior review of warranties, regardless of the product, under the provisions of the Magnuson-Moss Warranty Act. RV dealers are required by law to post a written notice—usually in the showroom area—that tells consumers that copies of all warranties are available. If those warranties are not on the premises, the dealer must provide the information necessary to obtain the warranty from the manufacturer.

A Warranty Checklist

In addition, the federal law also provides some significant warranty guidelines and restrictions that have taken the fine print and a good deal of the mystery out of the warranty process.

Warranties now must be much more specific about the duration of the coverage offered, as well as any items that might be excluded. Here are some of the other things you should consider when reviewing a warranty:

- Any expenses that are excluded from coverage. For example, some warranties may state that the owner must pay labor charges.
- What the consumer must do to obtain repairs. Does the RV or component have to be serviced by the selling dealer or a factory-authorized service center? If so, does the warranty provide sufficient information for the owner to contact the factory or appropriate facility to get repairs authorized and completed? Does it require the owner to pay for shipping charges if the item has to be returned to the factory for repairs?
- If a component fails, what will the manufacturer do? Does the warranty call for replacement or repair?
- Does the warranty cover **consequential damages?** Most warranties do not, which means that the manufacturer will not pay for any damage the product caused, or for your time and expenses in getting the damage repaired. For example, if the refrigerator in your RV breaks down, the refrigerator maker will not pay for food that spoils. Or, if the RV must go in for repairs while you are on the road, the factory will not reimburse you for motel expenses.
- Are there any conditions or limitations on the warranty? Some warranties will only provide coverage if you maintain or use the product as directed.

Spoken Warranties

Frequently during the negotiations for the purchase of a tow vehicle, trailer, or motorhome, the salesperson will make an oral promise to the buyer. For example, the buyer may be told that a piece of equipment will be changed, specific modification will be made, or free maintenance and repairs will be offered for a certain period of time. Such promises constitute **spoken warranties**. However, the warranties are not binding unless put in writing on the sales contract. If the salesperson makes such offers, insist that they be written into the sales agreement before you sign. If the request is refused, don't expect to get what you were promised.

Implied Warranties

Although a written warranty is not required by law, **implied warranties** are. These are warranties that are created by state law, and all states have them. Almost every purchase you make is covered by an implied warranty. The most common type of implied warranty is called a **warranty of merchantability.** This means that the seller promises that the product will do what it is supposed to do, for example, a motorhome will run, your rig's air conditioner will cool, or the furnace will heat.

Another type of implied warranty is the **warranty of fitness for a particular purpose.** This applies when you buy a product on the seller's advice that it is suitable for a particular use. For example, if an auto manufacturer assigns a tow-capacity rating to a given vehicle, and the dealer sells it based on the fact that it will be suitable for towing your trailer, that constitutes this type of warranty.

Even if the item you purchase does not come with a written warranty from the manufacturer, it is still covered by implied warranties unless the product is marked "as is," or the seller states in writing that no warranty is given. Kansas, Maine, Maryland, Massachusetts, Mississippi, Vermont, West Virginia, and the District of Columbia do not permit "as is" sales.

If problems arise that are not covered by the manufacturer's written warranty, you should investigate the implied warranties that might exist under your state's laws. Implied-warranty coverage can last as long as four years, but the length of coverage can vary greatly from state to state. Check with your local state consumer affairs office or the state attorney general's office to obtain information on implied warranties.

Resolving Warranty Disputes

The checklist on the opposite page outlines some steps to follow when faced with problems involving the interpretation or extent of warranty coverage.

If none of these actions resolves the problem, or if the dispute involves a significant amount of money, you can file a lawsuit through an attorney, basing your case on the Magnuson-

> *Even if the item you purchase does not come with a written warranty from the manufacturer, it is still covered by implied warranties unless the product is marked "as is," or the seller states in writing that no warranty is given.*

Moss Warranty Act. The provisions of this law allow you to sue for damages or for any other type of relief the court awards, including legal fees. You should also know that the law provides that only the maker of the warranty can be sued. However, some state statutes also allow dealers or distributors to be named in a warranty suit. Your lawyer will generally be able to advise you as to whether or not you have a claim under Magnuson-Moss. However, despite the fact that the law was enacted some years ago, some lawyers remain unaware of all of the remedies possible under that act. If you have a warranty case, it is best to inquire beforehand whether the lawyer has had experience in handling warranty cases.

How to Resolve Warranty Disputes

Read. Read the product warranty carefully before buying. After the purchase, file your sales contract or sales slips with the factory warranty.

Discuss. If a problem arises, discuss the problem with the retailer first. If you cannot reach an agreement with the dealer or retailer, write the manufacturer. Send all letters by certified mail and keep copies.

Complain. If you do not get satisfaction after corresponding with the manufacturer, contact your local consumer-protection agencies. Most importantly, recognize that the manufacturer cannot stall a resolution of your problem until the warranty runs out. If a problem exists before expiration of the factory warranty and there is a written record of a complaint, the manufacturer is obligated to resolve the problem according to the terms of its warranty. It should also be noted that at this point in the dispute it may be helpful to contact either *Trailer Life's* "RV Action Line" or *MotorHome's* "Hot Line" for assistance. Since both of these columns specialize in handling RV-related problems at no charge to readers, either of them can be a good resource for assistance before proceeding with more time-consuming and costly legal proceedings.

Arbitrate. Inquire about any dispute-resolution organizations that the company may use. The company may be willing to submit the problem to an arbitrator rather than face the prospect of formal legal action.

Litigate. If legal action becomes your next option, consider small-claims court if the amount of money involved is small—usually less than $1,000 to $1,500. The costs to file a small-claims-court action are low and the procedures are simple. The clerk of the small-claims court will be able to assist you with the filing of the lawsuit.

State Lemon Laws

As noted earlier, lemon-law coverage for RVs varies widely from state to state, and in many states may be nonexistent. However, lemon laws in most states are amended yearly, and it is possible that at least the chassis portion of a motorhome is covered under your state's law. Tow-vehicle owners will find the law provides fairly comprehensive coverage for their vehicles.

Basically, lemon laws represent an extended warranty granted by the state. Amendments in recent years, besides attempting to offer some relief for RV owners, have tended to focus on an extension of the manufacturer's warranty period. For example, many state lemon laws now provide fairly extensive coverage up to 24 months and/or 24,000 miles.

Under the lemon-law statutes, a vehicle manufacturer is usually given a specific number of opportunities to remedy a defect, in a given amount of time, before the law is triggered. Once the process is set in motion, it does not—contrary to popular belief—automatically assure that the vehicle will be bought back and/or replaced by the manufacturer. The consumer must present his or her case before a state arbitrator who rules on the merits of the case. Thus, the importance of maintaining comprehensive records of repairs and repair attempts is obvious.

Given the fact that lemon laws have been in effect for a number of years, resulting in a number of vehicle buybacks, it's reasonable to ask the question, "Where have all those lemons gone?" The answer is that the manufacturers take them back, repair them, and then try to recoup a portion of their expenses by offering them for sale as used vehicles on their dealers' lots. Because that practice is now prevalent, many states have either passed lemon-law amendments or have amendments pending that require the dealer to notify a prospective purchaser of the history of the vehicle.

Service Contracts/Extended Warranties

For most RVers, buying a **service contract,** or extended warranty as they are sometimes called, is buying peace of mind from repair costs and hassles. Given the fact that most RV

Bear in mind that one of the most important things a prospective RV buyer can do is review and compare the various warranties before the purchase.

*Service contracts
are now offered by
virtually every RV
dealer—and some
manufacturers—on
products ranging
from the RV itself
to the various
components and
appliances inside.*

breakdowns happen on the road, far from your selling dealer, a service contract can indeed appear to be very attractive insurance when you consider that such a breakdown may not only be expensive, but also result in the need for hotel or motel accommodations and rental of other transportation. On the other hand, service contracts can be expensive headaches for the unwary.

Service contracts are now offered by virtually every RV dealer—and some manufacturers—on products ranging from the RV itself to the various components and appliances inside. Cost of those contracts may begin at around $100 for a component and run as high as $3,000 or more for coverage on the RV, depending upon the length and amount of coverage provided.

Just as they can vary greatly in coverage, service contracts can also vary greatly in reliability. RV buyers should remember also that the contracts are a high-profit item for dealers, and that competition in the service-contract business is fierce because of its cash-flow potential. As a result, in addition to having a number of reputable companies, the service-contract arena is populated by many companies and underwriters who are on shaky financial ground, if not simply con artists.

Therefore, regardless of whether you are buying new or used, if the deal involves a service contract, consider the following:

What does the contract offer?

A service contract, like a warranty, provides repair and/or maintenance for a specific time period. Warranties, however, are included in the price of the the product, while service contracts cost extra and are sold separately.

What is covered by the contract?

Generally, the contract will be very specific in the parts and services that are covered. Read the contract carefully, and, if it does not list something specifically, then you must assume that it is not covered. Service contracts will specifically exclude any repairs resulting from misuse or a failure to service the product on an established maintenance schedule. Also, the product owner may be required to follow certain procedures, such as notifying the contract company before repairs are made. That requirement can be especially troubling for RVers unless the company maintains a 24-hour-telephone service for authorization of repairs.

What will the service contract give me that the manufacturer's warranty will not?

Before considering a service contract, make sure you know what your warranty covers. Carefully compare the contract's coverage with your warranty to determine if the contract is worth the extra expense.

What other costs will I have?

The contract may require that you pay a certain deductible on any repairs. Or it may call for an additional charge each time the contract is used. Also, some expenses may be limited or excluded. For example, your contract may not cover towing or rental-car expense. In addition, you may have to pay a transfer or cancellation fee if you sell the covered vehicle before the expiration of the contract. The RVer who may be buying a used unit that has a transferable service contract should leave nothing to chance. Besides following through with the selling dealer, you should contact the company directly to make sure the transfer has been made. If the seller charges you a transfer fee, be sure to get a receipt as proof of transfer.

Where can I get service?

If the service contract is underwritten by the RV dealer, you may find that the contract is very restrictive in its service requirements. In fact, it may be that service is only available at the dealer's location.

Who is responsible for the contract?

Again, if the contract is underwritten by the dealer, the contract will only be good if that dealer remains in business. Contracts that are offered by an independent company and underwritten by an insurer are the best choices.

Can I purchase the service contract later?

Most reputable dealers and service contract companies now allow RV buyers to defer the decision to purchase a service contract. For example, the dealer may tell you that the service contract can be purchased at a later date, as long as it is within 30 days of the purchase of your RV. If that is the case, take the time to get a copy of the contract and read it carefully before signing.

Secret Warranties

The term **secret warranty** stems from the fact that, in some cases, manufacturers have ceased notifying consumers directly about a defect in their vehicle. Instead of issuing a recall notice to individual owners, the manufacturer relies on the dealer to correct the defect at the next service interval, or the manufacturer issues a press release, assuming notice of the defect will be widely circulated by the media. Because the consumer is not notified directly and is only offered the repair free of charge when, and if he or she eventually learns of the defect, consumer advocates and state attorneys general have dubbed the process *secret warranty.*

The bottom line is that if a defect is discovered by the manufacturer, but that defect is not determined to be safety related, then it is up to the manufacturer to determine how the vehicles' owners will be notified.

The bottom line is that if a defect is discovered by the manufacturer, but that defect is not determined to be safety related, then it is up to the manufacturer to determine how the vehicles' owners will be notified. The result can be a Catch-22 situation for the owner. The simple fact is there is usually no way for the owner to know that a reimbursement is offered on the repair unless he or she knows it is covered, and the owner is not going to know the problem is covered unless there is some kind of notice from the manufacturer.

To correct the problem, the National Association of Attorneys General has urged state legislators to adopt legislation to outlaw secret warranties and require individual notification of owners, regardless of the defect. Several states are now considering adoption of such legislation, but none have been signed into law as yet.

While vehicle manufacturers agree that they do have a responsibility for correcting factory defects, they argue that the manufacturer should not have to go to unreasonable lengths to get the problem resolved. A spokesman for the Motor Vehicle

How to Complain to Your Dealer or Manufacturer

The following is a suggested format to follow when writing a letter of complaint to your dealer or manufacturer:

Date
John Doe, president
Acme RV, Incorporated
Address

Dear Mr. Doe:

I am writing concerning a problem I have with my new (year, make, model), which was purchased on (date). The vehicle identification number is (   ).

I experienced my first breakdown with my (vehicle) on (date) and have had repeated problems with it since then. The major problem at this point is (description). As a result of this problem we have been unable to use our (vehicle) since (date), and have spent (amount) thus far trying to get it repaired and back on the road. I attempted to get help through (service manager, dealership) on several occasions, but the (vehicle) remains unrepaired and is not roadworthy. The following is a list of the repair attempts:

(date) (problem # 1)
(date) (problem # 2)

Attached are copies of work orders and receipts, plus receipts for (incidental expenses, towing, etc.). A reply at your earliest convenience would be appreciated.

Sincerely,

Your name and address

cc: *Trailer Life* RV Action Line (or)
    MotorHome Hot Line (or)
    Good Sam Action Line

Manufacturers' Association (MVMA) notes, "Laws that would require notification of individual owners for every factory defect would be extremely costly, with very questionable benefits. The cost would have to be passed on to the consumers, and we would see yet one more regulation that adds to the cost of a vehicle."

RECALLS

While on the subject of factory defects, it seems appropriate to provide a few basics about the recall process. You should know that recalls are either voluntary on involuntary. A **voluntary recall** is self-explanatory: The manufacturer of the vehicle or product discovers a defect and notifies owners by mail or through the media that a recall has been initiated.

An **involuntary recall** usually originates when complaints, breakdowns, or accidents occur in sufficient numbers to alert a government agency—usually the National Highway Traffic Safety Administration or the Federal Trade Commission— that a problem exists in sufficient numbers to merit further investigation. That investigative process generally has a number of steps, and, depending upon the seriousness of the problem, can take months or even years before the government agency orders the manufacturer to initiate a recall. Because the time factor can be crucial, representatives of both NHTSA and the FTC urge consumers to contact them as soon as possible if they feel their vehicle or product has a safety-related or other type of defect.

A couple of important things to remember about recalls is that, even though a factory defect has been discovered, there can be limitations regarding the company's legal responsibility. Federal regulations do not permit companies to assign arbitrary cutoff dates on recalls, but a cutoff is provided for in the law. In the case of a voluntary recall, a company's financial responsibility ends eight years from the purchase date of the product. If the recall is safety related, there is no cutoff date.

SOURCES OF ASSISTANCE

Many manufacturers, particularly automobile/truck builders and builders of motorhome chassis, assign service personnel to offer advice and/or assistance in correcting problems, including suggesting locations of local dealers. The following is an address and telephone list for many such companies, as well as other agencies and associations offering assistance.

To file a **complaint,** report a vehicle **safety defect,** or to inquire about a vehicle **recall,** contact:

U. S. Department of Transportation
National Highway Traffic Safety Administration
Office of Defects Investigation
400 Seventh Street, S. W.
Washington, D. C. 20590
(800) 424-9393
In the District of Columbia area, telephone (202) 366-0123

To report **warranty problems** or inquire about your **warranty rights,** contact:

Federal Trade Commission
6th Street and Pennsylvania Avenue, N. W.
Washington, D. C. 20580
(202) 326-2000

Or, check your phone book for the nearest Federal Trade Commission regional office.

For information on **emissions equipment** and **emissions equipment warranties,** contact:

Environmental Protection Agency
401 M Street, S. W.
Washington, D. C. 20460
(202) 382-2090

To file a **complaint** with a consumer-advocate service, or for **assistance in resolving a dispute,** contact:

Trailer Life's "RV Action Line" or
MotorHome "Hot Line" (by mail only):
29901 Agoura Road
Agoura, California 91301

The Center for Auto Safety
20001 S Street, N. W., Suite 410
Washington, D. C. 20009
(202) 328-7700

AUTOSOLVE
American Automobile Association (AAA)
1000 AAA Drive
Heathrow, Florida 32746-5063
(407) 444-7740

AUTOCAP
8400 Westpark Drive
McLean, Virginia 22102
(703) 821-7144

Recreation Vehicle Industry Association
1896 Preston White Drive
Reston, Virginia 22090
(703) 620-6003

Recreation Vehicle Dealers Association
3251 Old Lee Highway, Suite 500
Fairfax, Virginia 22030
(703) 591-7130

To contact **major auto companies** and/or **chassis suppliers,** check your owner's manual for customer-service addresses and telephone numbers, or refer to *Trailer Life's Towing Guide.*

Remember, in dealing with service problems, a positive attitude is your biggest asset. Beyond that, the procedures and methods described here can help make you a victor rather than a victim.

Index

OTHER BOOKS BY TRAILER LIFE

Trailer Life's RV Repair & Maintenance Manual
Edited by Bob Livingston

All-new, updated edition presents recreational vehicle owners with all the practical knowledge needed for diagnosing problems, making repairs, communicating with mechanics. Detailed troubleshooting guides for all RV systems, hundreds of comprehensive illustrations and photographs, step-by-step instructions for repairing, replacing, and maintaining systems.
8½ x 11, 336 pages
$29.95 ISBN 0-934798-12-5

RVing America's Backroads

California	*New York*	*Idaho/Montana*
Florida	*Arizona*	*Texas*

Six information-packed, four-color travel guidebooks designed *specifically* for recreational vehicle owners! Each book takes you on spectacular backroads tours, lavishly illustrated with gorgeous color photography by award-winning photojournalists. Clear, accurate maps of suggested backroads tours show easy access from the major interstates…fact sheets list annual events, museums, restaurants. Don't plan an RV vacation without these exciting new books.
8½ x 11, 128 pages
$15.95 each

Full-time RVing: A Complete Guide to Life on the Open Road
Bill and Jan Moeller

The answers to all the questions anyone who dreams of traveling full time in an RV may have can be found in this remarkable new source book. *Full-time RVing* takes the mystery out of fulltiming and makes it possible to fully enjoy this once-in-a-lifetime experience.
7¼ x 9¼, 352 pages
$14.95 ISBN: 0-934798-14-1

The Good Sam RV Cookbook
Edited by Beverly Edwards and the editors of *Trailer Life*

Over 250 easy and delicious recipes, including 78 prize-winners from the Good Sam Samboree cook-offs around the country. Also contains tips, ideas, and suggestions to help you get the most from your RV galley.
7¼ x 9¼, 252 pages
$14.95 ISBN: 0-93478-17-6

These books are available at fine bookstores everywhere. Or, you may order directly from Trailer Life Books. For each book ordered, simply send us the name of the book, the price, plus $2 per book for shipping and handling (California residents please add 6½% sales tax). Mail to:

Trailer Life Books, P.O. Box 4500, Agoura, CA 91301

You may call our customer-service representatives if you wish to charge your order or if you want more information. Please phone, toll-free, Monday through Friday, 6:30 A.M. to 5:30 P.M.; Saturday, 7:30 A.M. to 12:30 P.M. Pacific Time, **1 (800) 234-3450.**